D1596147

JAPAN–CHINA RELATIONS IN THE MODERN ERA

From before the dawn of recorded history, there has been a rich flow of interaction between Japan and China. Japan has long learned many things from Chinese civilization, and since the modern era China began to learn from Japan. In the twenty-first century, however, China surpassed Japan in terms of GDP in 2010 to become the world's second largest economy. Amid this rapid rise of China and what has been called a power-shift in Japan–China relations, there are signs that bilateral tensions are rising and that the image each country has of the other is worsening.

This volume provides a cogent analysis of the politics of the bilateral relationship in the modern era, explaining the past, present, and future of Japan–China relations during a time of massive political, social, and economic changes. Written by a team of internationally renowned Japanese scholars and based on sources not available in English, this book is essential reading for students and scholars of Japan–China relations, Japanese international relations, and the politics and international relations of East Asia.

Ryosei Kokubun is President of the National Defense Academy of Japan.

Yoshihide Soeya is a Professor in the Faculty of Law, Keio University, Japan.

Akio Takahara is a Professor at the Graduate School of Law and Politics, University of Tokyo, Japan.

Shin Kawashima is a Professor at the Graduate School of Arts and Sciences, University of Tokyo, Japan.

Keith Krulak worked for over fifteen years as an international economist for the U.S. government before becoming a translator.

JAPAN–CHINA RELATIONS IN THE MODERN ERA

Ryosei Kokubun, Yoshihide Soeya,
Akio Takahara, and Shin Kawashima

Translated by Keith Krulak

LONDON AND NEW YORK

First published 2017
by Routledge
2 Park Square, Milton Park, Abingdon, Oxon OX14 4RN

and by Routledge
711 Third Avenue, New York, NY 10017

Routledge is an imprint of the Taylor & Francis Group, an informa business

Originally published in Japan by Yuhikaku Publishing Co. Ltd., in 2013

English translation rights arranged with Yuhikaku Publishing Co. Ltd.
through Japan Publishing Industry Foundation for Culture (JPIC)

English translation copyright © Keith Krulak, 2017

British Library Cataloguing in Publication Data
A catalogue record for this book is available from the British Library

Library of Congress Cataloging in Publication Data
A catalog record for this book has been requested

ISBN: 978-1-138-71491-5 (hbk)
ISBN: 978-1-138-71460-1 (pbk)
ISBN: 978-1-315-22905-8 (ebk)

Typeset in Bembo
by Wearset Ltd, Boldon, Tyne and Wear

MIX
Paper from
responsible sources
FSC® C013056

Printed and bound in Great Britain by
TJ International Ltd, Padstow, Cornwall

CONTENTS

ILLUSTRATIONS

Figures

Maps

Table

BOXES

PREFACE TO THE ENGLISH EDITION

Relatively little of the writing and research concerning the bilateral relations between Japan and the People's Republic of China (PRC) has been available in English until now. The primary reason may be that mastery of both the Japanese and Chinese languages is necessary in order to undertake high-level research of Japan–China relations, a tremendous challenge. However, another reason comes to mind: Japan–China relations are quite apt to be overlooked because they wind up overshadowed by the large international relationship between the United States and China. All too often, Japan–China relations are viewed as moving in accordance with U.S.–China relations; rarely are they viewed as operating independently.

After the conclusion of World War II and the PRC's founding, Japan in 1952 recovered its sovereignty, joined the U.S.-led Western bloc, and normalized diplomatic relations with the Republic of China in Taiwan under the Cold War system. And yet, private and quasi-governmental exchanges between Japan and China were rather frequent throughout the 1950s and 1960s. Consequently, Japan normalized diplomatic relations with China in 1972, six and a half years before the United States, and concluded the Treaty of Peace and Friendship in 1978, ahead of U.S.–China normalization of relations. The country most actively pulling China into the international economy, including with its assistance (ODA) to China starting in the 1980s, was Japan. And again, it was Japan foremost that felt the growing international frictions brought about by the rapid progress of China's rise, particularly from the latter half of the 1990s. In the twenty-first century, the United States had been most concerned about the intense frictions between Japan and China, yet presently there has been a sudden increase of friction between the United States and China. In reflecting on the past in this way, it seems that postwar Japan–China relations have consistently preceded U.S.–China relations.

We must point out one more reason for the paucity of research on postwar Japan–China relations in English: Japanese scholars had not actively been taking part in research activities in English, perhaps because of the language handicap. The four authors of this volume take pride in being scholars representing Japan in this field of knowledge. Concerned that there were few balanced textbooks on the modern history of Japan–China relations amid growing difficulties in their bilateral relationship at the start of the twenty-first century, the four authors teamed up to write the Japanese edition, published in 2013. This English edition has been revised and updated with new developments since the original book. In short, this volume is a textbook in which Japanese scholars have depicted the history of Japan–China relations in the modern era as objectively as possible by shedding light on the policy factors of both Japan and China.

A note on the rendering of personal names in this volume. Except for the four authors, the names of people from Northeast Asia are in the traditional order, that is, family name first (e.g., Yoshida Shigeru). Also, for the names of people from China and Taiwan, pinyin is used (e.g., Zhou Enlai) except when a special spelling is widespread for prewar figures (e.g., Sun Yat-sen), postwar Taiwanese (e.g., Lee Teng-hui), or in cases where they themselves used a special notation (e.g., Tung Chee Hwa of Hong Kong).

The publication of the English language edition arises from the opportunity of a new project that the Japan Publishing Industry Foundation for Culture (JPIC) started in 2014, the JAPAN LIBARY. Based on the decisions of a selection committee of seven experts, JPIC will select, translate, and publish 100 books representing the history, culture, society, and other facets of Japan so that the people around the world can discover outstanding books from Japan. The selection committee chose this volume as one of 14 "extremely outstanding" works in the first round.

This English language edition would not have been realized without the assistance of many people and organizations. First, we would like to express our sincere gratitude to Routledge for accepting JPIC's proposal and taking on the task of publishing the book. We would also like to thank the translator, Mr. Keith Krulak, for readily agreeing to the difficult job of translating the Japanese edition into English and for conscientiously working with the authors. A word of thanks is due as well to Mr. Benjamin Self of The Maureen and Mike Mansfield Foundation for introducing Mr. Krulak to us.

Also, Mr. Yasushi Seikai of Yuhikaku Publishing, who has been helping us since the original Japanese edition, forged a path for us on the publication of this English language edition. Updates for the English edition would not have been possible without the enormous cooperation of Mr. Yasuyuki Sugiura. Mr. Seiji Shirane helped proofread the translation of the Chronology of Key Events. Our deepest thanks go to all three gentlemen.

On behalf of all the authors
Ryosei Kokubun
Summer 2016

PREFACE

From before the dawn of recorded history, there has been a rich flow of interaction between Japan and China. Japan has long learned many things from Chinese civilization, and since the modern era China began to learn from Japan. In the twenty-first century, however, China surpassed Japan in terms of gross domestic product (GDP) in 2010 (Heisei 22) to become the world's second largest economy. Amid this rapid rise of China and what has been called a power-shift in Japan–China relations, there are signs that bilateral tensions are rising and that the image each country has of the other is worsening.

Looking back through history, there is a growing number of situations in today's Japan–China ties that were never experienced in the past. Politically, frictions and verbal sparring are endless. Economically, the two countries are intimately linked by trade and investment driven by the development of globalization; interdependence and the interpenetration of people, goods, and capital have advanced considerably. Consequently, in contrast to the past when Japan–China relations were mainly driven by the elite—politics, big business, and intelligentsia—now we are breaking into an era of people-to-people exchanges, including the Internet, study abroad, and travel. Moreover, though competition tends to steal the spotlight in today's Japan–China relations, in a certain sense, it is also the first time in history that there has ever been such an equal relationship.

Who could have predicted what today's Japan–China relationship would look like at the time of normalization of diplomatic relations in 1972 (Showa 47), just a mere 40 years ago? The future relationship probably will encounter many other opportunities and challenges. In particular, Japan and China both have entered a period of political transformation domestically and, in the context of these changes, bilateral relations will be undoubtedly affected.

The planning for this volume was born of the strong belief that one must have a firm grasp of history in order to secure an unshakable vantage point for the stunning changes happening in Japan–China relations. Our Japan–China relations—where did they come from, where are they now, and where are they heading? We must understand the events before us historically, not as separate points but rather as a series of points on a line. The history addressed by this volume is, in principle, that of the bilateral relationship since the foundation of the People's Republic of China in 1949. However, from the standpoint of historical continuity, it starts with Japan–China relations since the mid-nineteenth century.

The plan for this book was conceived in August 2004 (Heisei 16). The project began when, under the worsening conditions of Japan–China relations, Mr. Yasushi Seikai, an editor at Yuhikaku Publishing, willingly took on my idea. For the publication of a history of Japan–China relations in the modern era to meet the expectations of everyone interested in the trends happening today, I hoped to assemble the best lineup to showcase the current standard of Japanese academia. And so I sought the participation of Yoshihide Soeya, professor at Keio University, Akio Takahara, professor at the University of Tokyo, and Shin Kawashima, then associate professor at the University of Tokyo, who all willingly and graciously agreed.

How to depict the history of Japan–China relations in the modern era? Various perspectives are possible: economic history, social history, cultural history, intellectual history, personal history. This volume is essentially a history of political relations, and in that sense, it is mainly a history of relations between the two states. It is the specialty of the authors.

All things considered, it took almost ten years—a long time. This volume would never have seen the light of day without the determination of Mr. Seikai, who with much patience and persistence and masterful editorial work helped guide it to publication. We would like to express our heartfelt gratitude to him.

The writing of this volume benefited from the valuable advice of three scholars: Masaya Inoue, Yutaka Kanda, and Yasuyuki Sugiura. We want to recognize and thank them.

We hope that this book will be widely used as a standard text for the modern history of Japan–China relations.

On behalf of all the authors
Ryosei Kokubun
November 1, 2013

ABOUT THE AUTHORS AND TRANSLATOR

Ryosei Kokubun (Chapters 5, 6, and 7)

1953: born in Tokyo.

1976: B.A. from the Department of Political Science, Faculty of Law, Keio University; 2002: Ph.D. from Keio University.

Previously served as Professor and Dean at Keio University's Faculty of Law, *inter alia.*

Currently: President of the National Defense Academy of Japan (areas of specialty: Contemporary Chinese Politics/Diplomacy, International Relations of East Asia).

Selected publications: *Ajia Jidai no Kensho: Chugoku no Shiten kara* [Examination of the Asian Era—from China's Perspective] (Tokyo: Asahi Shimbun, 1996)—awarded the *Mainichi Shimbun*'s Asia-Pacific Prize Honorable Mention; *Chuka Jinmin Kyowakoku* [The People's Republic of China] (Tokyo: Chikumashobo, 1999); *Gendai Chugoku no Seiji to Kanryosei* [Politics and Bureaucracy in Contemporary China] (Tokyo: Keio University Press, 2004)—awarded the Suntory Prize for Social Sciences and Humanities.

Yoshihide Soeya (Chapters 2, 3, and 7)

1955: born in Ibaraki Prefecture.

1979: B.A. from the Department of English Language and Studies, Faculty of Foreign Languages, Sophia University; 1987: Ph.D. from The University of Michigan.

Previously served as Associate Professor at Keio University's Faculty of Law, *inter alia.*

Currently: Professor at Keio University's Faculty of Law (areas of specialty: International Politics, International Relations of the Asia-Pacific, and Japanese Diplomacy).

Selected publications: *Nihon Gaiko to Chugoku 1945–1972* [Japanese Diplomacy and China: 1945–1972] (Tokyo: Keio Tsushin, 1995); *Japan's Economic Diplomacy with China, 1945–1978* (Oxford: Clarendon Press, 1998); *Nihon no "Midorupawa-" Gaiko* [Japan's "Middle Power" Diplomacy] (Tokyo: Chikumashobo, 2005).

Akio Takahara (Chapters 4 and 7)

1958: born in Kobe.

1981: L.L.B. from Faculty of Law, The University of Tokyo; 1988: D.Phil. from the University of Sussex.

Previously served as Assistant and Associate Professor at J. F. Oberlin University's School of International Studies and Associate Professor and Professor at Rikkyo University's Faculty of Law, *inter alia*.

Currently: Professor at the Graduate School of Law and Politics, The University of Tokyo (area of speciality: Contemporary Chinese Politics).

Selected publications: *The Politics of Wage Policy in Post-Revolutionary China* (Basingstoke: Macmillan Press, 1992); co-author, *Mo Takuto, To Shohei soshite Ko Takumin* [Mao Zedong, Deng Xiaoping, and Jiang Zemin] (Tokyo: Toyo Keizai Shinposha, 1999); co-editor, *Nitchu Kankei Shi 1972–2012 I: Seiji* [A History of Japan–China Relations 1972–2012, Vol. I: Politics] (Tokyo: University of Tokyo Press, 2012); co-author, *Kaihatsu Shugi no Jidai e 1972–2014* [Towards an Era of Developmentalism 1972–2014] (Tokyo: Iwanami Shoten, 2014).

Shin Kawashima (Prologue, Chapters 1 and 7)

1968: born in Yokohama.

1992: B.A. from the Department of Chinese Studies, Faculty of Foreign Studies, Tokyo University of Foreign Studies; 2000: Ph.D. from The University of Tokyo.

Previously served as Associate Professor at Department of Politics, Faculty of Law, Hokkaido University, *inter alia*.

Currently: Professor at The University of Tokyo's Graduate School of Arts and Sciences (areas of specialty: Modern and Contemporary History of China, History of Asia's Politics/Diplomacy).

Selected publications: *Chugoku Kindai Gaiko no Keisei* [The Formation of Modern Chinese Diplomacy] (Nagoya: University of Nagoya Press, 2004)—awarded the Suntory Prize for Social Sciences and Humanities in 2004; *Kindai Kokka e no Mosaku 1894–1925* [Exploring a Modern State in China, 1894–1925] (Tokyo: Iwanami Shoten, 2010); co-editor, *Higashi Ajia Kokusai Seiji Shi* [The History of East Asian International Politics] (Nagoya: University of Nagoya Press, 2007).

Translator

Keith Krulak has degrees in Japan Studies and International Relations/ International Economics. Before becoming a translator, he worked for nearly 16 years as an international economist for the U.S. government.

PROLOGUE: JAPAN–CHINA RELATIONS BEFORE 1949

Between competitive coexistence and confrontation

FIGURE 0.1 At the Cairo Conference: (from the left) Chinese Generalissimo Chiang Kai-shek, U.S. President Roosevelt, UK Prime Minister Churchill, and at far right, Madame Chiang, Song Meiling (November 22, 1943).

Source: ©Jiji Press.

This chapter summarizes Japan–China relations from the early modern period up to 1949, focusing on political and diplomatic relations. Meiji Japan and Qing Dynasty China, both major powers, had concluded an equal treaty in the latter half of the nineteenth century. But after the First Sino-Japanese War, they concluded a revised, unequal treaty favorable to Japan, and moreover, Japan became a colonial empire holding sovereignty over Taiwan (Formosa) and the Penghu (Pescadores) Islands. Thereafter, Japan–China relations became diversified, comprising Japan's relations with mainland China and with its colonies. Even as those relations grew extremely close, it ultimately ended in all-out war. The history of the prewar period is both the basis for and the source of postwar Japan–China relations.

1 The start of relations between sovereign states

Early modern Japan–China relations

Early modern Japan–China relations were primarily between Japan under the Tokugawa shogunate and China under the Qing dynasty. These were not relations between sovereign states, and the various territories they governed also differed after the advent of the modern period. The Ryukyu Kingdom was in Okinawa; Ogasawara (the Bonin Islands) and Hokkaido, called Ezochi, were not always under the rule of the shogunate in Edo. On the Chinese side, too, Taiwan and Xinjiang were added to the regions ruled by the Qing Empire in the seventeenth and eighteenth centuries, respectively. And yet, in contrast to Africa and the Americas where territorial boundaries were drawn artificially through the process of colonization by the West at the start of the modern era, in East Asia in this period, nations took shape as prototypical early modern nations, fostering a relative uniformity of language and culture.

A discussion of early modern relations between Japan and China must begin with the official trade relations that were limited to Nagasaki. Official relations between Japan and the Qing dynasty consisted of engaging in frontier market trading (*hushi*) at Nagasaki, not tributary relations (*cefeng* or *chaogong*) predicated on the Qing bestowing titles in exchange for Japan bringing tribute. However, various indirect and unofficial relations also existed, such as relations with the Chinese mainland from the feudal domains facing the East China Sea and the Ryukyus or from Ezochi through Karafuto (Sakhalin Island). Also, the Ryukyu had relations with the Satsuma domain at the same time it was in a tributary relationship with the Qing—which is understood as dual subordination.

Economic ties were important for both Japan and China. Copper imported from Japan became the raw material for copper coins in the early Qing Empire; Japan imported white sugar in addition to books and written materials from China. Furthermore, Japan exported *tawaramono*—primarily dried seafood from Tohoku and Ezochi wrapped in straw bales—in exchange for silver from China. The Tokugawa shogunate was careful to avoid an increase in the outflow of silver.

In terms of political ideology, Japan absorbed Confucianism and an accomplished samurai was familiar with the Four Books and Five Classics of Confucianism as well as the historical works *Shibashi Lüe* and *Zizhi Tongjian*, and learned *nanga*.[1] In contrast, Japan's cultural influence on China was extremely limited. Japan was a recipient of Chinese culture as a member of the Chinese character/East Asian cultural sphere along with Joseon Korea, the Ryukyu Kingdom, and Vietnam. As it processed this culture, Japan generated complex sentiments toward China, as in Motoori Norinaga's concept of *karagokoro* ("Chinese spirit") in his book *Tamakatsuma*, ultimately fostering a sense of Japanese identity in opposition to China.

Mid-nineteenth century East Asia

Western ships began to appear in growing numbers in East Asian waters in the first half of the nineteenth century. The Qing, which had been trading with Western countries at Guangzhou (Canton) since about 1757, was asked to increase the number of treaty ports by Britain toward the end of the eighteenth century. Japan had been trading with the Dutch at Nagasaki, but was asked by Western countries and Russia to open treaty ports at the start of the nineteenth century. Then, the Opium War between China and Britain broke out in 1840 over the issue of the import of opium into China by Britain and other foreign countries. Britain won a lopsided victory by using overwhelming firepower and steamships unaffected by winds or tides, and the Treaty of Nanking (1842) was concluded. The Qing's defeat came as quite a shock to Japan. Arguments for coastal defense and expelling the barbarians developed vigorously, spurred by the many foreign vessels appearing in Japanese coastal waters—Commodore Perry's fleet in 1853 foremost—but, in the end, Japan decided to open up. In 1859, following on the conclusion of the Japan–U.S. Treaty of Amity and Commerce (1858), Nagasaki and four other ports were opened to Western trade, thus completely changing Japan's foreign relations through Nagasaki.

The important point is that, in the case of China, even after having lost the Opium War and concluded the Treaty of Nanking, there were no major changes in the Qing's long-standing tributary relations with neighboring states; those existing foreign relations coexisted alongside its foreign trade relations with Western countries. Whereas in Japan's case, opening the country to the West essentially changed its foreign relations entirely. Once Nagasaki became one of the treaty ports, Chinese merchants there branched out to Kobe, Yokohama, Hakodate, and the other ports, even though they were not what is known as "treaty port citizens" because there was no Japan–China treaty. At those ports, they directly engaged in trade hitherto conducted at Nagasaki, such as Ezochi dried seafood, and sent it to Shanghai, which was becoming a center of foreign trade in China's coastal region. The Tokugawa shogunate lost the benefits from Nagasaki trade, so to remedy the situation, the Nagasaki and Hakodate magistrates petitioned for trade and consular facilities and sent the *Senzai-maru* and other Western vessels of the shogunate to try to ship the products directly to Shanghai, but the Meiji Restoration arrived before they could obtain favorable results (Okamoto and Kawashima 2009).

Meiji Restoration and Qing reforms

The Meiji government that was established in 1868, seeking to become a modern state with centralized power, abolished the feudal domains in 1871 and instituted a centralized authoritarian system, with a capital city and prefectures ruled directly by the central government. The samurai largely lost their privileged status because the new government promulgated a universal conscription law and disposed of their stipends. Also, the new government made "rich nation, strong army" (*fukoku kyohei*) and encouragement of new industry (*shokusan kogyo*) its policy tasks, and it promoted "civilization and enlightenment" (*bunmei kaika*) aimed at Westernizing, even in terms of lifestyle. However, the burden to enact these policies weighed heavily on the populace, sparking protests throughout the country, and the deep discontent of the former samurai led to numerous uprisings, such as the Satsuma Rebellion (Seinan War). Since the government expended a great deal to suppress these disturbances, public finances were severely squeezed. To deal with this, Finance Minister Matsukata Masayoshi attempted a turnaround in public finances through a policy of deflation, but deflation meant a real tax increase. This policy, combined with other tax burdens, left the people in poverty, and the number of tenant farmers increased in the rural districts. In this way, the Meiji government faced rather rough sailing early on and was criticized by the Qing and Joseon for Westernizing hastily. Even after the Constitution of the Empire of Japan was promulgated in 1889 and the first Imperial Diet was convened the following year, the conditions were such that it was hard to call Japan's "modernity" as a constitutional monarchy a success. It is likely that the Meiji Restoration came to be called the model of Asian modernization after Japan's victories in both the First Sino-Japanese and the Russo-Japanese wars.

In contrast, the Qing dynasty implemented reforms, called the Tongzhi Restoration, from the 1860s through the first half of the 1870s. Although institutional reform was raised, the government explored ways to Westernize aspects of the military and industry to start with, and so it promoted new industries centered around the treaty ports and reconstituted the Beiyang Army as a modern army. In terms of domestic and foreign affairs, the Qing tried to build relations with the West and make use of Western conveniences while maintaining the existing institutions. Such things associated with relations with the West were called *Yangwu* ("Western affairs"). It was at the end of the nineteenth century, after the First Sino-Japanese War, that the Qing considered institutional reforms in earnest and tried to introduce a constitutional monarchy along the lines of Germany or Japan.

What greatly differed between nineteenth century Japan and China was their attempts at treaty revision. In the case of Japan, the government hastened preparations of the legal system, promulgating the Criminal Code (1880), the (Old) Civil Code (1890), and the Constitution of the Empire of Japan (1889). In addition to this legal preparation, the government attempted to revise the treaties through various institutions as a modern state, a series of "civilization and enlightenment" policies, as well as diplomatic negotiations. Ultimately, the Diet's establishment was the springboard for agreement with Britain to abolish extraterritoriality laws in 1894 (taking effect in 1899). Some in Japanese society argued that the abolition of extraterritoriality was unnecessary since it was implemented at the same time that foreigners were permitted to live among the general populace.

In the case of China, some believed that it must also undertake that kind of treaty revision, but adopting this as a policy happened in the period from the last half of the 1890s to the start of the twentieth century, when the Qing removed tributary relations from its framework of foreign relations and unified its treaty relations.

Sino-Japanese Friendship and Trade Treaty

The Meiji government, seeking to enter into diplomatic relations with the Qing dynasty, continued its contacts with Peking via Shanghai. As a result of negotiations, Japan–China relations became institutionalized once again after the Sino-Japanese Friendship and Trade Treaty was concluded in 1871 and the arrangements surrounding the Nagasaki trade were relaxed.

To state the conclusion first, this treaty was the sole equal treaty for both countries, which had concluded unequal treaties with Western countries. Yet, negotiations were clearly driven by the Qing and the content of the treaty's preamble was advantageous to China. For instance: "Article VI. In official correspondence, China will use the Chinese language, and Japan will use either the Japanese language accompanied by a Chinese version, or a Chinese version alone, as may be found on her side preferable." Such parts indicated that, even considering Japan's strong ability to read Chinese, China was in a superior position (Okamoto and Kawashima 2009). Furthermore, both sides acknowledged the authority of consular courts. But, one should be cautious about saying this indicated that Japan and China were forging relations based on the Western style. Qing China's relations with Japan differed from both its tributary relations and relations based on the unequal treaties with Western countries.

Japan and China established legations based on the Sino-Japanese Friendship and Trade Treaty. Since many personnel at the Qing's diplomatic missions at the time were bureaucrats who had passed the higher civil service examinations ("Mandarins") or had received a traditional education, this has become known as the "cultural exchange of literati." A notably well-known example of the written communications passed between Japanese intellectuals and Chinese officials is that of Okochi Teruna with He Ruzhang and Huang Zunxian. This was a kind of information collection operation by the Qing legation in Tokyo, but it also assisted China in shaping Japan's understanding. Huang, who worked at the legation in Tokyo, penned his *History of Japan* (published in 1895) after his return home. Meanwhile, Japan, after establishing its legation in Peking, sent students to China to address a problem with Peking Mandarin language comprehension. Odagiri Masunosuke was one of these early students to China. There are also instances of Qing bureaucrats who went to Japan and (re)discovered Chinese classics that had already been lost to China, which they collected and brought back home.

Early in the 1870s, soon after the opening of diplomatic relations, a telegraph line was laid between Nagasaki and Shanghai using Denmark's The Great Northern Telegraph Company (Det Store Nordiske Telegrafselskab A/S); telegraph messages went back and forth, and a sea route was opened. Regarding trade, both Japan and China were on the silver standard; Japan exported products such as seafood and copper and China exported soybeans, spun cotton, and sugar to Japan. It was after the First Sino-Japanese War that machine-made cotton manufactures were exported from Japan. To a certain degree, Japan and China began to hold commercial standards in common, at least in terms of trade rules and the management systems for public health and disease control (Mitani et al. 2009).

Demarcation of national borders

Japan and Qing China both defined their national boundaries through negotiations with Western countries in the latter half of the nineteenth century. In the north, Japan waived its claims to Karafuto (Sakhalin), which had become a mixed settlement, and gained sovereignty over the Chishima (Kuril) Islands in the Treaty of Saint Petersburg of 1875.[2] In the south, Japan declared the Ogasawara its possession in 1876 and incorporated Minami-Torishima (Marcus Island) into it in 1898. In the west, Japan turned the Ryukyus into Okinawa Prefecture in 1879, as is mentioned below, and made the Daito Islands a territory. The contours of modern Japan were complete. Japan incorporated the Senkaku Islands into Okinawa Prefecture by a cabinet decision during the First Sino-Japanese War and incorporated Takeshima (Korean: Dokdo) into Shimane Prefecture by a similar cabinet decision during the Russo-Japanese War.

China defined its national borders through wars and negotiations with the Western great powers, such as with Russia along the Amur River (Heilongjiang) and the maritime lands (Ussuri krai—most of modern day Priamurye and Primorye) by the Treaty of Aigun (1858) and Treaty of Peking (1860), and in Xinjiang and Central Asia by the Treaty of Saint Petersburg (also known as the "Treaty of Ili" 1881). Negotiations with Britain and France largely settled China's borders with Tibet, Burma, and French Indochina. But this still left many territorial issues unresolved.

Whereas modern Japan's national borders were demarcated larger than the area under its control in the Edo Period, China (in the sense above, at least) saw its national borders reduced slightly from the Qing's territory.

Ryukyu and Korean peninsula issues

Unlike Japan, which by and large had comprehensively changed its framework for foreign relations with the opening of five treaty ports, China had opened treaty relations with Western countries while maintaining its tributary relations. It adopted a framework for external relations that was close to a double standard. The number of tributary states quickly decreased after the 1880s because the countries in southeast

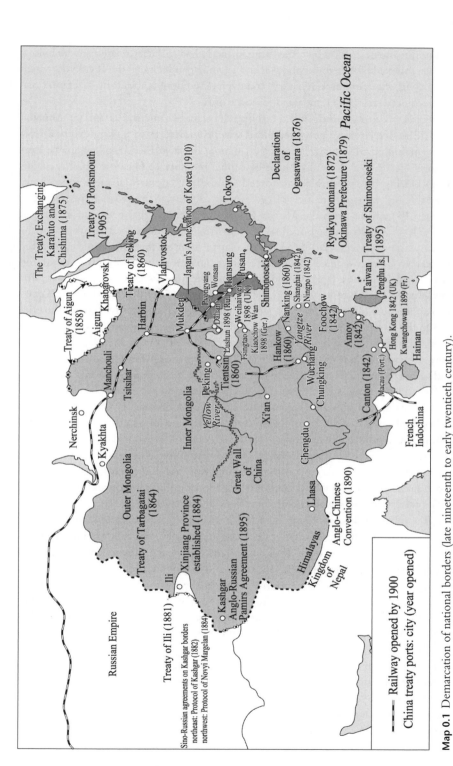

Map 0.1 Demarcation of national borders (late nineteenth to early twentieth century).

Source: Adapted by Mr. Ienaga Masaki from Kawashina, Hattori, eds. 2007, Map 1, p.2.

and northeast Asia with which the Qing formerly had tributary relations were colonized or annexed by Western countries and Japan. Japan included the Ryukyus, which was a Qing tributary, in its territory, and even raised doubts about the suzerain-vassal relations between Qing China and Joseon Korea.

The Ryukyu Kingdom of the early modern era became the "Ryukyu domain" in 1872 under Japanese pressure, and it was prohibited from having external relations, including tributary relations with China. It was turned into "Okinawa Prefecture" in 1879; the Ryukyu king became a member of Japanese nobility at this time. During this process, Japan forced China to recognize Japanese sovereignty over the Ryukyus when it deployed troops to Taiwan in 1874. It justified this Taiwan Expedition with the Mudan (Botansha) Incident that occurred in Taiwan in 1871, in which local aboriginal Paiwan tribesmen massacred Ryukyuan fisherman castaways who had gone ashore. Japan asserted that the Qing considered Taiwan to be *terra nullius*. There were also negotiations in the 1880s to divide up three Ryukyu islands: Japan would have ceded territories west of Miyako-Yaeyama to China in exchange for revising the Sino-Japanese Friendship and Trade Treaty into an unequal treaty favorable to Japan. But no agreement was reached in the end.

On the Korean peninsula, the Joseon (Yi Dynasty) had maintained suzerain-vassal relations with the Qing based on a tributary relationship, but in 1874 Japan pressured the Joseon to conclude the unequal Japan–Korea Treaty of Amity (Treaty of Kanghwa) and forced them to accept it. Meanwhile, employing its "Korean Stratagem" (*Chaoxian Celüe*) and other measures, China encouraged the Joseon to enter a treaty with the United States and strengthened its influence over its vassal's domestic and foreign affairs. In the wake of the Imo Incident and the Gapsin Coup in the 1880s, Japan and China both withdrew their troops from Korea under the 1885 Tianjin Convention, but the Qing were fundamentally in a superior position. Fukuzawa Yukichi wrote "*Datsu-A Ron*" ("An Argument for Leaving Asia [for the West]") in reaction to Japan's inferior status in Korea, but his newspaper editorial was not read widely at the time, rather it became well known after World War II (Sakai 2007).

The relations Joseon Korea had with the Qing are characterized as both a dependency and an independent state. Even as a vassal under the tributary relationship, it was possible to have an independent diplomacy. There were a range of possible interpretations between vassal state and independence. But, it is certain that the Qing used modern international relations theory to strengthen its power of influence over the Joseon (Okamoto 2004). And as China expanded its power of influence over Korea, it increased its military power. After the 1886 Nagasaki–Qing Navy Incident, in which sailors from four Beiyang Navy warships incited a riot in Nagasaki, Japanese society was left with the impression that Japan was in an inferior position militarily. In 1888 Japan reorganized its army structure from a system of regional commands into a system of divisions with potential for foreign campaigns. The Diet began to accept military budget increases in the 1890s and the foreign policy argument that became mainstream held that Japan had to secure Korea in order to protect itself from the Russian and Chinese threats—like that of Yamagata Aritomo's "Line of Interest" theory (Tobe 1999).

2 "Modernity" and nationalism

First Sino-Japanese and Russo-Japanese wars and Japan's rise

At the turn of the twentieth century, in the period when Japan was victorious in the First Sino-Japanese and Russo-Japanese wars—this was the beginning of Japan's ascent to contest China as the major power in East Asia and to surpass it. Japan and China both sent troops to Korea in 1894, triggered by the Donghak Rebellion; hostilities commenced between China and Japan, which had not withdrawn its troops after the revolt was ended and had demanded the Joseon enact domestic policy reforms. This First Sino-Japanese War ended in a Japanese victory. By the Treaty of Shimonoseki concluded in 1895, Japan came to have the same standing in China as the great powers; this unequal treaty became the basis for Japan–China relations. China ceded Taiwan and the Penghu Islands to Japan and Japan became a colonial empire. The indemnity of 200 million taels (then worth about 310 million yen) that Japan acquired became the basis for construction of the Yawata Iron and Steel Works and the transition to the gold standard in 1897. By adopting the same gold standard as Europe and the United States, Japan could more easily raise capital through government bonds and other means.

BOX 0.1 JAPANESE RULE OF COLONIES, OCCUPIED LANDS

Through the 1895 Treaty of Shimonoseki, Japan gained possession over Taiwan and the Penghu Islands and established Japanese concessions (*znjie*) in Soochow (Suzhou) and Hangchow (Hangzhou). After the Russo-Japanese War, it also came to rule the Kwantung Leased Territory with Port Arthur (Lüshunkou) and Dalian, and the South Manchurian Railway Zone. Furthermore, Japan exercised indirect rule in all its occupied lands in China in the 1930s through collaborationist governments, and not just by founding Manchukuo.

There are two views regarding the Japanese rule of Taiwan: although one can praise the points that brought about modernity, such as infrastructure improvements in the Taiwanese interior, respect for law, and the modern notion of time, one can criticize the policies of imperialization and assimilation. But, there are difficulties in a dualistic understanding of the positives and negatives of Japanese colonial rule, as the following points show. Even if a native were to try to get an education and adopt Japanese as his mother tongue, his existence as a colonial subject would be systematically distinct from a Japanese. The infrastructure constructed was fundamentally for the convenience of Japanese rule.

In China, the pro-Japanese collaborationist governments such as Manchukuo are labeled as "pseudo" and are not rated as legitimate dynasties or governments in Chinese history. This is a criticism of Japanese aggression as well as of the "traitors to their race" (*hanjian*), Chinese who ingratiated themselves with

Japan. Furthermore, leasehold lands, concessions, and railway zones were all fundamentally the invasion points for imperialism and became the subject of Chinese movements to recover national sovereignty. Recently, however, we are beginning to see positive interpretations of the leasehold lands and concessions, even in China, because economic activity and culture were emphasized in them.

The First Sino-Japanese War, unlike the Second Sino-Japanese War, did not bring with it intense "anti-Japanese" or "anti-Chinese" sentiment because it was not a war under general mobilization and it occurred before the formation of "China" as a modern state and sense of nationalism. On the other hand, anti-Russian sentiment worsened in Japan, evident in such sayings as "suffer privation for the sake of revenge," because the "Triple Intervention" by Russia, France, and Germany forced Japan to return the Liaotung (Liaodong) Peninsula to China, land that had been ceded to it in the Treaty of Shimonoseki in 1895.

China's loss to Japan spurred the great powers to divide up the country, establishing leaseholds in the coastal regions and defining spheres of influence for almost the whole country, and within China, anxiety about saving the country grew in intensity. When Social Darwinist concepts touting that "the strong always win, the weak lose" became popular in China, Japan was accorded a place as if it were a model modern state under a constitutional monarchy, having absorbed Western modernity. Japan came to be viewed as rich and strong.

However, Chinese political changes went through many twists and turns. The Boxer Rebellion occurred in 1900–01, stemming from an anti-foreign movement in northern China by the *Yihetuan*, a quasi-religious secret society (known in English as the Boxers). The great powers' attack on the Dagu Forts triggered China's declaration of war, which it fought against all of the great powers. A Japanese diplomat was killed, and the Japanese army provided the main force of the eight-nation alliance contingent. In the Boxer Protocol (Xinchou Treaty), the defeated Qing promised to pay a huge indemnity, the legations of the great powers including Japan came to exercise influence as a group of creditor nations, and they gained the right to base troops stationed in the coastal regions near Peking and Tianjin. (On the basis of this provision, Japanese troops based in Tianjin became the Northern China Expeditionary Army.) Also, the great powers temporarily set aside their competition to acquire concessions and decided to build cooperative relations among themselves, to include the recent arrivals on the international political stage concerning China, the United States and Germany.

However, Russia, which had occupied Manchuria (the northeastern part of present day China) during the Boxer Rebellion, did not withdraw its troops after the war. It was the start of deeper Russian confrontation with the great powers, especially with Japan over the Korean peninsula. Wary of Russia's policy of southward expansion, Britain concluded the Anglo-Japanese Alliance in 1902. In a backlash against Russia's occupation of Manchuria, China showed a neutrality favorable toward Japan when Japan and Russia began to fight in 1904, even though the battlefield was Manchuria—Chinese territory, the very birthplace of the Qing dynasty. Japan won the war, paying a heavy cost in human life; though it did not get any war reparations from Russia, it acquired Russia's concessions in South Manchuria with China's acquiescence in the Treaty of Portsmouth.

Japan's new Manchurian concessions and "first-class power" mentality

In Japan, there was the Northern Expansion Doctrine—confront Russia with Britain's backing—and the Southern Expansion Doctrine—Japan would secure Korea and try to expand its interests mainly in the Hokkien (Fujian) area near Taiwan in exchange for leaving Manchuria to Russia; ultimately the Northern Expansion Doctrine became the mainstream view, resulting in the Russo-Japanese War. Although the war ended in a Japanese victory, Japan failed to get reparations and domestic public opinion dissatisfaction grew, as demonstrated by the Hibiya Incendiary Incident.

What Japan acquired in the Russo-Japanese War in exchange for an enormous human cost were the concessions that Russia held in South Manchuria. Specifically, concessions related to the South Manchurian railway and the Kwantung Leased Territory, which included Port Arthur (Lüshunkou) and Dalian (for a period of 25 years from 1898). In the leasehold, Japan established the Kwantung Governor-General and troops that were later known as the Kwantung Army. It created the South Manchurian Railway Company (Mantetsu) to manage the railway and develop mines. For the army, it was these South Manchuria concessions that compensated for the lives lost in the war; pre-WWII Japan later stood up to Russia, the United States, and China in order to protect and maintain these very South Manchuria concessions.

After the Russo-Japanese War, Japan allied with Russia and concluded the Japan–Russia ententes to secure its position in its South Manchuria concessions and, in a sense, check the emergence of the United States that was pursuing an open door policy. In terms of its policy toward China, Japan as before kept in lockstep with Britain and the other great powers, a relationship of mutually recognizing each others' interests (Chiba 2008). From China's perspective, it was as if Japan had inherited Russia's South Manchurian concessions.

Meanwhile, there was a growing sense in Japan that, having beaten Russia in the war, the country was a major world power, a first-class nation. Furthermore, the power of the army and navy grew stronger; when Saionji Kinmochi's second cabinet refused the army's demands for two additional divisions, the Minister of the Army used the military's right for direct appeal to the Emperor to resign, thereby toppling the cabinet. Seeing Japan, a constitutional monarchy, beat Imperial Russia, an autocracy, spurred China to switch to a constitutional monarchy; in 1908 it proclaimed the *Qinding Xianfa Dagang* (*Principles of a Constitution*).

Modern state and nationalism

Defeated in the Boxer Rebellion, Qing China in the early twentieth century sought to become a modern constitutional state by introducing Western institutions. Germany and Japan, with their respective emperor systems, became the models. Many Chinese students abroad studied "the West/modernity" in Japan. Attendant on the abolition of China's civil service examination system, foreign degrees, in addition to academic degrees from the new style domestic schools, became the new qualifications for employment in the bureaucracy.

BOX 0.2 CHINESE STUDENTS ABROAD AND JAPAN

Many of the Chinese students who went abroad starting at the end of the nineteenth century went to Japan. With the reform of the Chinese higher civil service examinations, obtaining an academic degree was quicker, and the once lowly regarded Japan was favored. But looking over the longer term, the fact that Japan was viewed in China as a model for Westernizing and becoming a rich and powerful nation was probably a factor. The period with the most Chinese students was the start of the twentieth century when their number reached about 10,000. Basically, these students were more interested in "the West/modernity" that Japan had assimilated rather than in Japan itself, yet they brought back to China a Japanese "sense of values" and "wisdom." While living in Japan with its different culture, the Chinese students were stimulated and surprised by "Japan" itself. For instance, one student was surprised at the sight of women doing housework barefoot at a boarding house in the Hongo neighborhood of Tokyo and became aware of the problem with the Chinese tradition of foot-binding. Although he felt some inconvenience with his life in Japan, Chiang Kai-shek said that his time at the Tokyo Shinbu School (an Imperial Japanese Army Academy preparatory school for Chinese students) and military life with the 13th Division's 19th Field Artillery Regiment became the basis for his disciplined lifestyle later.

Also, Japan, especially Tokyo, became the base for national movements from various countries and regions at the start of the twentieth century; some Chinese students became involved in these movements. Activists from China, Vietnam, the Philippines, Korea, and other countries carried out reform and independence movements; the debate between Chinese calling themselves Constitutionalists or Revolutionaries is widely known. It was also in Tokyo that Sun Yat-sen rallied the groups advocating revolution that were regionally divided to create his *Tongmenghui* (China Revolutionary Alliance) in 1905. Among the Japanese, too, there were proponents of Chinese activists and quite a few supporters of the Xinhai Revolution.

However, the number of Chinese students that Japan invited after the start of the Second Sino-Japanese War, in the context of seeking to construct the

Greater East Asian Co-Prosperity Sphere, roughly matched the number at the start of the twentieth century. Japan was expecting to invite students from Asia, its own sphere of influence, to teach them Japanese language and "Japanese spirit" together with Japan's advanced status in Western civilization so that after graduation they would become a bridge between Japan and their own societies. These students experienced first-hand the war on the Japanese mainland and evacuations to flee from U.S. air raids, yet when Japan's defeat became very likely, instead they feared that they would be recognized as being Japanese collaborators by their own home countries and regional societies. After the war, their local communities did view them as Japanese collaborators, they became embroiled in the political battles and independence struggles of their local societies, and the Japanese government did not protect them.

Japan offered one model of "modernity" to China. Many Western books translated into Japanese were translated into Chinese, and the vocabulary of translated words—such as economy, society, law, and communism—flowed from Japan to China. This is perhaps part of the intellectual foundation shared between the two countries. Japanese school textbooks also had a large influence on China's; Japan's perceptions of China became one of the patterns for China's perceptions of itself.

Furthermore, the start of the twentieth century was the germination period for Chinese nationalism. The consciousness of "China" as a nation and the identity as Chinese were fostered among intellectuals (Yoshizawa 2003). Students abroad strengthened their consciousness as "Chinese" in Japan, which gave rise to the anti-Russian movement, which opposed Russian occupation of Manchuria after the Boxer Rebellion, and the Anthropology Pavilion Incident with a movement protesting the negative characterization of the Chinese "on display" at the National Industrial Exhibition in Osaka. Such nationalism and patriotic consciousness later became a big issue latent in East Asia.

Japan's annexation of Korea and diversifying Japan–China relations

Japan placed the Korean Empire in its sphere of influence, in accord with the mutual recognition of interests among the great powers and its victory in the Russo-Japanese War. Japan and Korea concluded agreements over two periods. The second Japan–Korea agreement deprived Korea of its diplomatic sovereignty, established the office of Korea Resident-General, and Korea became a protectorate. Next, the Korean military was disbanded under the third Japan–Korea agreement of 1907 and afterwards Japan strengthened its control. Ito Hirobumi, the first Resident-General, was assassinated by An Chung-gun, Japan annexed Korea under the Japan–Korea Annexation Treaty in 1910, established the office of Korea Governor-General, and the royal family of Joseon was included as a part of Japanese nobility.

As a result of taking possession of the Korean peninsula, Japan faced issues concerning its authority to govern the ethnic Koreans resident in Manchuria and in the border area between Manchuria and Korea (Gando issue). At the same time, with Japan's possession of Taiwan, Taiwanese-registered citizens holding Japanese passports were active in China, enjoying privileges that Japanese citizens held, such as extraterritoriality. In this way, "Japan–China relations" became further diversified through Japan's possession of Taiwan, the acquisition of the leasehold territory, and the annexation of Korea.

Some among the Korean intellectuals who opposed Japanese control engaged in anti-Japanese movements in China or actively sought assistance from the Chinese. There were some Taiwanese, too, who were active in China and engaged in opposition movements against Japan.

From Xinhai Revolution to First World War

After the Russian Revolution of 1905, the concept of socialism flowed into East Asia and the emperor system was called into question; in Japan, the High Treason Incident occurred. In China, too, there was a debate over whether to have a republic or an emperor-centered constitutional system, proposed by the Qing. Ethnic Han Chinese were strongly critical of a system of constitutional monarchy in which the Manchus would play a central role. Further, the Qing's heavy-handed policies to centralize power provoked a backlash in local communities, especially in the provinces. The Wuchang Uprising that took place in Wuchang, Hubei Province on October 10, 1911 was the catalyst for the Xinhai Revolution (Chinese Revolution of 1911). The Republic of China was established on January 1, 1912; the Qing dynasty perished the following month. Even as Japan supported the Qing dynasty in principle, it had a tendency to try taking an active China policy, seeking to acquire its own concessions, following Britain's lead. Yet, it was not as if Britain partnered with Japan; Britain decided to try and mediate between the Republic of China and the Qing.

During the Xinhai Revolution, Ijuin Hikokichi, the minister of Japan's legation to China, requested to use "(Country of) Shina" for China instead of *Qingguo* ("Country of Qing") that had been used until then. This was an attempt to use a word corresponding to the designation of "China" used in Western languages that was unnecessary to change with every dynasty. It was accepted and thereafter "Shina" became the diplomatic designation. In 1913 when Yuan Shikai was officially installed as president, Japan recognized the Republic of China, calling it "the Republic of Shina."

China was neutral when World War I started in 1914 (Taisho 13), but the second Okuma Shigenobu cabinet used the Anglo-Japanese Alliance as the rationale for Japan to enter the war. Japan attacked Germany's Jiaozhou Bay leasehold territory in China's Shandong (Shantung) Province and occupied the whole provincial area that had been Germany's sphere of influence. In addition, Japan presented the Twenty-One Demands to the Peking government in January 1915, intending to further secure its South Manchurian concessions that it acquired from Russia in the Russo-Japanese War and to become the legal successor to the German concessions in Shandong it had newly acquired. These demands not only provoked an extremely strong backlash from the Chinese, but also raised doubts about Japanese intentions among the United States and other powers. But Japan sent its final notice on May 7 and got China's acceptance on May 9. That day is known in China as the "Day of National Humiliation."

In 1916, Yuan Shikai, who opposed the concept of a republican state with a strong legislature, schemed to become emperor but failed and died. After that, the Republic of China entered WWI in 1917 and participated in the Siberian Expedition. Meanwhile, the United States concluded the Ishii-Lansing Agreement that sought joint mediation with Japan and recognized Japanese interests in China. The Terauchi Masatake cabinet tried to strengthen Japan's ties to China by providing the Nishihara loans to the Duan Qirui administration unilaterally—instead of joint loans from the great powers—and furthermore, it concluded a Japan–China military agreement.

Japan and China both participated as victor nations at the Paris Peace Conference in 1919. China expected the return of the German concessions in Shandong and the abolition of the Twenty-One Demands. However, by tying up with Britain and France, Japan succeeded to the German concessions in Shandong. The anti-Japanese May Fourth movement occurred in Peking as a reaction to this, and the residence of a diplomat responsible for negotiations with Japan was attacked. This May Fourth Movement historically is highly acclaimed in China as an anti-Japanese movement, and the attack is even affirmed as a use of violence for the purpose of justice backed up by nationalism. The Republic of China delegation refused to sign the Versailles Peace Treaty at the Paris Peace Conference; it concluded a separate peace treaty with Germany in 1921. Also, as victor nations, Japan and China both became founding members of the League of Nations. Japan became one of the four permanent members of the Council; after 1920 China was a candidate for a nonpermanent member seat and was elected several times.

The 1910s was a period in which China's anti-Japanese sentiment worsened, and it was a turning point in which Japan bore the brunt of Chinese nationalism's opposition to aggressors. The context for this was Japan's attempts to get deeply involved in China without keeping in lockstep with the other great powers. In this period, movements to boycott Japanese-made products occurred frequently and propaganda materials advocating against Japan were widely disseminated in society. In fact, the first history textbook issue that arose between Japan and China happened in the 1910s. In this incident, it was the Japanese side that protested that a Chinese textbook (in actuality, a supplementary reader) was anti-Japanese. After that, the Japanese started to criticize Chinese textbooks as being anti-Japanese (Kawashima 2010).

"Washington System" and Japan–China relations

The Washington Conference was held from 1921 to 1922 for the purpose of adjusting concessions in China and the Pacific left unresolved by the Paris Peace Conference, and to adjust and reduce naval forces. The conference was also linked to the issue of the continuation of the Anglo-Japanese Alliance, which was set to end in 1921. At the conference, the Nine-Power Treaty concerning China, the Four-Power Treaty concerning the Pacific, and the Five-Power Treaty concerning naval forces were concluded. This is said to be the start of cooperative relations between Japan, Britain, and the United States, primarily. The existence of this Washington System of cooperation is understood to have restrained antagonism between the three countries. There are many who believe that the slide to war finally happened because this antagonism intensified when this cooperation broke down owing to events such as Japan's Shandong Expedition and the Manchurian (Mukden) Incident in 1931.

Yet, this "Washington System" framework did not include the Soviet Union, Germany, or China's government in Guangzhou, which had succeeded in conquering the government in Peking with the Northern Expedition. The Chinese government in Peking, which had signed the Nine-Power Treaty, had sought to hold an assembly on the tariffs that were indispensable to its support and continuation. But French opposition delayed the assembly, the Peking government fell into a financial crisis, and recovering tariff autonomy became a task for the next government of China.

Meanwhile, the goal of the diplomacy of Shidehara Kijuro, the foreign minister in the Kenseikai-Minseito cabinet who shouldered Japanese diplomacy in the first half of the 1920s, was to maintain Japan's South Manchurian concessions and expand its economic interests in China based on cooperation with the United States and Britain. Moreover, "Shidehara diplomacy," as it was designated, also sought conciliation between Japan and China through cultural projects with China. However, there were active anti-Japanese boycott movements as well as movements seeking the return of the Kwantung leasehold territory, which was scheduled for reversion in 1923 under the original 25-year lease period. These movements stopped temporarily around the time of the Great Kanto Earthquake in Japan. But anti-foreign movements grew active once again, sometimes coupled with activities of the Chinese Communist Party (CCP,[3] established in 1921), after 1924, the year the Nationalist Party of China (established in 1919; hereafter, Kuomintang [KMT]) held its First National Party Congress in Guangzhou. The May Thirtieth Movement that occurred in Shanghai in 1925 evolved into a broad anti–British, anti–imperialism, and national sovereignty restoration movement to recover lost territory and concessions. This is considered the exemplary movement for Chinese nationalism. The KMT, while backing this movement, deployed the Chinese National Revolutionary Army on the Northern Expedition; under pressure to renounce its concessions, Britain returned some of them to China.

BOX 0.3 GREAT KANTO EARTHQUAKE AND JAPAN–CHINA RELATIONS

Japan's Great Kanto Earthquake of September 1, 1923 was widely reported in China, too, as Chinese evacuees sent back vivid news reports. Anti-Japanese movements and boycotts of Japanese products were actively occurring in 1923, the period when the Kwantung leasehold territory was to be returned, but they were resolved before summer. The great disaster that befell Japan completely changed the anti-Japanese mood up to that point in China, and generated an attitude to assist Japan. Central political and business communities as well as various local groups carried out fund drives for Japan; for instance, Canton intellectuals sent Chinese books for the rebuilding of the Tokyo Imperial University library, which had burned down. However, this attitude to assist Japan gradually lost steam, owing in part to the revelation that hundreds of Chinese laborers in Japan were massacred at the time of the earthquake, and Wang Xitian, the man who set out to investigate this massacre, was also killed.

Many of the Chinese laborers murdered after the earthquake were peasant farmers from the area around Wenzhou, Zhejiang Province who went to Japan to earn money to send home since they were unable to earn a living at home because of natural disasters. It is not clear if they were murdered by a vigilante band because of an issue related to keeping the peace (as were many ethnic Koreans), or if it was a confrontation with Japanese laborers over the daily struggle for jobs. Whichever it may have been, over 400 were murdered in the Ojima neighborhood of Tokyo's Koto Ward as well as in Ashigara, Kanagawa; Wang Xitian, a member of a mutual aid society for overseas Chinese in Japan who was out investigating the massacre, was murdered by the police.

This incident once again caused anti-Japanese sentiment in China to worsen and China dispatched an investigation team to Japan. Although the Japanese side recognized the fact of the murders, it steadfastly maintained that it was an unforeseen accident and refused to pay any indemnity. This event became an unresolved case, in effect, along with other cases in which the Japanese side sought reparations from China. Instead of being an opportunity to improve Japan–China relations that had deteriorated, the disaster ended by becoming a source for future troubles.

The Immigration Act of 1924, which excluded Japanese immigration to the United States, became a bilateral issue in the 1920s, and Japan's anti-American sentiment grew. Chinese immigration to the United States was restricted originally by an 1882 immigration law, which gave rise to China's anti-American movement at the start of the twentieth century. Under the 1924 Act, immigrants from Japan and China received the same treatment; being treated the same as Chinese rankled many in Japan.

Greater Asianism Lecture and Shandong Expeditions

And so, Japan–China relations in the 1920s were already in a severe state of affairs. On his way to Peking, Sun Yat-sen gave what is known as his Greater Asianism Lecture in Kobe, explaining a partnership of China–Japan (and the USSR) against the great powers. However, because Sun extolled Japan's victory in the Russo-Japanese War, the content of his speech was later made a basis for Japan's advance into Asia (Chin and Yasui 1989).

Japan–China relations encountered new developments in the second half of the 1920s. The Seiyukai took power in Japan, replacing the Minseito administration that had restrained the use of military power in China up to that point. When the National Revolutionary Army, headed by Chiang Kai-shek, went north from Guangzhou to topple the Peking government in 1926 and called for the recovery of national sovereignty from the great powers (Northern Expedition), the cabinet of Tanaka Giichi of the Seiyukai carried out the first Shandong Expedition in May 1927 (Showa 2) and decided on a policy to secure the South Manchuria concessions by holding the Far East Conference in June. The Tanaka cabinet deployed troops to Shandong twice in 1928 and clashed with the KMT government (Jinan Incident). The Japanese consulate in Nanking (Nanjing) in 1927 and Japanese nationals in Jinan, Shandong in 1928 were exposed to danger in the course of the National Revolutionary Army's Northern Expedition, and Japanese sentiment toward China worsened. On the Chinese side, too, Japan–China relations hit rough straits in terms of the political and diplomatic aspects, as suggested by Chiang Kai-shek starting to mark "vindicate one's honor" every day in his diary concerning the Japanese intervention. China's nationalism movement also viewed Japan—and not Britain—as the representative imperialist country.

Furthermore, the "Tanaka Memorial," said to be what Tanaka Giichi submitted to the Emperor at the time he formulated his China policy, is a forgery and does not exist. However, it is a historical fact that private Chinese groups treat the memorial as if it were real in order to criticize Japan and, in turn, the government came to use the text for propaganda (Hattori 2010).

With Peking under its control, the Nationalist government in Nanking ended the Northern Expedition in 1928. After Japan's Kwantung Army blew up a train and killed Zhang Zuolin, who had left Peking to return to Fengtian, his son, Zhang Xueliang, fell in behind Chiang Kai-shek and the Nanking government became a unified administration that included the Northeast region. The great powers recognized the Nationalist government in Nanking and its right to tariff autonomy. Japan was slower than the other great powers, recognizing the Nationalist government in 1929 and its tariff autonomy in 1930. However, it did not move its legation to Nanking because the legation in Peking was in an area where stationing the Japanese army was permitted, but in Nanking it was not.

Great Depression and Asia's economies

Although a confrontational state of affairs arose in the political and diplomatic aspects of Japan–China relations in the 1920s, Japan–China economic and human relations advanced rapidly, as seen in the development of *"zaikabo"*—the cotton spinning industry in China with Japanese capital—and the inauguration of the Nagasaki-Shanghai sea route.

The Great Depression began in 1929 in the United States, which was replacing Britain as the center for global finance. However, the Hamaguchi Osachi cabinet lifted the ban on the export of gold at the start of 1930. The subsequent outflow of gold and ensuing financial panic were accompanied by deflationary pressures that were an enormous blow to the Japanese economy (Showa Depression). Raw silk thread and silk, the leading Japanese exports to the United States before the panic, took a huge hit, but exports of cotton yarn and cotton textiles to Asia increased, and, at the same time, trade with Manchuria and imports of machinery and metals from the United States grew. As a result, Japan's industries began to take shape: the heavy and chemical industries, dependent on machinery from the United States and raw materials from Asia; and light industry, dependent on Asian markets and competing with British and Indian products.

The Chinese economy also felt the impact of the global financial panic. The notable problem faced by China, on the silver standard, was the huge outflow of silver abroad caused by the advanced countries abandoning the gold standard. Eventually, China's finances settled down when, with the help of Britain and the United States in the mid-1930s, it reformed its currency and issued a paper currency based on the silver standard that became the legal tender.

3 The age of war

From the Manchurian Incident to the Second Sino-Japanese War

The level of tension in Japan–China relations continued to rise as the 1930s dawned. The Manchurian (Mukden) Incident broke out suddenly on September 18, 1931. The Kwantung Army, which was behind the railway bombing incident at Liutiaohu, claimed the Chinese caused it and in short order took control of all Manchurian land along the rail line. Zhang Zuolin's son, Zhang Xueliang, was away from Fengtian at the time in order to maintain the peace in the countryside. Zhang and KMT leader Chiang Kai-shek took the policy of *Ānnèi Rǎngwài* (pacify internal disorder before resisting foreign aggression): they lodged protests against Japan on the diplomatic front, appealing that Japan had violated the Nine-Power Treaty and the Covenant of the League of Nations, at the same time they avoided all-out conflict with the Japanese military. On the other hand, the KMT integrated the regional military forces in China's interior, and advanced preparations for resistance against Japan while engaging in a war to seek out and destroy the CCP.

The Lytton Commission was organized at the League of Nations on the basis of the Chinese side's suit and was dispatched to the Far East. The Commission visited China and Japan and both countries submitted materials that became the basis of their claims. The Lytton Report that the commission drew up, in addition to recognizing China's sovereignty over Manchuria and acknowledging Japan's special interests there, proposed placing Manchuria under international control. The Japanese government did not accept the contents of the report, since it repudiated Manchukuo, which had been founded in 1932, and Japan withdrew from the League of Nations in 1933. Meanwhile, the Republic of China, which had been actively receiving the League's assistance since before the Manchurian Incident in such aspects as public health, education, and economics, maintained its close partnership.

Quite a few initiatives for peace between Japan and China were put forward after the Tanggu Truce of 1933. In particular, the diplomacy advanced by Foreign Minister Hirota Koki—notwithstanding the Amo statement, called the "East Asian Monroe Doctrine"—generally followed a conciliatory policy to avoid war, and raised the status of the Japanese legation in China to an embassy. Yet, he dashed the hopes of the Chinese by bringing up "Hirota's Three Principles" at the 1935 Japan–China peace talks. In this period of Hirota diplomacy, Japan strengthened its advance into northern China bordering Manchuria and reinforced its Northern China Expeditionary Army.

In 1936, Chiang Kai-shek, who was intensifying pressure on regional military powers at the same time as undertaking a search-and-destroy war against the CCP, was arrested in Xi'an by Zhang Xueliang, who had cooperative relations with the CCP (Xi'an incident). Chiang was eventually released, but this incident is considered to be the catalyst in the formation of the united front by the KMT and CCP against Japan. Even today, China takes a view of history that praises the KMT's and Chiang's anti-Japanese posture after the Xi'an incident.

A skirmish broke out, triggered by a shooting incident in the environs of Lugouqiao on the outskirts of Peking on July 7, 1937 (the Marco Polo Bridge Incident). Neither the Japanese nor Chinese thought at the time that this incident would become the start of the Second Sino-Japanese War. Yet there was a series of small incidents in northern China after this, and tensions grew, turning into an all-out war with the Second Shanghai Incident on August 13.

There are two views on the course of events from the Manchurian incident to the Second Sino-Japanese War: (1) the post-Manchurian incident efforts groping towards peace failed, resulting in war; or (2) war was inevitable, so both sides were postponing its start but tensions kept rising. Moreover, some seek the cause leading up to war in the Japanese military's reckless actions that the government affirmed after the fact. Yet one cannot overlook such aspects as the radical news reporting by the various Japanese media organizations and the public's indignation. Although under wartime controls, there was censorship and control of public opinion and media organizations, there was also aspects of the media and the public that supported the military in the stages before the start of the war.

After the Second Shanghai Incident on August 13, international public opinion initially leaned toward Japan because the Chinese military shelled the wrong targets, causing casualties among the many foreigners in the jointly held concessions. But, the situation changed when the Japanese army pushed ahead with the Battle of Shanghai in order to march on Nanking. Elite troops of the Chinese army who had been trained by commissioned German officers were inserted into the Battle of Shanghai, forcing the Japanese army into a hard fight. Yet, after the amphibious landings at Hangzhou Bay and other maneuvers, the Japanese army marched on Nanking, the Republic of China's capital. Breaching the city's fortified walls, the Japanese army entered Nanking on December 13, and carried out what is called the Nanking Massacre, and many noncombatants and prisoners of war were killed. This was picked up by international media organizations and Japan started being criticized internationally. Afterwards in China, this incident came to symbolize Japanese aggression in China and the brutality of the Japanese army.

Mass mobilization and occupation rule

At first, neither Japan nor China made a declaration of war in the Second Sino-Japanese War. One reason was to avoid the application of U.S. Neutrality Acts banning the trade of war materiel with belligerent nations. Japan, which officially was not at war with China, established local administrations made up of Chinese in its occupied territories (puppet governments).

The Republic of China government that had been in Nanking left the city before it was occupied by Japan, moving its base to Chungking (Chongqing) in the interior of Szechuan (Sichuan) Province. Sichuan Province was chosen not only because it was well-situated to receive foreign countries' assistance via Southeast Asia, it was also a model province directly controlled by the KMT (Iechika 2012). The Nationalist government in Chungking continued the war of resistance, which became protracted. Each country adopted a general mobilization system and began mobilizing every aspect of the daily lives of their people for war regardless of gender or age, as can be seen from Japan's National Mobilization Law and National Service Draft Ordinance. Japan further strengthened its control over its colonies on the Korean peninsula and Taiwan, and it implemented an imperialization policy to assimilate the people still more with Japan. The Chungking government declared war on Japan on December 9, 1941—after the Japanese attack on Pearl Harbor (mentioned later)—but Japan did not admit to being "at war with China" until it accepted the Potsdam Declaration.

Japan and China held various peace talks after the Nationalist government moved to Chungking, but in January 1938, Japan issued the first Konoe statement saying that it "thereafter would not deal with the KMT," recalled its ambassador, and cut formal diplomatic channels with the Chungking government. Japan indirectly ruled its occupied territory in China through collaborationist administrations and utilized local resources and materiel for the Japanese army's prosecution of the war. By means of the second Konoe statement, Japan successfully helped Wang

Jingwei (born Wang Zhaoming) to escape from Chungking. After it had Wang, a central figure in the KMT on par with Chiang Kai-shek, organize a Nationalist government in Nanking, Japan folded all of its collaborationist governments in mainland China into it, and recognized it as the Government of the Republic of China. Japan, Manchukuo, and Wang's regime were called the Japan–Manchuria–China bloc and the New Order in East Asia before finally being positioned as the foundation for the Greater East Asian Co-Prosperity Sphere. Even today in China, Japan's collaborationist governments are called "pseudo" governments and those involved with them are criticized as *hanjin*—traitors to their race.

Mainland China became a place where many political bodies ruled—the Nationalist government in Chungking, the CCP, the Japanese Army, as well as Japan's collaborationist governments—all waging a vigorous propaganda war using radio and various reporting media (Kishi et al. 2006). For instance, before 1937 and the outbreak of the Second Sino-Japanese War, there was a "Japan research" boom centered in Shanghai, and many journals related to Japan were published, but after the war started, views critical of Japanese aggression were circulated by the Chinese side. Meanwhile, Japan strengthened its propaganda in its occupied territory on the Chinese mainland and revised school textbooks, deleting portions that criticized Japan.

From Second Sino-Japanese War to world war

The situation transitioned quite significantly, from the Manchurian Incident into the Second Sino-Japanese War, and then into World War II. Yet, it was not evident that, whether at its start or even when war broke out in Europe in 1939, the Second Sino-Japanese War would wind up becoming part of a world war, with the Axis Powers (Japan–Germany–Italy) facing off against the Allied Powers (the United States, Britain, China [and later, the Soviet Union]). The Tripartite Pact between Japan, Germany, and Italy was concluded in 1937, yet it was not immediately linked to the Second Sino-Japanese War. A cooperative relationship existed between China and Germany; Japan–China peace efforts were made through Germany. In 1939, the Japanese army commenced large-scale aerial bombing of Chungking, Chiang Kai-shek's base, and Chiang was expecting Japan to start a war with either the United States and Britain or with the USSR. That year, the Nomonhan incident occurred: the Soviet army clashed with the Japanese Kwantung Army and Manchukuo's army in the border between Manchuria and Mongolia, and the Japanese side was defeated. However, instead of war, they concluded the Japan–Soviet Neutrality Pact in April 1941.

World War II began in September 1939 with Germany's invasion of Poland. But, it was not as if that tied the wars in Europe and East Asia together right away. Japan's confrontation with the United States and Britain over China and Manchuria did intensify. In 1939, America announced its withdrawal from the Treaty of Commerce and Navigation between Japan and the United States (taking effect in 1940) and implemented economic sanctions against Japan with Britain, China, and the Dutch—commonly called the "ABCD encirclement" in Japan. Chiang Kai-shek's administration in Chungking received foreign assistance via the Burma Road from Hanoi in French Indochina to Yunnan. Seeking to interdict this aid, Japan occupied northern and southern French Indochina in 1940 and 1941. At the time, France was under German control, yet because the Japanese army's movements were actions hostile to Britain and *France Libre*, the links between the wars in Europe and in East Asia were growing stronger.

Japan embarked on war on December 8, 1941, attacking Pearl Harbor in Hawaii (December 7, local time) and the British-ruled Malayan Peninsula and declaring war against the United States and Britain. The Chungking government, too, declared war on Japan on December 9. This is where the war in Europe was tied to the Second Sino-Japanese War, truly making it a "world war."

The tides of war and postwar structure

Because Japan started war against the United States and Britain, the Republic of China government in Chungking, which had joined the Allied camp with the United States and Britain, signed the Declaration by United Nations in January 1942 and came to be treated as one of the Big Four Allied powers. The Chinese war front, comprising China, Vietnam, and Thailand, then became the China theater, one of the theaters of war established globally, and Chiang Kai-shek was appointed as Supreme Allied Commander of the China theater. In this way, the Second Sino-Japanese War became part of the World War. U.S. President Franklin D. Roosevelt—who strongly emphasized the front against Japan so as to join the war on the basis of the Japanese attack on Pearl Harbor as well as China's geographical position on that front—made Joseph Stilwell Chief of Staff of the China theater to reinvigorate support to Chiang. Before long, an air route from India's Assam region replaced the Burma Road as the route to provide Chiang aid.

At the start of 1942, Japan defeated the British army and occupied Singapore, making the city-state its southern base (Syonan-to). The Japanese army massacred the Chinese diaspora in every region of Southeast Asia, becoming a source of troubles after the war. Defeated at the Battle of Midway in June 1942, Japan lost its primary carrier battle group. The United States, together with Australia, moved northward from the South Pacific to New Guinea and the Philippines, adopting a strategy of pressuring Japan. U.S. forces occupied the island of Saipan in July 1944, thereby enabling direct air raids on Japan's capital region. With the war at a virtual standstill on the Chinese mainland, the Japanese army, the Nationalist army, and CCP guerrilla forces everywhere became embroiled in a free-for-all. In 1944, Japan executed Operation Ichi-go, a "cross-through strategy" running north to south through the heart of mainland China. Although it was able to strike a blow against the Chinese side, Japan was unable to change the overall battle situation.

At the end of 1942, China began preparations to seek reparations from Japan. The Cairo Conference was held in 1943 at Roosevelt's invitation, with British Prime Minister Winston Churchill and Chiang Kai-shek. Chiang incurred British

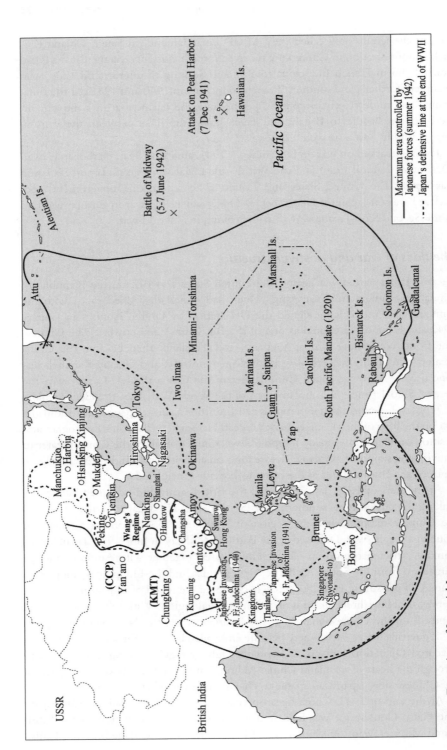

Map 0.2 Expansion of Imperial Japan.

Source: Adapted by Mr. Ienaga Masaki from Kawashima, Hattori, eds. 2007, Map 3, p.113.

displeasure by dropping by India and showing understanding for its independence movement. But, with Roosevelt's intercession, the conference results were released as the Cairo Declaration. The conference touched on such topics as the disarmament of Japan, the prosecution of war criminals and those affiliated with its "puppet" regimes, and reparations for war damages; the issue of the Emperor system was left up to a decision by the Japanese people. Further, the declaration stated:

> Japan shall be stripped of all the islands in the Pacific which she has seized or occupied since the beginning of the first World War in 1914, and that all the territories Japan has stolen from the Chinese, such as Manchuria, Formosa, and The Pescadores, shall be restored to the Republic of China.

It also mentioned the independence of Korea. The Cairo Declaration is not a signed document; it does not hold sufficient validity as a diplomatic document. Yet, because its essence was incorporated into the Potsdam Declaration and subsequent peace treaties, it has been ranked among the important documents denoting the East Asian postwar structure.

As one of the Big Four Allied powers, China also occupied an important role in establishing the allied nations as a postwar peacetime organization, that is, the United Nations (UN). It influenced the enactment of the Charter and associated rules and regulations, and it took a seat as a permanent member of the UN Security Council (UNSC) established in October 1945.

However, China's strategic position fell once the United States occupied the Philippines, Guam, and Saipan, making direct air raids against Japan possible. China's standing in the Big Four also declined relatively because of discord between Stilwell and Chiang as well as American distrust of the KMT; China was excluded as cooperation increased between the United States, Britain, and the Soviet Union. And then, with the Soviet Union entering the war against Japan in August 1945, the USSR occupied Manchuria, which was supposed to be China's according to the Yalta Conference between the United States, Britain, and the USSR.

Japan decided to accept the Potsdam Declaration, issued by the United States, Britain, China, and the USSR, on August 14, 1945 and signed the instrument of surrender on September 2. The formal ceremony of surrender of Japanese forces in the China theater took place in Nanking on September 9. Regarding Taiwan, Japan's control ended October 25, and the Republic of China, as a representative of the Allied nations, succeeded to its administration. But of the territory the Republic of China claimed in its constitution, Soviet influence increased in Manchuria and Xinjiang, and China ended up agreeing to the Sino–Soviet Treaty of Friendship and Alliance, signed August 14, that set the rules of reversion for Manchuria as well as settled the disposition of Outer Mongolia by plebiscite of the Outer Mongolian people.

Japan had not declared war against China, but its acceptance of the Potsdam Declaration meant that it also surrendered to China. Yet, perhaps because of the nuclear bombs dropped on Hiroshima and Nagasaki, Japanese society remembers the significance of surrender to the United States more strongly than defeat to China.

4 Japan's defeat and restructuring East Asian international relations

Japan's defeat

A defeated Japan came under occupation rule by the Allied nations. China, being one of the important Allied nations, also joined the occupation. Not just a founding country of the Far Eastern Commission and the Allied Council for Japan, it also established a Republic of China delegation in Japan and sent a judge to the International Military Tribunal for the Far East (Tokyo Trials) to judge Class A "crimes against peace." At the trials that opened on May 3, 1946, the Chinese judge relentlessly pursued responsibility for war crimes. All 25 defendants were found guilty, except for the two who died of illness before the trial and one against whom charges were dropped; seven, including Tojo Hideki, received the death sentence.

In addition, regional trials were held for officers and enlisted men linked to atrocities during wartime (Class B and C war crimes); such trials were held at ten locations in China. Those linked to the Nanking Massacre were prosecuted there, and yet, there were also cases in which the crimes were reduced for Japanese soldiers who cooperated with the KMT in the Chinese Civil War. Besides this, the Japanese who had been imprisoned when Soviet forces invaded Manchuria were extradited from the Soviet Union to the People's Republic of China after its founding in 1949 and were prosecuted in Shenyang and Taiyuan in 1956.

In a radio broadcast to his people at the end of the war, the Republic of China's Chiang Kai-shek declared victory while proposing a policy of magnanimity "to repay violence with virtue," in the sense of quietly repatriating the Japanese in China without exacting revenge. There were two aims behind this policy: to rid the continent of the Japanese army, still the largest military force in mainland China at the time of Japan's defeat; and (it was Chiang's intention) to make use of Japanese soldiers and technicians, responding to necessity. Chiang also advocated the dichotomy of militarists and the people—in other words, an argument that put the onus for the war on a small group of militarists while holding the people blameless. Nevertheless, he advanced preparations for demanding reparations. In fact, it was after the 1950s, when reparations demands had already been waived, that the waiver was included in the "repay violence with virtue" policy.

At the time, it was decided that Japan would provide reparations in kind to China. The Pauley mission dispatched by U.S. President Harry S. Truman had decided that half of the industrial machinery production capacity, all facilities related to aircraft production and naval shipyards, and iron and steel production capacity should be removed from Japan and provided to China. Part of this plan was implemented. Also, weapons and other items left behind, including the navy's warships, were transferred to the Republic of China as reparations.

In addition, the deployment of two divisions from China to occupy the Nagoya region was studied but not implemented; China's request to General Douglas MacArthur to jointly rule Okinawa was denied. As it sought to inhibit Japan's remilitarization and resurgence as a major (economic) power, China tried to request Japanese reparations, being a country that had suffered great damage from Japanese aggression.

There was also Chinese representation on the Far Eastern Commission, which was set up in the United States; this representative played a definite role in the process of creating the Constitution of Japan. For instance, the Chinese representative raised doubts about the Ashida amendment that opened the path to authorizing the maintaining of self-defense military power, had the civilian clause (Article 66 Clause 2) inserted into the draft, and joined the USSR representative to debate the matter. Also, it is thought that China rarely took the initiative in the decision-making process for specific occupation policies. Yet, China consistently insisted that the appellation "Shina" carried a sense of contempt for China and should be removed from official documents and publications. In fact, the word fell out of use in official documents and was censored or deleted from publications.

In occupied Japan, citizens of the Allied nations including China were not subject to the Imperial Constitution of Japan and enjoyed extraterritoriality. However, from Japan's standpoint, the people of Taiwan were still subject to this constitution, for once Japan had renounced the territory, they had become residents of a land with an undetermined affiliation. But, the Chinese side objected, and so, provided they registered at the Chinese representative office in Tokyo, people of Taiwanese descent also came to enjoy special rights such as extraterritoriality.

Chinese Civil War

At the conclusion of the war against Japan, the KMT's true strength greatly exceeded the CCP's. The start of 1948, it is said, was when the CCP sensed that it had become a national political power; until then, it was nothing more than a regional power setting up bases in the regions. Right after winning the Anti-Japanese War, Mao Zedong flew to Chungking from Yan'an, the CCP base, met repeatedly with Chiang Kai-shek, and issued the so-called "Double Tenth Agreement" (Summary of Conversations Between the Representatives of the KMT and CCP) on October 10, 1945. In the agreement, the two sides shared a fundamental sense of direction on the basic policies for peacefully founding the country, democratizing politics, and opening a national people's assembly. The disposition of Manchuria after the one-year Soviet occupation, however, became a point of contention. The USSR and the CCP schemed of turning Manchuria into a CCP base, but the KMT sought to return Manchuria to its own hands. U.S. special envoy George C. Marshall tried but failed to reconcile the KMT and CCP; they each released statements attacking the other side in August 1946, a year after winning the war.

The Nationalist government at the time was criticized at home and abroad as being authoritarian, corrupt, and contrary to "democracy" and "liberty." So in

November 1945, it held a national assembly to enact a constitution with the aim of transitioning from "political tutelage" of the KMT guiding national politics to "constitutional rule," implementing constitutional politics. But, the CCP did not take part. (The constitution was promulgated January 1, 1947 and took effect December 25.) The KMT had sought to show its own initiative toward "democracy" and "liberty" by enacting constitutional rule, but it failed. In 1948, in fact, it declared martial law and suspended constitutional rule. Also, through the enactment of constitutional rule, the designation "Nationalist government" was no longer used officially.

Though the KMT army occupied Yan'an in March 1947, the CCP recaptured it in April 1948; the CCP army also overwhelmed the KMT army in Manchuria in September, and the war situation gradually leaned in favor of the CCP. The KMT's corruption and its divergence from the basic concepts of "democracy" and "liberty" increasingly became a problem in the United States, which had been providing the KMT with enormous sums of assistance, hoping for a united and democratic China; arms assistance was blocked and economic assistance became the focus. Also, the priority of economic assistance to China fell with the 1947 Truman Doctrine, which emphasized assistance to Western bloc countries in Europe.

Changes in occupation policy of Japan

U.S. policy for Japan's occupation began changing in 1947–48, in the context of "containment" in Europe and changes in the Chinese situation. Already, the Supreme Commander for the Allied Powers (SCAP, generally referred to in Japan as the GHQ) had issued an order stopping the general strike of February 1, 1947, and that summer it tacked toward lifting the economic embargo and authorizing foreign trade, hoping to revive Japan's economy. Consequently, Japan–China trade was also restarted, provoking a large backlash within China.

U.S. Secretary of the Army Kenneth Royall announced a change of policy for Japan's occupation in San Francisco in January 1948 and spoke of moving from the demilitarization and democratization stage to the economic revival stage. Japan had received GARIOA funds (Government Aid and Relief in Occupied Areas) in 1946 and received EROA funds (Economic Rehabilitation in Occupied Areas) in 1949. Meanwhile, the authorities sought to stabilize the economy by implementing a nine-point economic stabilization plan at the end of 1948 and the Dodge Line after March 1949, and then taking contractionary financial and monetary policies. Demands for Japanese reparations stopped during this time, perhaps owing to U.S. involvement. China had already received naval warships and industrial facilities from Japan as reparations in kind, and so it temporarily ceased demanding reparations. George Kennan, the designer of the policy of containment, played a large role in this policy change. Kennan thought that the United States should rehabilitate Japan politically and economically so that it held sufficient industrial power as a member of the free world.

The Chinese government could hardly have welcomed this policy change; it had been planning to seek reparations from Japan as the country that had suffered the most damage. But in fact, reparations under the Pauley plan had already been discontinued.

Kuomintang's defeat and founding of the People's Republic of China

In 1949, Chiang Kai-shek resigned and was succeeded by Li Zongren, who groped for peace with the CCP but failed. The United States released a "China White Paper" in August that attributed the KMT's gross incompetence as the primary cause for its defeat. U.S. distrust of the KMT reduced Chinese influence in the issues concerning peace with Japan.

The KMT's loss in the civil war became decisive in 1949. The first plenary session of the Chinese People's Political Consultative Conference (CPPCC) was held in September, with the CCP playing a central role. The CPPCC adopted the Common Program, specifying the government's structure as socialist and making Beijing the capital, and elected Mao Zedong chairman of the CPPCC's national committee. The People's Republic of China (PRC) was founded on October 1 and was recognized successively by the Soviet Union and Eastern European countries. Thus, two Chinese governments were created—the PRC government and the Republic of China (ROC) government—and countries around the world were confronted with the issue of which China to recognize, a situation that remains unchanged today.

The ROC government moved from Chengdu to Taipei in December 1949. The "228 Incident" occurred in Taiwan on February 28, 1947, causing discord to grow between the KMT and the Taiwanese people. However, the KMT government enacted the Temporary Provisions Effective During the Period of Communist Rebellion in 1948 and proclaimed martial law again in 1949. These two actions placed Taiwan under long-term martial law, constrained the political participation of the Taiwanese people, and concentrated power in President Chiang Kai-shek by not placing term limits on the president and not holding elections for members of the Legislative Yuan, the parliament. The provisions were maintained until 1991, and the KMT government exercised authoritarian politics under the slogan of "recover the mainland."

At that stage, the United States had not yet decided to defend the ROC government that had moved to Taiwan or the Taiwan Strait, and it was groping about to maintain existing relations with the CCP. This was apparent in the Acheson Line in early 1950. Despite calls for an early return of occupied Japan to international society, it was difficult to achieve. One would have to await the outbreak of the Korean War in June 1950 for the framework for Japan–China relations in East Asia to be decided and for the disposition in the Taiwan Strait to be set.

Notes

1 *Sibashi Lüe* (*Summary of Eighteen Histories*) is a compendium of 18 Chinese histories for children. *Zizhi Tongjian* (*Comprehensive Mirror for Aid in Governance*) is an epic history of China prior to the Song Dynasty (960–1279). *Nanga* is (typically monochrome land-scape) painting in the China's Southern School style (*nanzonghua*).
2 In Japanese, "The Treaty Exchanging Karafuto and Chishima."
3 Though generally referred to as the Chinese Communist Party (CCP) in the English-speaking world, the People's Republic refers to it as the Communist Party of China (CPC).

Cited and referenced materials

Chiba Isao, 2008, *Kyugaiko no keisei* [The Configuration of the Old Diplomacy], Keiso Shobo.

Chin Tokujin, Yasui Sankichi, eds., 1989, *Sombun, "koen daiajiashugi" shiryoshu* [Sun Yat-sen: Collection of Documents from the "Pan-Asianism Lecture"], Horitsu Bunka Sha.

Cho Iyu [Zhang Weixiong], 1999, *Bunjingaikokan no meiji nihon* [The Meiji Japan of the Literati Diplomats], Kashiwa Shobo.

Hattori Ryuji, 2010, *Nitchu rekishi ninshiki* [The Perception of History in Japan and China], University of Tokyo Press.

Iechika Ryoko, 2012, *Shokaiseki no gaikoseisaku to nitchusenso* [Chiang Kai-shek's Diplomatic Strategy and the (Second) Sino-Japanese War], Iwanami Shoten.

Kawashima Shin, 2010, "Nitchu gaikokenan toshiteno kyokashomonda [The Textbook Issue as a Pending Issue for Japan–China Relations]," in Namiki Yorihisa, Osato Hiroaki, Sunayama Yukio, eds., *Kindaichugoku, kyokasho to nihon* [Early Modern China, Text-books, and Japan], Kenbun Publishing.

Kawashima Shin, Hattori Ryuji, eds., 2007, *Higashiajia kokusai seijishi* [The History of East Asian International Politics], University of Nagoya Press.

Kishi Toshihiko, Kawashima Shin, Son An Suk, eds., 2006, *Senso, rajio, kioku* [War–Radio–Memory], Bensei Publishing.

Mitani Hiroshi, Namiki Yorihisa, Tsukiashi Tatsuhiko, eds., 2009, *Otona no tameno kingen-daishi: 19 seikihen* [Early Modern/Modern History for Adults: The 19th Century], University of Tokyo Press.

Okamoto Takashi, 2004, *Zokkoku to jishu no aida* [Between Tributary and an Independent State], University of Nagoya Press.

Okamoto Takashi, Kawashima Shin, eds., 2009, *Chugoku kindaigaiko no taido* [The Quicken-ing of China's Early Modern Diplomacy], University of Tokyo Press.

Osato Hiroaki, Son An Suk, The Society of Humanities at Kanagawa University, eds., 2002, *Chugokujin nihonryugakushi kenkyu no gendankai* [The Present Stage of Historical Research on Chinese Exchange Students in Japan], Ochanomizu Shobo.

Sakai Tetsuya, 2007, *Kindainihon no kokusaichitsujo ron* [Early Modern Japan and the Theory of International Order], Iwanami Shoten.

Tang Chi-hua, 2010, *Bei "Feichu Bupingdeng Tiaoyue" Zhebi de Beiyang Xiuyueshi (1912–1928)* [Treaty Revision Policy of the Beijing Government, 1912–1928: Out of the Shadow of the "Abrogation of Unequal Treaties"], Social Sciences Academic Press: China.

Tobe Ryoichi, 1999, *Nihon rikugun to chugoku* [The Japanese Army and China], Kodansha.

Yoshizawa Seiichiro, 2003, *Aikokushugi no sosei* [The Creation of Patriotism], Iwanami Shoten.

1

JAPAN–CHINA RELATIONS OF THE 1950s

Forming relations with the "two Chinas"

FIGURE 1.1 Signing the Peace Treaty between Japan and the Republic of China: Kawada Isao, Plenipotentiary of Japan (on right) and Yeh Kung-ch'ao, Plenipotentiary of the Republic of China (April 28, 1952, Taipei).

Source: ©The Mainichi Newspapers.

Japan–China relations of the 1950s developed as the Cold War/hot war in East Asia took shape. The Korean War in 1950 clarified U.S.–China confrontation. Also, Japan returned to international society as a member of the Western bloc. In 1952, Japan made peace and entered into diplomatic relations with the Republic of China in Taiwan, likewise in the Western bloc. The People's Republic of China strengthened its ties to the Soviet Union as a member of the Socialist bloc. Japan and China maintained economic relations at the private level. Postwar Japan's "Japan–China" relations started as a triangular relationship with the so-called "two Chinas."

1 "Two Chinas" and Japan regains independence

Early postwar map of East Asia

The end of World War II brought about major revisions to the map of East Asia. But it was in the mid-1950s after the Korean War that national borders were shaped roughly as they are today. These events also meant that the Cold War had spread to East Asia; it was in this region that the Cold War exhibited armed clashes and other "hot war" conditions. Japan rejoined international society as a member of the Western bloc and concluded the Japan–U.S. Security Treaty at the start of the 1950s. The United States also concluded security pacts with the Republic of China (Taiwan), the Republic of Korea (ROK or South Korea), the Philippines, and other countries, thereby constructing the "hub & spoke" alliance system. Except for Japan, which was then under democratic rule, the other countries listed were founded as anti-Communist authoritarian regimes and received U.S. economic and military aid. Within the Eastern bloc, countries such as China, the Democratic People's Republic of Korea (DPRK or North Korea), and North Vietnam undertook socialist construction on the economic and military fronts under the heavy influence of the Soviet Union and stood in opposition to the West.

From a global perspective, East-West confrontation underwent a relative moderation in the mid-1950s, even as small-scale conflict continued in East Asia in the Taiwan Strait and on the Korean Peninsula. This did not mean that there were no interactions whatsoever between the two blocs: each side carried out influence operations on the enemy camp's population to emphasize its own legitimacy and sought to expand economic ties. Yet relations generally were unstable (Shimotomai 2004). Moreover, there were instances of peoples being divided between the East and West blocs, as in Hong Kong and Macao (between the PRC and the ROC).

As well, the 1950s can be called the period when the patterns of international politics in modern East Asia were formed. This is the case for Japan–China relations, as Japan commenced its ties with the two Chinese governments, the Republic of China and the People's Republic of China. These relationships stood at the center of the overlap of complex international relations, including Japan–U.S.–PRC, Japan–PRC–ROC, and Japan–U.S.–USSR–PRC.

Founding of the People's Republic of China and continuation of the Chinese Civil War

The People's Republic of China was established in Beijing on October 1, 1949. Communist victory in the Chinese Civil War derived not just from the CCP's military superiority backed by Soviet support. The CCP also garnered popular support through propaganda efforts casting it as more ably embodying "democracy" and "liberty" and by attempts to break up vested interests, such as by proclaiming land reform and redistribution in agricultural villages. Thus, in the early construction of the country, the CCP was not a one-party dictatorship but a coalition government comprised of various democratic parties.

Around the time of the PRC's founding, the Nationalist government moved constantly throughout China's south and west, opposing the CCP. But by December, the Nationalists had shifted their base from Chengdu, Sichuan Province to Taipei, Taiwan. By representing the Allied Powers, the Nationalists had already claimed Taiwan from Japan, which had relinquished it after accepting the terms of the Potsdam Declaration. It is generally said that the Chinese Civil War ended on October 1, but the KMT clinched a victory in the Battle of Guningtou at Kinmen (Jinmen; widely known in English as Quemoy) Island, Fujian Province that began on October 25, 1949. Thereafter, the two sides fought for legitimacy, and the civil war continued until the early 1990s.

As a consequence of this political struggle between the Beijing and Taipei governments, every country in the world, at the moment it officially recognized China, confronted the issue of Chinese right of representation, that is, whether to view Beijing or Taipei as the sole legitimate government to represent China (Ishii 1985). Founded as a socialist country, the PRC was recognized by the USSR and the Eastern bloc, moreover gathering the support of African and Asian countries, such as India. Even in the Western bloc, Britain—from the viewpoint of maintaining its Hong Kong colony, which bordered on the PRC's Guangdong Province— recognized the PRC government in January 1950 and dispatched a chargé d'affaires *ad interim* to Beijing. It also maintained consular relations with Taiwan. Japan, too, would later be confronted with the issue of Chinese representation at the UN; at the time of the PRC's founding, it was not an independent nation, but under the occupation of the United States and the Allied nations. Nevertheless, efforts were made to maintain some sort of official relations with the Beijing government since there existed within Japanese society a strong sympathy for socialism and communism as well as deep-rooted economic expectations for China, with its enormous population.

In the meantime, the Sino-Soviet Treaty of Friendship, Alliance, and Mutual Assistance concluded in February 1950 between China and the USSR designated Japan as the hypothetical enemy and had the objective of "prevent[ing] a repetition of aggression or breach of the peace by Japan or any other state which might directly or indirectly join with Japan in acts of aggression." This, of course, had the United States in mind as the "other state which might … join with Japan."

BOX 1.1 RESTART OF POSTWAR HONG KONG AND HONG KONG INFORMATION

Though occupied by Japan with the outbreak of the Second Sino-Japanese War, Hong Kong was again ruled by Britain after the war. To maintain its Hong Kong colony, Britain recognized the People's Republic of China, which ruled the neighboring Guangdong Province, in 1950.

Because a socialist country was founded in China, capitalists in Shanghai and elsewhere on the mainland shifted their capital to Hong Kong, and artists and authors, intellectuals, and leading figures in the political and financial communities moved to Hong Kong to live. Hong Kong especially became a base of activity for various democratic parties during the Chinese Civil War and even after the PRC's founding.

Hong Kong, which had been Britain's trading base even before the war, seized a new opportunity for development with the influx of this kind of human and financial capital. There were also times when the control of the border between Hong Kong and China was relaxed and many Chinese immigrants from Guangdong and other parts flowed into Hong Kong. Hong Kong was also a seaport on China's southern hinterlands.

In terms of transportation, Hong Kong became a transit hub connecting the Eastern and Western blocs in East Asia, as there were no direct flights between the two blocs. This was also true for the antagonistic governments in Beijing and Taipei. Hong Kong became the front line for obtaining information on China, hidden behind the "bamboo curtain," because of the concentration of much human talent and capital owing to its strategic position in transportation. BBC Hong Kong had the role of monitoring Chinese domestic transmissions, in addition to its broadcasting function. Japan's Hong Kong Consulate-General, too, had an information collection function and Hong Kong information became important intelligence. As observable in its cinema, Hong Kong also became a base for propaganda from the West targeting the Chinese community, including the diaspora in Southeast Asia.

Postwar Hong Kong successfully developed as a financial center because of Shanghai capital and British investment, but this happened in the political and cultural context of it being a key node for both Eastern and Western blocs.

Furthermore, with the establishment of two Chinese governments, overseas Chinese in Japan found themselves pressured to choose the nationality of one or the other. Complicating the situation, there were some people born in Taiwan who chose PRC nationality.

Outbreak of the Korean War

On the Korean Peninsula, Japanese colonial rule ended on August 15, 1945, the Soviets advanced into the area north of the 38th parallel, and the Americans advanced into the south. The Democratic People's Republic of Korea, with Kim Il-sung as its leader, and the Republic of Korea, with Rhee Syngman as its leader, were founded in 1948.

And yet, the United States had not yet made the decision to prevent, even by the use of force, the liberation of Taiwan by the Chinese People's Liberation Army (PLA); around the time of the PRC's founding, the United States had a harsher view of the KMT administration. In other words, one could think that the United States would have accepted the CCP's liberation of Taiwan. The "defense perimeter" that Secretary of State Dean Acheson outlined in January 1950—the line connecting the Aleutian Islands, Japan, Okinawa under U.S. military administration, and the Philippines—was the defense perimeter for the United States, and the 38th parallel and Taiwan Strait were not mentioned in this "Acheson Line."

However, the Korean War broke out on June 25, 1950 when DPRK forces crossed the 38th parallel and went south. It is even said that Acheson's declared defense perimeter invited North Korean aggression. Yet, two days later, on June 27, President Truman issued a "Statement on the Situation in Korea," in which he said "the occupation of Formosa by Communist forces would be a direct threat to the security of the Pacific area and to the United States forces performing their lawful and necessary functions in that area." The United States dispatched the Seventh Fleet to the Taiwan Strait, effectively neutralizing it.

As for the war situation, North Korea was winning even after the UN forces, with U.S. forces playing the largest role, landed on the Korean peninsula. But the situation changed completely after MacArthur's Incheon landing, and North Korea lost its advantage. But, when UN forces reached the Yalu (Amnok) River at the end of October, the PRC sent the Chinese People's Volunteer Army into Korea to assist the DPRK army, which had become numerically inferior. The direct standoff between the United States and the People's Republic of China, beginning with the neutralization of the Taiwan Strait, clarified the boundaries of the Cold War in East Asia. One reason for China's entry into the war, it is thought, was its attempt to gain Soviet assistance for the liberation of Taiwan (Gyu 2007; Shu 2004).

In the course of the Korean War, Japan was tied ever firmer to America's Western bloc. U.S.-administered Okinawa and the Japanese main islands that based the U.S. military became front-line bases for American forces in the Korean War. At the same time, the Japanese economy, which had been in a slump owing to the Dodge Line (contractionary financial and monetary policies under the direction of Joseph Dodge), faced increased production for textiles, machinery, and metals and began to heat up from the special demand from the Korean War. Further, to fill the vacuum made by the movement of U.S. troops based in Japan to the war front, the Japanese Coast Guard was strengthened, a National Police Reserve was established, and de facto remilitarization had begun. The immediate postwar policies of demilitarization and restraining economic growth were revised (the so-called reverse course), and the National Police Reserve became the National Safety Forces in 1952.

With the Korean War, the Cold War had fully arrived in East Asia. Unlike the Cold War in Europe where nuclear weapons loomed in the background but no actual combat took place, the conditions in East Asia should be called a hot war, involving actual combat.

San Francisco Peace Conference

Peace with Japan was a matter of great interest, even for China, one of the Big Four allied powers. However, because of the developments of the Chinese Civil War and the Korean War that followed, there were difficulties actualizing the postwar structure that had been envisioned before the war ended, which could be called the Yalta system. The United States tried to advance peace with Japan through the Far Eastern Commission, composed of the Big Four (United States, Britain, Soviet Union, and China) as well as the Netherlands, Australia, New Zealand, France, the Philippines, and India. The Soviet Union, though, proposed making decisions through the Council of Foreign Ministers of the Big Four. Taking a pro-Soviet policy already, the PRC government supported the USSR proposal, at least until the Korean War. Of course, the Beijing government insisted that it be the one to represent China, not the Taipei government. Within the Western bloc, opinion was divided between the United States, which supported the Taipei government's participation in the peace talks, and Britain which supported the Beijing government's. On the issue of Taiwan's affiliation, too, Britain sought to clarify that it belonged to China, whereas the United States decided to leave the matter as it was expressed in Japan's renunciation. But John Foster Dulles, then a consultant to the U.S. State Department responsible for the Japan peace treaty issue, had talks with British Foreign Secretary Herbert Morrison in June 1951, and the United States and Britain decided not to invite either the Beijing or Taipei governments to the peace conference and to let Japan, itself, determine its relations with China (the recognition issue). PRC Foreign Minister Zhou Enlai protested this move on August 15, saying that it "was dividing the allied nations that fought against Japan and creating a new aggression bloc in the Far East."

In Japan, there were two opposing arguments: a separate peace, which prioritized peace with the countries in the Western bloc, and a comprehensive peace, which held that Japan must make peace with all the belligerent countries. The third Yoshida Shigeru cabinet chose the separate peace argument (Watanabe and Miyazato 1986).

The Peace Conference was held in San Francisco in September 1951, in the midst of the Korean War. Not only did the two governments of China and North and South Korea not attend, neither did India nor any other Asian country. Furthermore, the USSR and Eastern Europeans (Czechoslovakia and Poland) did attend but did not sign the treaty. Under Article 2 of the treaty, Japan renounced claims on Formosa (Taiwan), the Pescadores (Penghu) Islands, Spratly (Nansha)

Islands, and Paracel (Xisha) Islands. Regarding the reparations issue, Japan's obligations were discharged with Article 14(b), but several exception provisions were prepared. China reserved the right to seek reparations in Articles 10 and 14(a2). Forty-nine countries including Japan signed the treaty, and once it entered into force on April 28, 1952, Japan recovered its sovereignty and regained its independence.

BOX 1.2 SAN FRANCISCO PEACE TREATY AND OKINAWA, SENKAKU/DIAOYU ISLANDS

The United States, which was already exercising occupation rule, would assume the authority to govern Okinawa (the Ryukyu Islands and Daito Islands) under Article 3 of the San Francisco Peace Treaty and would end up administering Okinawa until 1972. The United States ruled by setting up a Ryukyu government in Okinawa. The Senkaku Islands were included within the governing area of this Ryukyu government—a point that the Japanese government makes a basis for Japanese sovereignty over the Senkaku Islands. At the time of the 1972 reversion of Okinawa, the authority to rule Okinawa reverted from the United States back to Japan, and the Senkaku Islands were also clearly included here. However, the Beijing government, following the Taipei government, made claims for sovereignty over the Senkaku Islands. Having returned administering authority, the United States hoped that the sovereignty issue would be resolved by the parties concerned.

Meanwhile, in the process of drawing up a statement protesting the San Francisco Peace Treaty, China drafted a document concerning territorial issues dated May 15, 1950. This document used the place names "Senkaku" and "Sento" not "Diaoyudao," acknowledged them as part of Okinawa (Ryukyu), and noted that "because they are so close to Taiwan, we must start an investigation into whether we cannot [separate them from Okinawa and] have them added to Taiwan" (Chinese Foreign Ministry Archives 1950). Yet, this language was not reflected in China's statements protesting the San Francisco Peace Treaty.

As for the issue of the Senkaku Islands, Taiwan began claiming sovereignty only after the UN Economic Commission for Asia and the Far East (ECAFE) pointed out the potential for undersea natural resources in the surrounding sea area in the latter half of the 1960s; China began its claims in response to Taiwan's. In 1970, Taiwan recast the Senkaku Islands as the Diaoyutai Island chain (Diaoyutai Lieu).

China issued a "Statement of the Ministry of Foreign Affairs of the People's Republic of China" on December 30, 1971 concerning the Senkaku Islands. It denounced the Japanese government's transfer of Diaoyu and other islands appertaining to Taiwan to the U.S. government after WWII, as well as the U.S.

government's declaration of "administrative authority" over these islands, as illegal. Furthermore, it recalled that PRC Foreign Minister Zhou Enlai criticized the imperialist United States on June 28, 1950 for dispatching the Seventh Fleet to Taiwan and the Taiwan Strait, and proclaimed the determination of the Chinese people to recover Taiwan and all territory belonging to China. "Now the U.S. and Japanese Governments have once again made an illicit transfer between themselves of China's [D]iaoyu and other islands. This encroachment upon China's territorial integrity and sovereignty cannot but arouse the utmost indignation of the Chinese people."[1]

China stated that the Senkaku Islands have been Chinese territory since the Ming Era and Japan's possession of the Senkaku Islands by cabinet decision of January 1895 was an invalid action taken during the First Sino-Japanese War.

Note
1 English translation from Peking Review: www.massline.org/PekingReview/PR1972/PR1972-01.pdf

Furthermore, together with the peace treaty, the United States and Japan concluded the "Security Treaty Between the United States and Japan." With this, the U.S. military in Japan could be stationed there even after Japanese independence. Japan had been designated as a base to contain North Korea, China, and the Cold War/hot war in East Asia that had been growing more definite with the Korean War.

Foreign Minister Zhou Enlai issued a statement on the San Francisco Peace Conference on September 18, 1951: "The People's Republic of China has not been participating in the preparatory process, the negotiations process, or even the signing of the San Francisco Peace Treaty, and so the Central People's Government considers it to be illegal and invalid."

Dulles-Yoshida correspondence

The Japanese government's stance regarding the "two Chinas" remained as uncertain as ever, even in the midst of the Cold War/hot war created by the Korean War. In an essay "Japan and the Crisis in Asia" that ran in *Foreign Affairs* (January 1951), Prime Minister Yoshida Shigeru wrote, "Red or white, China remains our next-door neighbor. Geography and economic laws will, I believe, prevail in the long run over any ideological differences or artificial trade barriers" (Yoshida 2001). Even in question-and-answer sessions in the Diet, Yoshida did not make entirely clear that Japan recognized the Government of the Republic of China in Taipei (ROC government). He was focused on the Chinese market rather than its socialist ideology, and he paid special attention to recognition of Beijing by Britain, a Western bloc member, Yoshida says in his memoirs. Yoshida remarked that Japan would establish a trade representative office in Shanghai even if it were to recognize the ROC government, on the premise of eventually building suitable relations with both the Beijing and Taipei governments.

However, the ROC government—unable to attend the San Francisco Peace Conference even though it was one of the Big Four allied powers—was hearing from the United States that Japan would recognize it, not the PRC government. Besides, neither government in Beijing or Taipei was going to accept either a simultaneous recognition of, or the building of limited relations with, both.

Prime Minister Yoshida tried to put off the recognition issue until after the issue of Chinese government representation was resolved internationally (Inoue 2010). But, the United States did not accept that. Reacting to State Department consultant Dulles' indication that the U.S. Senate's ratification of the San Francisco Peace Treaty would hit difficulties, Yoshida promised to recognize the ROC government. Asked to put that in writing, Yoshida sent what is called the "Yoshida letter" (Dulles' side had prepared the draft) to Dulles on December 24, 1951. In the letter, along with promising to recognize and conclude a peace treaty with the ROC government, Yoshida pointed out that the scope of applicability under the treaty to be concluded would not encompass the territory governed by the Beijing government: "The terms of such bilateral treaty shall, in respect to the Republic of China, be applicable to all territories which are now, or may hereafter be, under the control of the Nationalist Government of the Republic of China." This letter was made public in January 1952 and became the basis for Japan's position on the issue of "two Chinas." At the same time, it shows that Japan made cooperating with the United States and acceding to its request to conclude a peace treaty with the ROC government a priority over the issue of China's right of representation (Chin 2000).

The PRC government had a strongly negative reaction against the publicized Yoshida letter; Deputy Foreign Minister Zhang Hanfu stated that it was a "most serious, most brazen act of warmongering."

Japan–ROC Peace Treaty

Reacting to the Yoshida letter's publication, the Japanese government appointed former Finance Minister Kawada Isao as plenipotentiary representative for negotiations of the Peace Treaty between Japan and the Republic of China (Sino-Japanese Peace Treaty; hereafter, Japan–ROC Peace Treaty). Kawada and staff arrived in Taipei on February 17, 1952 and held negotiations with the ROC plenipotentiary Yeh Kung-ch'ao that lasted over two months. A peace treaty was indispensable for the purpose of putting an end to the state of war and building peacetime relations. And yet, over seven years had passed since Japan's defeat, and Japan–ROC economic relations had already restarted in reality through such agreements as the Sino-Japanese Trade Agreement, concluded in 1950 between Japan under SCAP (the GHQ) and the ROC. Also, given the outcome of the Chinese Civil War and the fact that the ROC government was not invited to the San Francisco Peace Conference, even the basic composition of roles—the ROC as the victor in war,

Japan as the defeated nation—was crumbling. The ROC position became disadvantageous, especially once the U.S. Senate ratified the San Francisco Peace Treaty in March 1952.

In the negotiations process, the ROC government sought to conclude the peace treaty as one of the principal victors, in conformity with the San Francisco Peace Treaty. It emphasized its own role as a victorious country. Further, the ROC government at first had not waived its rights to demand reparations. But, it accepted the Japanese assets in Taiwan and the reparations in kind that Japan had already made as adequate for this, and so it settled for wording concerning reparations in the form of labor services based on provisions conforming to the San Francisco Peace Treaty (In 1996).

Japan, meanwhile, tried to limit the treaty's scope of applicability to the territory under ROC government control, as was in the Yoshida letter. This was based on its plan to have relations with the PRC government in the future. Regarding the issue of territory, the ROC side demanded that Japan renounce claims to Taiwan and the Penghu Islands, as it had in the San Francisco Peace Treaty, and in addition, that it clearly renounce rights to islands in the South China Sea, such as the *Shinnan Gunto* (English: Spratly/Chinese: Nansha islands) and the *Seisa Gunto* (Paracel/ Xisha islands), but it did not raise the Senkaku Islands. Consequently, the Spratly and Paracel islands, along with Taiwan (Formosa) and Penghu (Pescadores), were listed as territories Japan renounced.

President Truman signed the letter of ratification for the Japan–U.S. Security Treaty on April 15, 1952, following the treaty's passage by the full Senate. By so doing, the date for the San Francisco Peace Treaty to enter into force drew nearer. The ROC government hated the fact that it was concluding a bilateral peace treaty through separate negotiations based on the provisions of the San Francisco Peace Treaty. Yet, it signed the draft peace treaty with Japan on April 28, right before and on the very day the San Francisco Peace Treaty entered into force. Thus, the state of war between Japan and the Republic of China was ended.

At least at this stage, however, it did not conclusively end the state of war between Japan and the People's Republic of China. The scope of applicability of the Japan–ROC Peace Treaty was recorded in an exchange of memoranda from plenipotentiary Kawada to plenipotentiary Yeh: "Concerning the Republic of China, it applies to all territories which are now, or may hereafter be, under the control of the Nationalist Government of the Republic of China." Regarding reparations, the ROC government stated that it also waived its right to reparations in labor service that the San Francisco Peace Treaty stipulated, and pledged to waive its right to demand reparations. It took a magnanimous stance regarding war criminals. The text from Article 11 of the San Francisco Peace Treaty was removed from the Japan–ROC Peace Treaty: "Japan accepts the judgments of the International Military Tribunal for the Far East and of other Allied War Crimes Courts both within and outside Japan, and will carry out the sentences imposed thereby upon Japanese nationals imprisoned in Japan." In other words, it meant that the treaty opened the path to releasing the war criminals.

On the other hand, this treaty was not merely a peace treaty; it also contained provisions concerning subsequent trade relations in peacetime—one of the treaty's special characteristics. Furthermore, the treaty's scope of applicability, which Japan had strongly emphasized at the time of concluding the treaty, was linked to Japan's posture of limited recognition of the ROC government. However, because the treaty also included substance associated with "all of China," such as the termination of the state of war and waiving the seeking of reparations, it is believed that the Japanese government afterwards gradually came to recognize that the treaty did not limit recognition but merely limited areas in which it would enter into force (Inoue 2010).

Japan–ROC/Japan–Taiwan relations and the issue of Taiwan's affiliation

As a result of this back-and-forth on the treaty's scope of applicability, it meant that the Japanese government did in fact recognize that the ROC government governed Taiwan, to which Japan had renounced claim. Regarding the status of Taiwan, one argument is that it is undetermined and the ROC's rule cannot be justified. The KMT takes the view that not only did the Cairo Declaration acknowledge the restoration of Taiwan and Penghu Islands to the Republic of China, Japan also recognized that the Republic of China governed Taiwan in the Japan–ROC Peace Treaty. Article 10 of the treaty stipulates that ROC nationals

> shall be deemed to include all the inhabitants and former inhabitants of Taiwan (Formosa) and Penghu (the Pescadores) and their descendants who are of the Chinese nationality in accordance with the laws and regulations which have been or may hereafter be enforced by the Republic of China in Taiwan (Formosa) and Penghu (the Pescadores).

Actually, this refers to both Taiwan's *benshengren* (people who lived on Taiwan since before the war) and *waishengren* (people who crossed over into Taiwan from mainland China after the war).

This treaty was concluded between the Japanese and ROC governments, an agreement that ended the war between victor and defeated and opened the pathway to a return to peacetime relations. At the same time, the treaty's subject also includes the people of Taiwan, over whom Japan ruled for 50 years. For that reason, an aspect of the treaty is a basic agreement for the purpose of de-imperialization/ decolonization, to derive a new relationship between the colonizing state and the colonial people. Postwar relations between Japan and Taiwan became a dual relationship: ties between Japan and the ROC government that had moved to Taiwan, and relations between Japan and the original people of Taiwan (Kawashima et al. 2009).

However, it means that Japan, the colonizing power, and Taiwan, the former colony, underwent this de-imperialization/decolonization process through an intermediary, namely the "Republic of China"—a phenomenon called *daiko datsu-shokuminchika*. And because Japan did not interact directly with Taiwanese society in the decolonization process that took place under this three-party relationship, the resolution of various issues was neglected. It was not just that Japan did not adequately compensate for such issues as the postal savings in Taiwan in the era of Japanese colonial rule. Military pensions, disabled veterans compensation, and compensation for Hiroshima and Nagasaki atomic bomb victims, all of which Japan started limiting to "holders of Japanese nationality" in the early postwar period, were not applicable to Taiwanese who had lost their Japanese nationality after the war, regardless of the fact that Japan had even applied military conscription to Taiwan immediately before the war's end and had also employed many Taiwanese as forced labor (Kawashima et al. 2009).

Beijing government's attitude

The Beijing government, needless to say, harshly protested the conclusion of the Japan–ROC Peace Treaty. Zhou Enlai stated that his government "firmly opposed the 'peace treaty' of Yoshida and Chiang Kai-shek, who openly disdain the Chinese people and regard them with hostility," calling this treaty a "crazy plot of U.S. and Japanese reactionaries," and he added that "[we] still cannot see any trace of remorse from Japan's reactionary leadership" and that the allied military stationed in Japan should withdraw (Kazankai 1998, p. 42). Perhaps the Beijing government reacted thusly because the treaty was concluded during the course of the Korean War, and because China did not accept Japan having formal relations simultaneously with both governments in Taiwan and Beijing, even if Japan had sought to leave open the possibility of formal relations with China by limiting the scope of applicability of the treaty with Taiwan.

The Japan–ROC Peace Treaty later influenced aspects of Japan–China relations leading to the 1972 normalization of Japan–China diplomatic relations, providing a basic framework for normalization; the Beijing government carried out diplomatic normalization based on the content of that peace treaty. Since the Japan–ROC Peace Treaty was concluded in the process that shaped the Cold War/hot war in East Asia, China denounced the "imperialist" United States and U.S.-allied Japanese government, even as it attempted to find "friends" among the Japanese people, as is stated later. Such operations toward Japan were part of a framework linked to Japan's "two Chinas" concept, a rivalry with the U.S.-allied ROC government for Japanese recognition as the government of China.

End of the Korean War and anti-Communist alliance

The Korean War was essentially in a state of ceasefire in 1952. The Eastern and Western blocs headed toward accommodation in 1953, as Dwight D. Eisenhower took office as president in the United States and Iosif Stalin died in the Soviet Union. An armistice agreement was concluded July 27 in Panmunjom between the

UN forces, represented by commander Mark W. Clark, and China and North Korea, represented by commanding general Peng Dehuai and Supreme Commander Kim Il-sung. (The armistice still exists at present.)

After the Korean War armistice, the United States began to build military alliances with the countries in East Asia. The Japan–U.S. Security Treaty and the Mutual Defense Treaty Between the Republic of the Philippines and the United States of America were both concluded in 1951. The Mutual Defense Treaty Between the United States and the Republic of Korea was concluded in October 1953, and it meant that U.S. forces would remain stationed in South Korea. Also, the United States concluded the Mutual Defense Treaty between the United States of America and the Republic of China in 1954, and pledged to defend the Taiwan Strait. Japan, too, concluded a Mutual Defense Assistance Agreement (MSA) with the United States in 1954, and its National Safety Forces were reorganized as the Self-Defense Forces (SDF).

The Eastern bloc including China, North Korea, the Democratic Republic of Vietnam (North Vietnam) came to contest the hub-and-spoke-shaped security framework that was created between the United States and its allies. Japan, including Okinawa under U.S. military administration, was given a central place in that Western bloc. Also, South Korea, the ROC government, the Republic of Vietnam (South Vietnam), and others were united repeatedly under the slogan of "Anti-Communism."

China pushed ahead with unification of its southern and southwestern regions during the Korean War, and after the Armistice, it fired artillery shells on Kinmen Island on September 3, 1954 (First Taiwan Strait Crisis) and "liberated" the ROC-controlled islands on the Zhejiang coastline in 1955. Consequently, ROC-ruled territory became Taiwan, Penghu, Kinmen, and Matsu (Mazu). Chiang Kai-shek still aimed to "recover the mainland" afterwards, but the Sino-American Mutual Defense Treaty, even though it pledged to defend the Taiwan Strait, did not support Chiang's aim (Matsuda 2006),

2 Operations toward Japan and separation of politics and economics

Cold War and commerce

As the confrontation between capitalism and socialism gradually took shape, there existed a strong tendency within Japan, situated on the capitalist side, to expect that mainland Chinese markets would serve to revive the postwar Japanese economy because of historical circumstances and geographical conditions. The Japan–China Trade Promotion Association (JCTPA) was already formed in May 1949, before PRC's founding that October. Organized by men such as Nosaka Sanzo, Hirano Yoshitaro, and Uchiyama Kanzo, it established and became the parent organization for the Japan–China Friendship Association. Also, the Diet Members' League for the Promotion of Sino-Japanese Trade was created as a non-partisan organization in 1949 by 90 Japanese lawmakers from both the House of Representatives and House of Councillors; its name was later changed to the Diet Members' League for the Promotion of Japan–China Trade (hereafter, Diet Members' League). In April 1950 the upper house passed a resolution on promoting Japan–China trade. Japanese parliamentarians, rather than the government, played the key role to promote Japan–China ties, as the countries did not have diplomatic relations. It also showed that the lawmakers most enthusiastic about Japan–China relations were those whose electoral constituents and supporters were hoping for developments in Japan–China relations, primarily the economic aspects.

With the start of the Korean War in June 1950, however, the U.S. policy of containment in Europe toward eastern Europe began to be applied to East Asia. Namely, the embargo list for COCOM (Coordinating Committee for Export to Communist Areas) was applied to relations with China, and the United States took measures banning strategic goods to China by the end of that year. Various sanctions measures were also taken at the UN in February 1951 in reaction to designating the People's Republic of China an aggressor. For instance, the resolution banning strategic materials to China and North Korea in May of that year fits the bill. After that, the West's trade controls against the Communist bloc were further strengthened and CHINCOM (COCOM's China Committee) was established in July 1952.

Japan had to balance this kind of U.S.-centric policy of containing China on the trade front with its domestic expectations for the Chinese market. However, the degree of difficulty increased with Japan's recognition of the Republic of China in Taiwan in April 1952. In the Far Eastern Trade Conference in the summer of 1952, Japan joined COCOM and tried to change its regulations on trade with China in the least possible way to clear the hurdles. Yet, it wound up that Japan had to implement controls on trade with China that added another 400 items to the COCOM list because of its provisional signature to the "Understanding between the United States and Japan regarding Communist China Trade Controls" that September.

Japan–China private trade agreements

During the Korean War, the PRC's policy toward Japan was extremely harsh in some aspects, yet a flexible side became visible in others, notably the "private level." In April 1952, on the occasion of the Moscow International Economic Conference that was designed to promote East-West economic exchanges, Premier Zhou Enlai ordered Nan Hanchen (Governor of the People's Bank of China) and Lei Renmin, who were head and deputy, respectively, of the Chinese delegation, to invite the Japanese Diet members attending the conference to Beijing. Those lawmakers were upper house members Kora Tomi and Hoashi Kei, and Miyakoshi Kisuke of the lower house. Kora and Miyakoshi were directors on the Diet Members' League. Hoashi was an executive of the Japan–China Friendship Association and advisor for the JCTPA.

At the Moscow conference, Nan stated his wish to "revive and develop normal trade relations between Japan and China," and thus, the three Japanese lawmakers went to Beijing from Moscow. What was concluded on June 1 at the end of negotiations was the first Japan–China Private Trade Agreement. Since the agreement was made under trade controls, the products to be traded were limited and trade was in barter form. The time period was six months, and the combined two-way value was 30 million pounds sterling. In that sense, the economic effect of this agreement was extremely limited. But, it had the symbolic meaning of blazing the trail to forge private economic ties without diplomatic relations, and the significance of providing the model for subsequent agreements. As a result of this agreement, China passed a "law on Japan-registered vessels coming to Chinese ports" in October 1952. The first Japanese ship reportedly entered China on April 27, 1953 under this law (Shimakura 2012).

Murata Shozo, an advisor to OSK Lines who attended the Moscow International Economic Conference with Kora and the others, organized the Japan Council for the Promotion of International Trade in April 1952, aiming to promote trade with the Eastern bloc including China and the USSR. Before long, Murata was joined by Ishibashi Tanzan, Kitamura Tokutaro, and Takasaki Tatsunosuke, who reorganized the council into the Japan Association for the Promotion of International Trade (JAPIT) in 1954.

The Second Japan–China Private Trade Agreement was concluded in October 1953. This one-year barter trade agreement for the same two-way value of 30 million pounds sterling was concluded between Diet members sympathetic to the PRC, represented by Ikeda Masanosuke, and the China Council for the Promotion of International Trade (CCPIT), chaired by Nan Hanchen. In addition, both sides agreed to establish trade representative offices in this agreement.

Militarists/people dichotomy

China needed to have a definite justification for its domestic audience regarding the reopening of economic relations with Japan, a country it had once waged war against and which still had very close relations with China's main adversary, the United States. What was emphasized then was the dichotomy of militarists and the people, an argument originally advocated by Chiang Kai-shek: first, make a distinction between Japanese militarism and the Japanese people, seeking responsibility for Japan's aggression from an executive group of militarists and considering the people as victims (Iechika 2011); then, even concerning the government, distinguish between the high-level officials involved in the policy decision-making process and public servants in general, and also with the military, distinguish between executive officers and the rank-and-file soldiers.

This dichotomy was tied on the one hand to the issue of past responsibility for the war and on the other tied to Chinese operations toward Japan of the 1950s, as shall be explained below.

The militarist/people dichotomy also influenced how the history of Japan–China relations is depicted. Thus goes the story: because of the "Continental

Policy" in Japan after the Meiji Restoration, the government and military leadership consistently maintained aggression against China. But, among the Japanese people were "friends," who sympathized with the Xinhai Revolution, and "mentors," who showed goodwill to Chinese students studying in Japan. The former is represented by Sun Yat-sen's circle of Japanese friends; the latter by "Fujino *Sensei*" (Fujino Genkuro), who was Lu Xun's mentor when he was an exchange student at Tohoku Imperial University. This manner of explaining China's Japan policy and Japan–China relations came to be maintained for a long time afterwards, too.

People's diplomacy

China began developing its Japan policy as private sector diplomacy buttressed by the militarist/people dichotomy. It was developed as part of people's diplomacy, which sought to have the "private sector leading the public" by developing Japan–China bilateral private diplomacy, then linking it to government-to-government diplomacy (Len 2001; Osawa 2011). Specifically, this meant expanding China's influence by increasing the number of "the Japanese people" who opposed their conservative "reactionary" government allied with "American imperialism" and building friendly ties to them through China friendship groups in Japan. It was also designated the "Japan neutrality" policy, among other names.

Of course, there was no way anything purely "private" should exist in China, and so this "private" diplomacy was developed through friendship societies under the control of the party and government. Yet, the private sector did exist on the Japanese side and such a policy had a definite meaning, since the proximity of even former politicians to the ruling party and administration varied.

Also, from the perspective of 1950s China, its own confrontation with the United States and the ROC government was serious, and so Chinese operations targeted Japan to drag it into the PRC's own bloc, even within Japan–U.S.–China or Japan–PRC–ROC relations. For that very reason, China denounced the Japanese government, which was thought to be tied to the United States and the ROC government, and it sought to make ties with the Japanese people, who had strong leftist ideas, and with the business community, which dreamed of forming economic relations. Furthermore, although Sino-Soviet relations were relatively solid in that period, it did not mean that the U.S.–USSR relaxation of tensions on the global scale was immediately linked to the easing of tensions within the East Asian region.

Hatoyama administration and the 1955 system

Relaxation of tensions between the Eastern and Western blocs became the trend after Stalin's death in 1953. The new leader of the Soviet Union guided the Korean War to an armistice. China at the time came to embrace the concept of the Five Principles of Peaceful Coexistence and brought a ceasefire to the war in Indochina by successfully persuading North Vietnam at the Geneva Conference in 1954. China began to shift away from its external hardline stance even as it did battle with the ROC government on the Zhejiang coast. Such a policy shift also had an impact on its Japan policy.

In October 1954, China and the USSR confirmed their cooperative posture toward Japan in a joint statement and clarified their willingness to normalize relations with Japan. Also, a Chinese Red Cross delegation headed by Defense Minister Li Dequan visited Japan at the invitation of the Japanese Red Cross. It was groundbreaking for a cabinet-level PRC official to visit Japan.

In December 1954, the Yoshida Shigeru cabinet, which had lasted for about seven years, resigned en masse in the face of rising criticism sparked by a shipbuilding scandal, and Hatoyama Ichiro, head of the newly created Japan Democratic Party, took office as Prime Minister. The next autumn, the Socialist Party, which had been split into left and right, united in large part because Hatoyama touted such policies as revising the constitution and militarizing the SDF. To oppose this united Socialist Party, the Liberal Party and Japan Democratic Party also merged in a "conservative union," creating the Liberal Democratic Party (LDP). Thus, what we call the 1955 system was formed in which the largest party, the conservative LDP, faced off against the second largest party, the reform-oriented Socialist Party.

In terms of foreign policy, the Hatoyama administration continued criticizing the Yoshida administration, advocated an independent diplomacy, and touted that the goal of foreign policy was to improve relations with the Communist bloc. China paid careful attention to such moves by Japan; in December 1955, the State Council's Diplomatic Committee and the United Front Work Department of the CCP's Central Committee (CCPCC) decided to bolster its study of Japan. Among China's organizations for Japan operations was the "Office for Japan Operations," reportedly created at the time of the 1952 Japan–China private trade agreement negotiations; subsequently, a Japan Group was formed to handle Japan operations. The "Committee for Japan Operations" was created in December 1955, becoming the section responsible for research and study of Japan as well as for the formulation and implementation of policy toward Japan. The senior officer was Guo Moruo and his deputies were Liao Chengzhi, Chen Jiakang, and Wang Yunsheng, yet in fact, Liao was said to be the main manager.

Principles and plans for policy and operations toward Japan

It seems that China began setting its policy toward Japan around the time of the Hatoyama administration's formation. First, an "initial concept on the four stages of normalizing Japan–China relations" was drafted. Next, as Zhang Xiangshan from China's International Liaison Department (ILD) has said, on March 1, 1955 after the Hatoyama cabinet's formation, the CCP Politburo adopted what would become the first systematic basic policy toward Japan, "On the Principles and Plans for Operations toward Japan in Keeping with the CCPCC's Japan Policy." Said to have been involved in drafting this document were Zhou Enlai, naturally, as well as Deputy Foreign Minister Zhang Wentian and Central ILD Director Wang Jiaxiang. Based on the involvement of the Politburo, this document can be thought of as holding more importance than one simply drafted by the responsible office (Cho 2002).

This document noted the cause of the change of prime ministers in Japan, compared the foreign policies of the Hatoyama and Yoshida administrations, and on that basis, stated the five fundamental principles for policy toward Japan:

1. withdrawal of the U.S. military from Japan and opposition to construction of U.S. military bases;
2. improvement in Japan–China relations based on equality and mutual benefit, and actualizing the normalization of diplomatic relations in stages;
3. promotion of friendship between the peoples of Japan and China;
4. pressuring the Japanese government, isolating the United States, and forcing the revision of Japanese policy toward China; and
5. exerting an indirect influence on and supporting movements of the Japanese people seeking anti-Americanism, independence, peace, and democracy.

In addition, it stated the principles and plans for future policies and operations toward Japan, as well as predictions for the future of Japan–China relations. It raised the following as the tasks going forward: expanding trade; resolving fisheries issues; strengthening cultural and friendship exchanges; developing legislative exchanges; resolving the issue of Japanese left behind in China and the war criminals issue; normalizing bilateral relations; and strengthening propaganda and public opinion operations for Japan. In line with these principles, China began to take a positive policy toward Japan under the Hatoyama administration.

Hatoyama administration's approach to separating politics and economics

All Japanese administrations took the policy of "separating politics and economics" in the course leading to normalization of Japan–China relations. It was understood that an expansion of economic relations was desirable even though there were no political or diplomatic relations with China. Yet, the interpretation and substance of this policy differed with each administration. The Hatoyama administration, more than the Yoshida or Kishi administrations, is viewed as having taken an impulsive policy from the point that it had sought to improve relations with the Communist bloc. Yet, there were multiple positions inside Hatoyama's administration: whereas Foreign Minister Shigemitsu Mamoru and others emphasized consideration toward the United States, Trade and Industry Minister Ishibashi Tanzan was hoping to expand trade with China. Ishibashi succeeded Hatoyama as prime minister. Once prime minister, however, Ishibashi kept unambiguously touting the separation of politics and economics in relations with China, but he recognized he could still expand trade with China in the sense of expanding private exchanges, which stayed within the boundaries tacitly recognized by the United States. One might say that China policy under the Hatoyama and Ishibashi administrations had been placed within the frameworks of Japan–U.S. relations or the Cold War/hot war in East Asia.

It was at negotiations for the Third Japan–China Private Trade Agreement in 1955 that the conflict between Chinese expectations for improved relations and the Hatoyama administration's "separation of politics and economics" came to a head. Foreign Trade Vice Minister Lei Renmin and his deputy Li Zhuchen (known as a native capitalist of China) led the large-scale, 38-member official delegation to Japan in March; an agreement was concluded in May between JAPIT, the Diet Members' League, and CCPIT. The details remained the same: a one-year barter trade of a total two-way value of 30 million pounds sterling. In addition, this agreement settled on holding exhibitions for both countries' products, and such fairs were in fact held in Harumi, Tokyo in October and Nakanoshima, Osaka in December of 1955. But the Chinese side sought more—the establishment of trade representative offices with diplomatic status and the direct settlement of trade accounts in both countries' currencies, for instance. Yet, these were not easy requests to bring to fruition. Notably, the United States had strong reservations about the growing relations between Japan and China.

Meanwhile, there was a growing sense of alarm within the Japanese government toward China's "private sector leading the public" policy that sought to enhance relations to the governmental level through private exchanges. Japan's Ministry of Foreign Affairs (MOFA), especially, appeared concerned that private exchanges were progressing and becoming multi-dimensional, and so it began to assume that it would take part in direct negotiations as a matter of course. Because negotiations would be of concern to the United States, MOFA decided that the agenda of talks should touch first of all on humanitarian issues, that is, the issue of repatriating Japanese left behind in China and the war criminals issue.

The Japanese government made an attempt at talks via its Geneva consulate general. China agreed to talks, however, it proposed starting negotiations on such agenda items as studying the whereabouts of Chinese laborers forced to go to Japan during the war, or trade promotion and freedom of passage between Japan and China conditional upon Japan seeking to normalize relations. The talks were carried out even as the United States showed it was concerned. Japan's so-called diplomacy of a "limited" approach to China did not bear much fruit.

Yet, even so, economic exchanges continued relatively smoothly. Certainly, what is called the "China differential" had arisen because although COCOM eased the embargo against the Communist bloc in August 1954, those changes were not applied to trade with China. (The "China differential" was eliminated in 1957.) However, in December 1955, the Japan–China Importers and Exporters Association (JCIEA) was established with financial assistance from the Japanese Ministry of International Trade and Industry (MITI). It was expected not only to promote Japan–China trade but also to be a unified point of contact for the existing private groups involved in Japan–China trade, such as the JCTPA, the Diet Members' League, and JAPIT.

Chinese leadership's positive policy toward Japan

China tried out various positive approaches toward Japan after the establishment of the Hatoyama administration, in addition to accumulating real accomplishments from exchanges through China's "private leading the public" policy and "gradualist approach." It is thought that these positive moves were a national-level policy that included the nation's leadership such as Mao Zedong and Zhou Enlai, not merely something drawn up by the section in charge of Japan policy.

Apart from negotiations on the Third Japan–China Private Trade Agreement, that positive policy was demonstrated twice. First, while attending the Asian-African Conference in Bandung, Indonesia in April 1955, Premier Zhou Enlai met with Takasaki Tatsunosuke, Director of Japan's Economic Council Agency, and remarked that it was possible to build friendly Japan–China relations even while Japan–U.S. ties were maintained. This position differed from China's Japan policy that originally demanded that Japan become free and independent from American imperialism. On other occasions, too, Zhou appeared to suggest that Japan–U.S. relations would not become an obstacle to Japan–China diplomatic normalization. Behind this change in policy may have been China's adoption of the Five Principles of Peaceful Coexistence or the evolution of positive diplomacy toward Western bloc countries except for the United States.

Second, Mao Zedong showed an attitude of appeasing Japan. In September 1955, when the first Diet delegation led by Kanbayashiyama Eikichi visited China to celebrate the anniversary of the PRC's founding at the invitation of the National People's Congress (NPC), Mao along with Zhou personally interviewed the delegation and, without harping on history issues, said that it was the future that was important and stated his expectation to normalize relations soon. The meeting lasted three hours and the Japanese delegation and NPC Chairman Peng Zhen adopted a "Joint Statement Concerning Diplomatic Normalization and Promotion of Trade."

China had difficulty implementing this kind of positive policy toward Japan, especially with the final objective of diplomatic normalization, under such policies of the Hatoyama administration as were laid out above.

Progress on postwar process

The diplomacy on humanitarian issues that MOFA had put forward was making steady progress, though it fell short of the negotiations for diplomatic normalization sought by China. Japan had asked China for an investigation into the whereabouts of 40,000 Japanese left behind in China after the war. China affirmed its magnanimous policy regarding war criminals, subjecting few to imprisonment and not sentencing anyone to death or life imprisonment at a CCP Politburo meeting at the end of 1955. In the summer of 1956, China released over 1,000 war criminals, who were repatriated to Japan in September aboard the *Koan-maru*. Of course, 45 criminals were prosecuted, but even so, the maximum sentence was for no more than 20 years.

But the issue of reparations had not reached a resolution at this stage. Certainly, China had adopted the "militarist/people" dichotomy, and there was already an argument that demanding reparations from Japan would cause its people to suffer. Quite a few judges from the Tokyo Trials had gone to the Chinese mainland, but China had not decided to waive its demands for reparations, calculated to exceed $50 billion. It is believed that it was 1964 when China decided to waive demands for reparations from Japan (Mori 2006).

Japan's Asia policy and China

After the second half of the 1950s, Japan tried to establish its own toehold in the Southeast Asian region after the withdrawal of the British and Dutch, as it was implementing the reparations to Southeast Asian countries under the San Francisco Peace Treaty. These very reparations became the starting point for Japan's official development assistance (ODA). This was an extremely important policy to economic revival in Japan, which could not build adequate economic ties with China (Miyagi 2004).

Having signed the Joint Declaration by Japan and the Union of Soviet Socialist Republics in October and become a member of the UN in December of 1956, Japan the following year began to set three objectives for its diplomacy (the three diplomatic principles): UN-centered; cooperation with the United States (and free world countries); and remain steadfast to the standpoint as a member of Asia. Yet, Japan's Asia policy was carried out in the context of America's Japan policy and the framework of the Cold War/hot war in Asia. Furthermore, its Asia policy faced many difficulties in the early postwar period, especially troubled by anti-Japanese movements of the ethnic Chinese diaspora.

Meanwhile, Southeast Asia was a focal point for the unfolding legitimacy battle between the governments in Beijing and Taipei and their various ongoing political struggles. Japan asked the ROC government to control its diaspora groups. The first Japanese prime minister to visit Southeast Asia after the war was Kishi Nobusuke, who succeeded Ishibashi. Kishi's diplomatic policy direction groped around for a new Asia policy, such as the Southeast Asian Development Fund concept. China, too, was providing support to communist organizations throughout the region, as it continued maintaining and strengthening its friendly ties to Indonesia, or to communist nations like North Vietnam.

3 Japan–China relations under the Kishi administration

Kishi administration and Asia policy

A cabinet headed by Kishi Nobusuke was formed in February 1957, succeeding the short-lived Ishibashi administration. The Kishi cabinet, aiming for a more autonomous and independent Japan, tried to develop an active diplomacy for Asia while endeavoring to be autonomous vis-à-vis the United States within the frameworks of the Japan–U.S. security alliance as well as the Cold War/hot war. Its first step was a tour around Southeast Asia, the first by a postwar Japanese prime minister. In addition to the purpose of improving ties between Japan and those countries that still bore the scars of war, the tour was intended to increase Japan's autonomy ahead of Kishi's visit to the United States. One aspect of the trip was Japan's attempt to act as an equal to the United States, for in a sense, the United States was a competitor to Japan in Southeast Asia, where the British and Dutch were pulling out.

Kishi stopped over in Taiwan on his return from this Southeast Asian tour. There, Kishi called for stronger ties with the ROC government and supported Chiang Kai-shek's policy to recover the mainland. Thus, Kishi is viewed as leaning toward Taipei and being anti-Beijing, but he was active in promoting economic relations with China (Kawashima et al. 2009). This was also apparent in Kishi's India policy: Kishi stressed the importance of Japan–India–China cooperation in an October 1957 meeting with Indian Prime Minister Jawaharlal Nehru, who was visiting Japan. Kishi's diplomatic line emphasizing Asia also extended to the Middle East; he showed a willingness to play the role of mediator at the time of the Lebanon Crisis. Yet, Kishi's Asian diplomacy did not always proceed smoothly and his image as being pro-American was fixed once he set about negotiations for the revision of the Japan–U.S. Security Treaty.

Group of pro-ROC lawmakers

There were quite a few Diet members, such as those in the Diet Members' League, who advocated the promotion of Japan–China relations; their number exceeded 350 at the end of the 1950s. On the other hand, there were many parliamentarians in what is called the "pro-ROC group" who sought to emphasize Sino-Japanese relations with the ROC government. Among them, the Japan–ROC Cooperation Committee played a central role; it was established in March 1957, spurred by Ishii Mitsujiro's 1956 visit to Taiwan. The point of this organization was friendship and cooperation between Japan and the ROC government and anti-communism. Yatsugi Kazuo, who acted as the Japanese chapter's executive director, was known to have enjoyed a close relationship with Kishi. Members included powerful LDP lawmakers such as Funada Naka, Ishii Mitsujiro, and Ono Banboku. The contact organization on the ROC side was the Committee for the Promotion of Sino-Japanese Cooperation. The two sides held meetings in both Japan and Taiwan and frequently sought to develop Japan–ROC relations while restraining the development of Japan–PRC relations.

The pro-ROC group of parliamentarians extolled the policy of magnanimity that Chiang Kai-shek took in terms of the repatriation of Japanese soldiers and reparations from the Japanese, and so they took his saying "to repay violence with virtue" as the slogan for their argument that Japan owed Chiang a debt of gratitude (*"on"*). This kind of movement continued even after Japan and the ROC government severed diplomatic ties.

Factions within the LDP formed gradually between 1955 and 1960. At that time, whether a faction was "pro-ROC" or "pro-China" was an indication of its key characteristics. The pro-ROC group was created in conjunction with the formation of these factions, and like two sides of the same coin, it was inseparable from the creation of the "pro-China" group.

Institutionalizing and developing Taiwan–Ryukyu relations

The ROC government began to develop an active diplomacy toward Okinawa under U.S. military administration in 1957. Kiyuna Tsugumasa, a man of Okinawan descent who went by the name Cai Zhang (Japanese pronunciation: Sai Sho), was already active in Taiwan; in Okinawa, too, his Ryukyu Revolutionary Comrades Association sought to bring the Ryukyus and the Republic of China closer together.

ROC operations for Okinawa were advanced by Fang Zhi or possibly Chen Chien-chung of the KMT Central Committee's Sixth Section (mainland operations). Li Guoqing of the Planning Commission for the Recovery of the Mainland visited Okinawa in 1957 and reported on the situation in Okinawa to Chiang Kai-shek.

Seeking to expand trade relations, Taiwan and Okinawa established the Sino-Ryukyuan Cultural and Economic Association as an ROC organization in 1958, setting up an office for the Ryukyus in Naha. Thereafter, the ROC government used this organization to conduct ROC-Okinawa commerce, to handle overseas Chinese diaspora business, and to recruit Okinawan exchange students to go to Taiwan. Finally, many exchanges started taking place among leading figures from both sides.

Fourth Japan–China Private Trade Agreement

The Kishi administration was not unenthusiastic about developing the economic relationship with China. However, China was critical of Kishi's political stance and so denounced him publicly on July 25, 1957 (the "Kishi criticism"), causing tensions to rise in Japan–China relations (Sugiura 2006). A Japanese commercial mission visited China on September 17, but negotiations on the Fourth Japan–China Private Trade Agreement hit an impasse over the number of people in the trade representative offices. Yet, this was not because the Chinese side firmly refused to conclude the agreement. Rather, it was trying to get feedback on its "Japanese neutrality" operation—to find comrades in Japan to loyally serve social-ism and communism and oppose the United States (Sugiura 2008).

Chen Yi took over as foreign minister at the start of 1958, and the Japan opera-tions group was created under him. A Nippon Steel delegation represented by Inayama Yoshihiro, the executive director of Yahata Steel, visited China that February. The delegation concluded a five-year, 100 million pound sterling barter agreement with the China Metals Import Corporation and China Minerals Corpo-ration. A memorandum was exchanged in March regarding the pending issue of establishing trade representative offices. Not only did the contents of the memoran-dum include approval to fly the flag at the office, it also bestowed diplomatic privi-leges on the trade representatives. This was the result of concessions by the Japanese side and the Chinese side stressed that it was the product of people's diplomacy. As the memorandum exceeded the scope of private economic exchange substance-wise, Japan–China relations was thought to be on the verge of transitioning "from private to public."

Although he did not approve of this agreement, Kishi appeared to take a posi-tion in support of cooperation. However, there were extremely strong negative responses from the United States and the ROC government. President Chiang Kai-shek protested by sending letters to Prime Minister Kishi and Foreign Minister Fujiyama Aiichiro, and followed with steps to cancel the Japan–ROC trade talks in mid-March and to halt the purchase of Japanese products. Reacting to this out-burst, the Japanese government said in a statement from Chief Cabinet Secretary Aichi Kiichi that it did not grant diplomatic privileges to the trade representative office that would be established by the Fourth Japan–China Private Trade Agree-ment, nor did it acknowledge the flying of the flag. Though the ROC government praised Japan's policy shift, China strongly denounced Japan.

Nagasaki flag incident

As this dangerous mood was brewing between Japan and China, an incident occurred on May 2, 1958 in which a youth tried to drag down the PRC's Five-star Red Flag that had been hung at an exhibit of Chinese products held in the fourth floor event space at the Hamaya Department Store in Nagasaki City. A certain degree of ROC government involvement was suspected in this incident (Yokoyama 2009). The Japanese police considered the case as property damage, that is, an insig-nificant crime, and soon released the perpetrator. China, however, took the inci-dent extremely seriously and reacted quite negatively.

Foreign Minister Chen Yi issued statement on May 9 that called it an insult to the People's Republic of China, a provocation to 600 million Chinese people; the next day, he declared that all economic and cultural exchanges with Japan would be cut off. It gave the impression that relations, which until that point had been gradually building up according to the "private sector leading the public" policy, had suffered a setback. After summer, China presented three principles for politics to Prime Minister Kishi: (1) cease all words and actions that regard China as hostile; (2) stop the plot aimed at making two Chinas; and (3) do not further obstruct normalization of bilateral relations.

Yet, this did not mean the complete cut-off of all Japan–China relations. The Chinese government had not discarded the militarist/people dichotomy; it took the position of "cut but not completely"—severing ties with the Kishi administration and those whom China viewed as "reactionary forces" while continuing exchanges with groups hostile to them, that is, political groups close to China. In a sense, this also demonstrated the limits of China's policy to seek out "friends" inside Japan, an operation toward Japan uninterrupted until then. In summary, this "cut but not completely" policy can be seen as hoping to further rouse "friends" to action by making the souring of ties with unfriendly people conspicuous (Sugiura 2008).

Changes in China's Japan policy

The Nagasaki flag incident is not thought of these days as having been a decisive factor for China when considering turning points in its Japan policy. The Chinese government had been making preparations before the Nagasaki flag incident to attack and criticize the Kishi cabinet for supporting Chiang Kai-shek's policy to recover the mainland and for accepting the U.S. and ROC requests at the time of the Fourth Japan–China Private Trade Agreement (Aoyama 2007). Also, looking at PRC foreign policy as a whole, one begins to see signs of China getting tougher abroad coinciding with the start of the Great Leap Forward movement at home. In summary, one cannot go so far as to conclude that the Nagasaki flag incident was a decisive turning point in relations.

The Chinese PLA commenced shelling Kinmen Island on August 23, 1958. Reportedly 500,000 artillery shells were fired over 44 days. The United States reiterated its full support for the ROC government. Dulles visited Taiwan in October and made an offer: the United States would continue its assistance if the ROC government limited its defensive line to Kinmen and Matsu. The frontline was fixed at Kinmen and Matsu after Chiang Kai-shek accepted the offer, even as he emphasized that he himself would not abandon the policy to recover the mainland.

As China was in this hardline external posture, former Prime Minister Ishibashi went there and met with Premier Zhou Enlai in September 1959. When Ishibashi insisted on a "Peace Alliance" (mutual non-aggression) among Japan, China, the United States, and the USSR, it is said that Zhou also agreed with the proposal. Also, the Japan–China Friendship Association and the Chinese People's Association for Cultural Exchanges with Foreign Countries concluded a fisheries agreement on emergency evacuation procedures in October 1959. The Japan–China Private Fisheries Agreement, concluded in 1955, had actually lapsed in 1958, and so Japanese fishing vessels operating in the vicinity of China were routinely in danger of being seized. The 1959 agreement designated the following ports of shelter:

Nagasaki and Tamanoura in Nagasaki Prefecture and Yamagawa in Kagoshima Prefecture in Japan; Lianyungang and Wusonggang in China.

Revision of Japan–U.S. Security Treaty and prelude to Sino-Soviet split

Under the Kishi administration, negotiations to revise the Japan–U.S. Security Treaty that started in 1958 reached agreement in January 1960, and the Treaty of Mutual Cooperation and Security between Japan and the United States was signed. The treaty incorporated a strengthening of Japan's defensive power along with America's responsibility for Japan's defense. An anti-security treaty movement arose within Japan that May, around the time ratification of the treaty was taking place in the Diet. China opposed this security treaty revision, and so it looked favorably on this anti-security treaty movement. Within China, large-scale mass demonstrations took place, in response to Japan's movement (Sugiura 2013). The underlying tone for people's diplomacy at this stage was also maintained, and China did not completely sever its ties to Japan even in the tense situation after the Nagasaki flag incident. The Kishi cabinet, after waiting for the ratification of the treaty, resigned en masse in July (Okabe 1971).

Meanwhile in China, the rift with the Soviet Union had been growing wider since 1959, and on June 20, the USSR announced the termination of the Sino-Soviet Agreement on New Technology for National Defense. The cause is said to be China's refusal of the Soviet requests to use communications facilities at Chinese ports and to organize a joint submarine force when the USSR provided China with a sample nuclear bomb in connection to its nuclear bomb development. Thereafter, the Sino-Soviet split would begin to exert a large influence on relations with Japan (Gyu 2007).

Cited and referenced materials

Aoyama Rumi, 2007, *Gendaichugoku no gaiko* [The Diplomacy of Contemporary China], Keio University Press.

Chin Chohin [Chen Zhaobin], 2000, *Sengonihon no chugokuseisaku* [Postwar Japan's China Policy], University of Tokyo Press.

Chinese Foreign Ministry Archives, 1950, *Duiri Heyuezhong Guanyu Lingtu Wenti yu Zhuzhang Tigang Caoan* [Draft Outline on Issues and Arguments on Parts Concerning Territories in the Peace Treaty with Japan], Archives of the Ministry of Foreign Affairs of the People's Republic of China, file number: 105–00090–05(1).

Cho Kozan [Zhang Xiangshan] (Suzuki Eiji, tr.), 2002, *Nitchu kankei no kanken to kensho* [Observations and Analysis of Sino-Japanese Relations], Sanwa.

Gyu Gun [Niu Jun] (Masui Yasuki, tr.), 2007, *Reisenki chugokugaiko no seisakukettei* [China's Foreign Policy Decision Making during the Cold War], Chikura Publishing.

Iechika Ryoko, 2011, "Chugoku niokeru 'sekinin 2 bunron' no keifu [The Genealogy of the 'Dualistic Image of War Responsibility' Argument in China]," in Soeya Yoshihide, ed., *Genzai chugokugaiko no 60 nen* [Sixty Years of Modern China's Diplomacy], Keio University Press.

In Engun [Yin Yanjun], 1996, *Chunichi senso baisho mondai* [The Issue of Reparations from the Sino-Japanese War], Ochanomizu Shobo.

Inoue Masaya, 2010, *Nitchu kokkoseijoka no seijishi* [Political History of the Japan–China Diplomatic Normalization], University of Nagoya Press.

Ishii Akira, 1985, "Taiwan ka Pekin ka [Taiwan or Beijing?]," in Watanabe Akio, ed., *Sengonihon no taigaiseisaku* [Postwar Japan's Foreign Policy], Yuhikaku Publishing.

Kawashima Shin, Shimizu Urara, Matsuda Yasuhiro, Philip Yang, eds., 2009, *Nittai kankeishi 1945–2008* [A History of Japan–Taiwan Relations 1945–2008], University of Tokyo Press.

Kazankai, 1998, *Nitchu kankei kihon shiryoshu 1949–1997 nen* [Collection of Basic Documents in Japan–China Relations, 1949–1997], Kazankai Foundation.

Len Jo [Lian Shu], 2001, "Chugoku no taigaiseisaku to nihon, 1953–1957 [China's Foreign Policy and Japan (1953–1957)]," in *Hogaku seijigaku ronkyu* [Journal of Law and Political Studies], Keio University Department of Law and the Department of Political Science, Editorial committee, No. 50.

Matsuda Yasuhiro, 2006, *Taiwan niokeru 1 to dokusaitaisei no seiritsu* [Establishment of One Party Autocracy in Taiwan], Keio University Press.

Miyagi Taizo, 2004, *Sengoajia chitsujo no mosaku to nihon* [Japan and the Search for a Postwar Asian Order], Sobunsha Publishing.

Mori Kazuko, 2006, *Nitchu kankei* [Japan–China Relations], Iwanami Shoten.

O Ihin [Wang Weibin], 2004, *Chugoku to Nihon no gaikoseisaku* [The Diplomatic Policies of China and Japan], Minerva Shobo.

O Setsuhyo [Wang Xueping], ed., 2013, *Sengo nitchukankei to Ryo Shoshi* [Liao Chengzhi and Postwar Japan–China Relations], Keio University Press.

Okabe Tatsumi, 1971, *Gendai chugoku no taigaiseisaku* [Contemporary China's Foreign Policy], University of Tokyo Press.

Okabe Tatsumi, 1976, *Chugoku no tainichiseisaku* [China's Japan Policy], University of Tokyo Press.

Okabe Tatsumi, 2002, *Chugoku no taigaisenryaku* [China's Foreign Strategy], University of Tokyo Press.

Osawa Takeshi, 2011, "Sengoshoki nitchukankei niokeru 'danzetsu' ki no saikento, 1958–1962 [A Reexamination of the Break in Japan–China Relations in the Early Postwar (1958–1962)]," in Soeya Yoshihide, ed., *Genzai chugokugaiko no 60 nen* [Sixty Years of Modern China's Diplomacy], Keio University Press.

Osawa Takeshi, 2012, "Zenshi, 1945–71 nen [Early History (1945–71)]," in Takahara Akio, Hattori Ryuji, eds., *Nitchu kankeishi 1972–2012 I: Seiji* [A History of Japan–China Relations 1972–2012, Vol. I: Politics], University of Tokyo Press.

Shimakura Tamio, 2012, "Kokkoseijoka izen no nitchu keizaikoryu [Japan–China Economic Exchanges Before Normalization of Diplomatic Relations]," in Hattori Kenji, Marukawa Tomoo, eds., *Nitchu kankeishi 1972–2012 II: Keizai* [A History of Japan–China Relations 1972–2012, Vol. II: Economy], University of Tokyo Press.

Shimotomai Nobuo, 2004, *Ajia reisenshi* [Asia's Cold War History], Chuokoron-Shinsha.

Shu Kenei [Zhu Jianrong], 2004, *Motakuto no chosensenso* [Mao Zedong's Korean War], Iwanami Shoten.

Soeya Yoshihide, 1995, *Nihongaiko to chugoku: 1945–1972* [Japanese Diplomacy and China 1945–1972], Keio Tsushin.

Sugiura Yasuyuki, 2006, "Chugoku no 'nihon churitsuka' seisaku to tainichi joseininshiki [China's Policy of 'Making Japan Neutral' and Perception of Japanese Conditions]," in *Hogaku seijigaku ronkyu* [Journal of Law and Political Studies], No. 70.

Sugiura Yasuyuki, 2008, "Chugoku no 'nihon churitsuka' seisaku to tainichi joseininshiki [China's Policy of 'Making Japan Neutral' and Perception of Japanese Conditions]," in *Ajia kenkyu* [Asian Studies], Japan Association for Asian Studies, Vol. 54 No. 4.

Sugiura Yasuyuki, 2013, "Tainichiseisaku toshiteno taishudoin no genten [The Origin of Mass Mobilization as a Policy Toward Japan]," in Kokubun Ryosei, Kojima Kazuko, eds., *Gendaichugoku seijigaiko no genten* [Origins of Contemporary Chinese Politics and Diplomacy], Keio University Press.

Tanaka Akihiko, 1991, *Nitchu kankei 1945–1990* [Japan–China Relations 1945–1990], University of Tokyo Press.

Watanabe Akio, Miyazato Seigen, eds., 1986, *San Fransisco kowa* [San Francisco Peace Settlement], University of Tokyo Press.

Yokoyama Hiroaki, 2009, "Nagasaki kokkijiken horon: Fuin ga tokareta nagasaki kokkijiken no 'shinso' [The Nagasaki Flag Incident Addendum: The Seal is Broken on 'The Truth' of the Nagasaki Flag Incident]," in *Toa*, Kazankai Foundation, No. 502.

Yoshida Shigeru (Foreign Affairs, Japan, ed. and tr.), 2001, "Kitarubeki tainichi kowajoyaku nitsuite [Japan and the Crisis in Asia]," in *Foreign Affairs kessakusen, 1922–1999 Jo* [Selected Essays from Foreign Affairs (1922–1999) Vol. 1], Asahi Shimbun.

2

JAPAN–CHINA RELATIONS OF THE 1960s

Caught between the "two Chinas"

Figure 2.1 Takasaki Tatsunosuke chats with Premier Zhou Enlai (on right) at a dinner party during his visit to China (October 11, 1960, Beijing).

Source: ©Photo: Kyodo News.

Japan–China relations of the 1960s were jolted by the reality of the "two Chinas." The Ikeda administration envisioned recognition of the People's Republic of China in the long term by seeking to preserve the status of the ROC government, whereas the Sato administration made approaches to both Taiwan and China, but was inclined toward dealing with the ROC government. Sato achieved the reversion of Okinawa but paid a price with the "Taiwan clause." On the trade front, Friendship Trade and LT Trade started, but they were shaken by ROC government interventions and were forced to restructure under the Great Proletarian Cultural Revolution.

1 Ikeda administration and "two Chinas" policy

Sino-Soviet split and China's independent path

International politics of the 1960s began with the Sino–Soviet split coming out into the open. Mao Zedong had started down an independent path in the latter half of the 1950s both in terms of a revolutionary line and a foreign policy line, advancing the Great Leap Forward policy while simultaneously criticizing the U.S.–Soviet peaceful coexistence line. Increasingly distrustful of China, the USSR took steps: in mid-1959, it unilaterally abrogated the 1957 "Agreement on New Technology for National Defense" with its commitment to provide China a sample nuclear bomb, and it gave sudden notice in July 1960 that it was recalling the technicians it had dispatched to China and canceling all of its contracts. The situation deteriorated further in October 1961 when State Council Premier Zhou Enlai, who was attending the 22nd Congress of the Communist Party of the Soviet Union (CPSU), criticized CPSU First Secretary Nikita Khrushchev over the Albania issue and returned home halfway through the assembly.

The Cuban Missile Crisis suddenly broke out in this context. The United States publicly announced in October 1962 that the Soviet Union was constructing a medium-range ballistic missile base in Cuba and demanded the Soviets remove it. Tensions hit a peak when the United States started a naval quarantine of Cuba while leaving open the option of bombing the missile base. The 13-day period starting from the analysis of imagery of the base taken by U.S. spy planes until the Soviets agreed to remove the base is said to be the closest the U.S.–USSR confrontation ever came to nuclear war.

U.S. President John F. Kennedy and Soviet First Secretary Khrushchev who resolved the crisis concluded that their decisions signified a triumph of reason, and progress was later made on institutionalizing some of the framework for U.S.–Soviet coexistence, symbolized by the conclusion of the 1963 Partial Nuclear Test Ban Treaty (PTBT) and the 1968 Nuclear Non-Proliferation Treaty (NPT). China furiously opposed this course of events, as it was intensifying its confrontation with both the United States and the Soviet Union. China scathingly criticized the Soviet response of compromise in the Cuban Missile Crisis as "defeatism" and accelerated its plans for independent nuclear development. So then, just after the Cuban Missile Crisis, China formally established the "Central Committee's Council of 15 Experts" in December 1962 responsible for nuclear development and set a goal for a nuclear test in 1964, the 15th anniversary of the PRC's founding (Iizuka 2011). As planned, it successfully carried out a nuclear test on October 16, 1964.

In this way, China at that time set off on an independent line while deepening confrontation with both the United States and Soviet Union. Under that arrangement,

China set forth the "intermediate zone" theory that placed strategic emphasis on cooperation with the independent developing nations of Asia and Africa as well as with Japan and Western European countries. China began moving to build trade ties with Japan and normalize diplomatic relations with France in the first half of the 1960s based on this kind of diplomatic strategy, as described below.

In addition, this diplomatic approach coincided with the failure of the Great Leap Forward policy, a situation that is said to have resulted in as many as 30–40 million deaths by starvation. That situation led to Mao Zedong's resignation from the presidency, followed by President Liu Shaoqi's criticism of the Great Leap Forward and Mao's self-criticism at an enlarged working conference convened by the CCPCC in January 1962. Liu later tried to revise the policies that caused such an enormous number of starvation deaths, but before long, the situation evolved into a fierce power struggle as Mao set the Cultural Revolution into motion.

With Mao in semi-retirement at the start of the 1960s and fixing the economy being the pressing issue, Deng Xiaoping emerged as Liu's right-hand man. Secretary-general of the Central Secretariat since 1956, Deng also lost his position with the coming of the Cultural Revolution. The one who dealt with foreign relations including Japan–China relations amid all the turbulence was Zhou Enlai, who had been premier of the State Council consistently since the country's founding.

"Two Chinas" and the issue of China's UN representation

As that was happening, the Ikeda Hayato cabinet was established in Japan in July 1960. Ikeda had been known for some time as a proponent of improving Japan–China relations, advocating the promotion of Japan–China trade. Japan, having attained its long-sought goal of UN membership in 1956 (Showa 31), also began to closely associate the China recognition issue with the issue of Chinese representation in the UN. Namely, the idea was to seek progress on the issue of China's UN representation first, and then, on the back of that, to aim for recognition of the PRC government. MOFA carried out a reexamination of Japan's China policy right from the start of 1961, a project that set the focus on the Japan–U.S. summit with President Kennedy during Prime Minister Ikeda's visit to the United States.

The reexamination, advanced under the direction of the Asia Bureau's China Division, laid out a blueprint to promote China's membership in the UN with the scope of its representation limited to the mainland, leaving the ROC government's seat there unchanged, and to eventually establish diplomatic relations with China. This approach mixed two mutually incompatible desires: one was the intention to try to maintain the ROC government's international status, the other was the desire to restore diplomatic relations with China. This was a de facto "two Chinas" policy, but the intent of the first point was not hostile toward China, and the desire of the second had not presumed a severing of relations with the ROC government.

And so for Japan, its "two Chinas" policy was like the proverb: he who runs after two hares catches neither. The policy had poor potential to be achieved and did not reflect any sort of grand strategy. At the same time, however, the "two Chinas" was an evident international political reality at that time. The Kennedy administration at its outset had been studying a "two Chinas" membership draft plan that would have let China succeed to the ROC government's status as the government representing China in the UN. Quite a few UN member states took "two Chinas" as a realistic premise for purposes of China becoming a UN member. As both China and the ROC government touted a "one China" principle, many countries struggled with the reality of "two Chinas."

However, looking at this same issue from a Chinese perspective, it seems that China came to interpret an ulterior motive hidden in Japan's "two Chinas" policy: "Taiwanese independence" (Chin 2000). Certainly, a desire for "Taiwanese independence" did exist in parts of Japan, as Chen Zhaobin clearly details. Although that desire formed one part of Japan's complex domestic political environment, it does not mean, however, that it dictated Japanese diplomacy toward China. Rather, Japan groped about for a plan for China's UN membership on the basis of a medium- to long-term goal of normalizing diplomatic relations with China in parallel with securing the status of the ROC government.

Concerning the issue of Chinese representation in the UN, the ROC government's seat had been protected since 1952 by passage of a U.S. proposal to shelve the matter by the UN General Assembly (UNGA). However, in the 1960s, when the ranks of developing member states swelled and expectations for China to join the UN gradually grew, even the U.S. position began to show signs of changing, as mentioned above. But, the PRC and ROC governments, naturally, remained vehemently opposed to idea of a de facto "two Chinas." At that point, the United States proposed a resolution at the 1961 UNGA designating the issue of China's UN representation an important question requiring the agreement of over two-thirds supermajority of the General Assembly, and it was passed. The Ikeda administration ultimately decided to co-sponsor that resolution.

Groping for a Japan–U.S.–Europe coalition

However, that fact did not mean that the Ikeda administration had changed its approach on the China issue. Even if it did not go so far as to change its fundamental position on recognizing the ROC government as the legitimate government representing China, for the time being, it firmly maintained its basic policy of pursuing "two Chinas" precisely in order to preserve the ROC government's seat in the UN. Specifically, it sketched out a blueprint to settle the ROC's international legal status by limiting it to the regions the ROC government actually controlled, thereby protecting its UN seat even if China were to also become a member. Ikeda then attempted to promote this concept by cooperating with not just the United States, but with Britain and Canada, too. The only one who could persuade the ROC government, which inevitably would oppose the concept, was the United States, so Ikeda's visit there was important in this sense, too.

In the summit with Kennedy during his June 1961 visit to the United States, Ikeda alluded to the importance of measures to determine the ROC government's status on the basis of the thinking above, to which Kennedy responded that, even if they were able to maintain the ROC government's status, there would be considerable opposition domestically to letting China join the UN. Foreign Minister Kosaka Zentaro, who was on the trip, had a deeper exchange in his meeting with Secretary of State Dean Rusk. Preserving the ROC government's status in the UN was more important than excluding China, Kosaka argued, and to that end, he stressed the importance of the United States in convincing the ROC government that it should recognize its own position, namely the reality that the area under its control was limited (Ikeda 2004).

Visiting Canada next, Ikeda asked that Canada take the initiative for the "two Chinas" policy at the UN in his meeting with Prime Minister John Diefenbaker. Soon after returning home from this trip to North America, moreover, Foreign Minister Kosaka made a trip to Europe on July 4. In meetings with British Foreign Secretary Alec Douglas-Home and Prime Minister Harold Macmillan, Kosaka explained Japan's "two Chinas" policy and requested that Britain exert its influence on the United States to persuade the ROC government and also sought British initiative in the UN on this matter (Inoue 2010). Although in all of these meetings Japan was able to gain agreement in principle from these countries on maintaining the ROC government's status and seat in the UN, it could not get their active cooperation to take concrete action, however.

Ikeda and Kosaka understood that announcing the "two Chinas" policy publicly to China, to the ROC government, and even to the Japanese at home was impossible. So, that is why they believed that Japan could not take the initiative openly. The situation, however, was actually the same for the United States, too. Japanese policymakers must have also understood that the probability of bringing Japan's idea to fruition was poor. Regardless, there was a sense of urgency in the Ikeda administration's movements.

From reading the relevant meeting records and historical archives, one can sense the feeling of impending crisis over losing the ROC government's UN seat, as the prospects for the 1950s resolution shelving the Chinese representation issue grew uncertain and the likelihood of China joining the UN increased. At the same time, however, the Japanese government at the time was also sketching out the blueprint to normalize Japan–China diplomatic relations if China were to join the UN. In the end, it could be said that the "two Chinas" policy attempted to simultaneously satisfy two incompatible desires, where there was no solution to begin with. Consequently, there was not always a coordinated linkage between the two aims as a diplomatic strategy.

China–France diplomatic normalization and frustration of the "two Chinas" policy

In November 1963, the situation in Vietnam suddenly became fluid after Ngo Dinh Diem, who had been president since the 1955 founding of the Republic of

Vietnam (South Vietnam), was assassinated in a military coup. Right after that, President Kennedy was assassinated on November 22 and was succeeded by his vice president, Lyndon Baines Johnson. Under Johnson, America's Vietnam policy tilted toward direct military intervention, and the Soviet Union and China began to provide full-scale military support to North Vietnam.

In that context, French President Charles de Gaulle, who had opted for an independent diplomacy and kept a distance from the U.S.–USSR confrontation and the Cold War, stunned the world by boldly moving to normalize diplomatic relations with China in January 1964. The move was in sync with China's diplomatic policy, which similarly was opposed to both the United States and the Soviet Union and saw strategic significance in aligning with Western European countries on the basis of the "intermediate zone" theory. The Japanese government, which had been groping for a de facto "two Chinas" policy, was keenly interested in how China–France diplomatic normalization dealt with the Taiwan issue.

The Japanese government was encouraged at first that President de Gaulle appeared intent on maintaining relations with the ROC government even after the normalization of China–France relations. Actually, France conveyed its intent to China in the course of diplomatic normalization negotiations that, even if it acknowledged the PRC government as the sole legal government, so long as the ROC government did not take steps to sever ties on its own, the French government would not take strong measures. Then, in a "secret agreement clause" concerning normalization of relations, France and China both agreed that if the ROC government were to withdraw its representative office in France, France, too, would recall its representation and institutions from the Republic of China.

As previously stated, the Ikeda administration, which was advancing a "two Chinas" policy, was trying to get the United States and European countries to persuade the ROC government to accept the reality that its legal standing was limited to the territory under its effective control. In that context, the normalization of China–France ties unexpectedly pressured the ROC government to decide whether to recognize the reality of "two Chinas" or not. Sensing the tide was turning in Japan's favor, Foreign Minister Ohira Masayoshi proposed bilateral policy consultations on the issue of Chinese representation in the UN to Secretary of State Rusk, who was visiting Japan in late January immediately after China–France diplomatic normalization was announced. Moreover, at the lower house budget committee on January 30, Prime Minister Ikeda first revealed that Japan also wished to recognize the Chinese government, were China to join the UN, a diplomatic policy that until then had not been announced publicly.

However, the Japanese government's fleeting expectations soon dissipated—the ROC government decided to cut ties with France on February 10. At that point, MOFA was pressed to reexamine its "two Chinas" policy. The result was issued as a "unified view on the China issue" dated March 5. It concluded that, provided China were to become a member of the UN, Japan would "consider" normalizing relations with China, but that diplomatic normalization with China "would mean severing all relations" with the ROC government. It meant the frustration of the "two Chinas" policy that had continued since the 1950s (Inoue 2010).

The China issue in Japanese domestic politics

Let us now turn to Japan's domestic politics regarding China and the Republic of China. As we saw in the previous chapter, Japan established diplomatic relations with the ROC government in 1952, after which it concluded four private trade agreements with China over the 1950s. The people engaged in promoting Japan–China trade in the 1950s were not only those affiliated with the Japanese Communist Party (JCP) and progressives, but included big business executives and conservative politicians in the pro-China group. Also, the Japan–ROC Cooperation Committee was established in 1957 with the ROC government for the purpose of promoting cooperative relations spanning the fields of politics, economics, and culture. No particular factional rivalries were at work at the start of this organization.

The Japan–ROC Cooperation Committee was held 14 times between April 1957 and October 1971. At first, the ROC side repeated its unilateral criticism of the Japanese side's "pro-Communist" attitude, but the Japanese and ROC positions both came to converge in the fifth session held October 1959. At that session, the number of Japanese participants more than doubled to 31, up from the dozen or more who had participated until then (Soeya 1995). The Nagasaki flag incident and the cutting of Japan–China exchanges the previous year had resulted in the creation of a pro-Taiwan group in Japan.

Naturally, the ROC government expected the members of the Japan–ROC Cooperation Committee to exercise some influence on the Japanese government. Powerful politicians were members of this committee: Kishi Nobusuke, Ishii Mitsujiro, and Ono Banboku were advisers and Funada Naka, Kaya Okinori, Fukuda Takeo, and Aichi Kiichi were members. In fact, they frequently did make proposals on behalf of the ROC government to the relevant ministries and agencies and sometimes directly to Prime Minister Ikeda concerning the issue of Export-Import Bank of Japan (JEXIM) financing of industrial plant exports to China, as discussed later.

Growing increasingly dissatisfied with the Ikeda cabinet's China policy, the pro-Taiwan group aimed to block Ikeda's bid to win a third term in the LDP presidential election of July 1964. Former Prime Minister Yoshida Shigeru was also worried about being used by progressives to attack a conservative administration, and thus became critical of Ikeda's efforts to bring Japan and China closer together, especially of his administration's arguments for recognizing China and for promoting its UN membership. However, Ikeda was reelected for a third term by barely garnering a majority; the voting results were: Ikeda Hayato—242 votes, Sato Eisaku—160 votes, and Fujiyama Aiichiro—72 votes. It is said that Yoshida had hoped for a transition of administration to Sato, but even so, he assessed the results as favorable, as Ikeda was boxed in (Inoue 2010).

2 Politics and diplomacy concerning Japan–China private trade

New circumstances of 1960 and the "three trade principles"

As described in the previous section, the Ikeda administration's de facto "two Chinas" policy tried to deal with the reality of a divided China by aiming to normalize relations with China while seeking to defend the ROC government's international status. This effort might be said to encapsulate what had been the general approach of Japan's postwar diplomacy of trying to find the best policy response to a given presumed reality. One can see in retrospect that Japan–China relations, and the progress made in the Ikeda era on institutionalizing Friendship Trade and LT Trade, also developed within the framework of such Japanese diplomacy toward China.

Immediately after the war, it was self-evident that Chinese markets would play an important role in the reconstruction of postwar Japan. However, the path for developing Japan–China economic relations was blocked by the establishment of a Communist China in 1949, U.S.–China confrontation after the outbreak of the Korean War in 1950, and the emergence of the Taiwan issue. However, it was also natural for the Japanese government, which began to grope for a de facto "two Chinas" policy from the 1950s, to promote Japan–China trade relations within a U.S.-centric framework. One might say that the Japanese government's response to the four Japan–China private trade agreements that had been concluded by private initiative in the 1950s was a result of trial and error on the basis of the assumptions laid out above.

Triggered by the Nagasaki flag incident of May 1958, the Chinese government took steps across the board cutting off Japan–China trade and people exchanges, as discussed in the previous chapter. China was trying to make waves right in the middle of Japan's general election scheduled for the end of May, the first since the LDP was established by a conservative union in 1955. The PRC's steps took place right as Mao Zedong's revolutionary line was becoming radicalized, as symbolized by the Great Leap Forward policy. However, the failure of the Great Leap Forward policy was clear. Also, amid the burgeoning Sino-Soviet split, China was forced to reconsider Japan–China trade policy in order to rebuild both its domestic economy and its foreign relations. It was in the midst of all this that the Ikeda cabinet began with impeccable timing on July 19, 1960.

At which point Zhou Enlai presented his "three trade principles" the following month when he met with officials from the JCTPA, a group that had been carrying on private Japan–China trade since the 1950s. Zhou's principles outlined three forms of trade between Japan and China: intergovernmental agreements, private contracts, and "individual considerations." As examples of the latter form, Zhou appealed to the group: "you should introduce trade that anyone would consider friendly, beneficial to both sides, and possible." Zhou designated the CCPIT—the organization that promoted trade with countries with which China did not have diplomatic relations—as the point of contact for the Chinese side (Soeya 1995).

Friendship Trade and LT Trade

Thus, the type of Japan–China trade called Friendship Trade began in 1960. Companies that received Chinese certification as friendship trading companies participated in the Canton Trade Fair held every spring and fall and carried out business negotiations on trade. A Friendship Trade protocol was exchanged in December 1962, institutionalizing the framework. It stipulated that "supporting the three political principles, the three trade principles, as well as the principle of inseparability of politics and economics in Japan–China relations that the Chinese government had put forward" was the basis for Friendship Trade. It was signed by CCPIT on the Chinese side and by three groups on the Japanese side: the JCTPA, JAPIT, and JAPIT Kansai Headquarters.

The three Japanese groups all had experience working with private Japan–China trade since the 1950s, but they had different histories. The JCTPA had strong ties to the JCP whereas the JAPIT groups were established by business executives who attached importance to trade with China. Consequently, the trading companies and firms that were introduced to China by the three groups and certified as friendship trading companies were diverse. They can be divided primarily into three types. The first were the specialist trading companies under the JCTPA's influence whose existence depended on trade with China. The total number of friendship trading companies exceeded 300 at their peak in the mid-1960s, with the majority being this first type. The second were so-called dummy companies that the general trading companies established for the purpose of trading with China; the third were the few instances where general trading companies engaged directly in Friendship Trade.

Ikeda was trying to find ways to improve relations with China within the framework of cooperation with the United States. So, although he generally welcomed the development of Japan–China trade, he was seeking methods different from the highly politicized Friendship Trade. In the spring of 1962, Ikeda sought the cooperation of All Nippon Airways President Okazaki Kaheita, who had participated in JAPIT's establishment in 1954 and continued making efforts to promote Japan–China trade thereafter. Okazaki submitted to the government a concept for a long-term comprehensive barter agreement with the direct participation of manufacturers and manufacturers' groups, what is called the "Okazaki plan." After the plan had been examined by the government, Okazaki presented it to Sun Pinghua when he came to Japan in July 1962; there was general agreement on the plan with Zhou Enlai when the LDP's Matsumura Kenzo visited China in September.

It was after these developments that Takasaki Tatsunosuke, a former president of Manchuria Heavy Industries and a minister in the Kishi cabinet, visited China in the latter part of October leading an economic delegation comprising the steel and chemical fertilizer industries. Takasaki and Liao Chengzhi, Zhou Enlai's appointed representative, signed the first five-year "Memorandum on Japan–China Comprehensive Trade" (1963–67) on November 9. It set the annual trade value at 36 million pounds sterling ($100 million); it was decided that Japan would export steel, chemical fertilizer, and industrial plant and China would export such items as coal, iron ore, and soybeans. This comprehensive trade between Japan and China was called LT Trade, taking the first letter of the last names of the men who signed the memorandum.

BOX 2.1 LIAO CHENGZHI AND THE JAPAN HANDS

China's diplomacy toward Japan during that period of the postwar when the two countries did not have diplomatic relations was unique, carried out entirely by Liao Chengzhi under the direct guidance of Zhou Enlai. Organized under Liao was a group of Japan hands, many who had experience studying in Japan before the PRC's founding in 1949. The most recent research by Wang Xueping and others have named these Japan hands "Liao's group." Notably active were the four called the "Four Guardian Kings": Zhao Anbo, Wang Xiaoyun, Sun Pinghua, and Xiao Xiangqian (O 2013).

Liao, whose name is etched in the LT Trade of the 1960s, was born in Tokyo in 1908 of parents who were both close to Sun Yat-sen and were executives in the KMT. His family returned home in 1919 (it is said Liao only understood Cantonese and Japanese at the time), but upon the assassination of his father in 1925, Liao went back to Japan where he studied at the Waseda First Higher School affiliated with Waseda University. He returned home in 1928, joined the CCP, and then was assigned to organizing strikes in Germany and the Netherlands. Expelled from both countries, he returned home in 1932 by way of Moscow, took the job of head of the propaganda section of the All-China Federation of Trade Unions, and later worked in a senior position in the party's propaganda department and earned the trust of Mao Zedong and Zhou Enlai.

By the time Japan had regained its independence under the San Francisco peace system and established diplomatic relations with the ROC government in the spring of 1952, Liao Chengzhi had attained the position as the man with administrative responsibility for Japan policy. Thereafter, he singlehandedly undertook policies for Japan and the Chinese overseas diaspora until he lost his position in the Cultural Revolution in 1967. Liao maintained a stance that was severe toward the barbarity of Japanese militarism and tolerant toward the ordinary Japanese people, in line with the PRC's Japan policy of distinguishing between the Japanese people and a group of militarists.

Naturally enough, over time Liao and many other Japan hands in China as well as Matsumura Kenzo, Takasaki Tatsunosuke, and others in Japan's group of China hands have left the stage of Japan–China exchanges. While the Second Sino-Japanese War has surely become an event of the distant past, memories of the war have now become an increasingly thorny issue, sowing confusion in Japan–China relations. Perhaps this recent trend is not unrelated to the departure of the Japan hands and China hands in both countries.

TABLE 2.1 Friendship Trade and LT/Memorandum Trade.

	(US$ millions)						
	1963	1964	1965	1966	1967	1968	1969
Friendship Trade	51	195	299	416	406	436	562
(% total)	37	63	64	67	73	79	90
LT/Memorandum Trade	86	115	171	205	152	114	63
(% total)	63	37	36	33	27	21	10
Total	137	310	470	621	558	550	625

Source: Soeya (1995, Table 6, p. 143).

Included in the memorandum was a clause calling for consultation on a deferred payment method for the export of industrial plant from Japan, which later caused a diplomatic row involving the ROC government. Furthermore, groups and enterprises with strong anti-establishment leanings within Japan played a central role in Friendship Trade, and this made for extremely politicized trade in a separate sense. As will be seen below, politics rocked both trade channels beginning in the mid-1960s, forcing their transformation. However, the two trade channels were mutually complementary economically, and because of that dual structure, Japan–China trade steadily expanded in the 1960s.

The JEXIM financing issue and Zhou Hongqing incident

As previously mentioned, industrial plant was included among the items for export from Japan in the "Memorandum on Japan–China Comprehensive Trade" signed in November 1962. What had been assumed was Kurashiki Rayon's vinylon plant. For that purpose, Japan and China concluded trade terms for the first year of LT Trade, but decided not to make it public. In the trade terms, they included an agreement to let China pay for the industrial plant export by deferred payment and set the interest rate at 4.5 percent annually. This was done at Takasaki's initiative, in a head-on challenge to the policy the Japanese government had indicated beforehand that industrial plant exports be omitted from that year's trade agreement.

Before the Takasaki delegation's visit, the Japanese government had approved a limited deferred payment method for industrial plant exports that would not involve the Japanese government and attached a condition that any guarantees would come from the Bank of China. However, the LT Trade's first year trade terms requested JEXIM financing for the industrial plant. The contract for the export of the Kurashiki Rayon vinylon plant, conditional upon JEXIM financing, was formally signed in July 1963. Though it had showed a cautious stance at first, the Japanese government, encouraged by Ikeda's forward-looking posture, ultimately deemed it acceptable in August, on the condition that the interest rate be raised to 6 percent.

The ROC government's negative response was quick and firm. On August 21—the day after Japan's foreign, trade and industry, and finance ministers met and agreed to allow JEXIM financing—Chang Chun, secretary general to the ROC president, firmly protested to Japanese ambassador Kimura Shiroshichi, carrying with him a message from Chiang Kai-shek. The next day, Chiang Kai-shek sent a telegram addressed to Yoshida Shigeru, expecting him to exercise pressure on Ikeda; his Ambassador in Japan Chang Li-sheng conveyed a protest to Foreign Minister Ohira. Ambassador Chang, carrying Chiang's telegram, dropped in at Yoshida's residence in Oiso on August 24. However, the Ikeda administration showed no indication of yielding to the ROC government. Losing its temper, the ROC government recalled its Ambassador to Japan on September 21.

Just then, an accidental event that had no direct connection to JEXIM financing caused Japan–ROC relations to sour further. Zhou Hongqing, then in Japan as the translator for a Chinese oil hydraulic machinery delegation, rushed into the Soviet embassy seeking asylum on October 7. When the Soviet embassy handed him over to Japan, Zhou changed the destination for his defection from the Republic of China to Japan, but in the end, he desired to go back to China. Eventually, the Japanese government decided to repatriate Zhou to China, and the Ministry of Justice issued written deportation orders on October 26.

Trying to cool rising Japan–ROC tensions, Ikeda dispatched LDP Vice President Ono Banboku to Taipei on October 30. However, the ROC government's attitude was obstinate; it opposed the JEXIM financing and sought to prevent Zhou's repatriation to China. In mid-November, Chen Chien-chung—an associate of Chiang Ching-kuo and in charge of special security missions—was unofficially dispatched to Japan, where he planned secret operations with the LDP's pro-Taiwan group to block Zhou's repatriation to China. The decision to repatriate Zhou to China was finalized at the end of December, since his detention limit was approaching (Zhou was repatriated on January 12, 1964). Once that happened, the ROC government in early January recalled its four embassy staff: the chargé d'affaires, two councillors, and a first secretary. Then it took steps to stop ROC government purchases that made up 40 percent of imports from Japan.

Yoshida's visit to Taiwan and the "first Yoshida Letter (1964)"

Thus, as Japan–ROC relations faced their biggest crisis in the postwar, a plan surfaced for Yoshida Shigeru to visit Taiwan. Chiang Kai-shek had already raised the issue of a visit by Yoshida with Ono when he was in Taiwan in late October 1963. Yoshida met with Chen Chien-chung as well as the resident chargé d'affaires in the latter part of December to convey his willingness to visit Taiwan. In early January 1965, Ikeda learned of Yoshida's intentions from Ishii Mitsujiro, who had also been in contact with the ROC government, and so Foreign Minister Ohira announced the Japanese government's position welcoming Yoshida's visit to Taiwan. Thus, Yoshida paid a call on the ROC government from February 23–27, and met with Chiang Kai-shek three times.

At the two previously scheduled meetings, Yoshida spoke of his expectations for Sato Eisaku as Ikeda's successor and basically agreed with Chiang Kai-shek's criticism of the Ikeda administration, striving to ease the ROC government's concerns. To that end, Yoshida sat and listened to Chiang speak for most of the meetings. One could say that Yoshida's visit to Taiwan achieved its original objective of reconfirming the overall situation of Japan–ROC relations in these meetings. But the ROC government requested an unscheduled third meeting with Chiang on February 26, the day before Yoshida was to return home. There, Chiang requested a halt to JEXIM financing for the export of industrial plant to China and presented three specific points as a conclusion to the meeting.

The three points were included in a "Draft Outline for Measures toward Communist China," that Chang Chun proffered to Yoshida, paying him a visit that night. The outline in total consisted of the following five points:

1.   the goal is to bring the people of mainland China into the Free World;
2.   to that end, Japan and the ROC government shall cooperate concretely;
3.   Japan shall provide spiritual and moral support for the ROC government's policy of recovering the mainland;
4.   Japan shall oppose the concept of two Chinas; and
5.   Japan–China trade should be limited to private trade, and the Japanese government shall abstain from economic assistance to China.

After Yoshida returned to Japan, Chang Chun sent the "Draft Outline" to Yoshida on March 4 with Chiang's approval and requested formal confirmation.

The research of Shimizu Urara and Inoue Masaya lays out the facts above in detail through a careful reading of the archives of both Japan and the ROC government (Shimizu 2009; Inoue 2010). Chang Chun mentions in his memoirs that Yoshida sent him a letter dated April 4, agreeing to the "Draft Outline for Measures toward Communist China" (Cho 1980). The contents of the letter was made public even before that, in *The Secret Records of Chiang Kai-shek* (Sankei Shimbunsha 1977). In that letter, Yoshida merely pointed out that there was only one difference of fact in the minutes of his meeting with Chiang that was enclosed with the "Draft Outline," stating that "other than that, the rest is correct." The letter itself, however, is not among the Japanese and ROC documents that have been made public, though diplomatic records do exist that reference a letter from Yoshida addressed to Chang Chun dated April 4, according to Inoue.

Whatever the case may be, there is no mistaking the fact that Yoshida's letter dated April 4 was sent to the ROC government, as mentioned above. Inoue attaches importance to this as the "first Yoshida letter (1964)." From the ROC government viewpoint, this letter was the very product of Yoshida's visit to Taiwan, equivalent to proof that Yoshida, who held influence over Ikeda and Sato, pledged to exercise his influence on the Japanese government. In fact, against the background of this "first Yoshida letter (1964)," what used to be known as "the Yoshida letter (1964)" came about amid the further souring of

Japan–ROC relations over the issue of industrial plant exports to China and JEXIM financing.

The "Yoshida Letter (1964)" and the Ikeda administration

Even as Ikeda pushed ahead on a response to the ROC government in its hardline position, there was fundamentally no change in his forward-leaning position on trade with China. In April 1964 soon after Yoshida's visit to Taiwan, Matsumura Kenzo and Okazaki Kaheita visited China and agreed to mutually establishing LT Trade liaison offices comprising five staff members as well as exchanging up to eight newspaper reporters, with the liaison offices as the point of contact (Furukawa 1988). Furthermore, Nichibo (formerly Dainippon Spinning) entered into a provisional contract with China in May to export a vinylon plant, signing a formal contract in September. Representatives from Nichibo and Kurashiki Rayon had joined the Takasaki Mission of November 1962 that had launched LT Trade. From the start, the Takasaki Mission's plan was to accomplish the export of both companies' vinylon plants to China. However, Takasaki thought to move first on exporting Kurashiki Rayon's smaller scale plant because of the difficulties that would arise from moving ahead with both plant exports simultaneously.

With the export of Nichibo's plant increasingly likely so soon after Yoshida's visit to Taiwan, a concerned ROC government sought to block it, again concentrating its negotiations with Japan on Yoshida. Chang Chun and Yoshida sought to reach a mutual understanding, exchanging letters several times through the Japanese Ambassador to Taiwan, Kimura. As a result, at the ROC government's request, Yoshida wrote up the points of understanding between the two countries in the so-called "Yoshida letter (1964)" addressed to Chang Chun dated May 7. There were two promises: to propose a study of private-sector financing for industrial plant exports to China, in keeping with the ROC government's wishes; and to not consider allowing the export of Nichibo's vinylon plant to China within that fiscal year.

The content of the "Yoshida Letter (1964)" was made known to Ikeda beforehand by Yoshida's close acquaintance, Kitazawa Naokichi. The letter was not made public, but Kurogane Yasumi, Ikeda's chief cabinet secretary, announced the very substance of the letter as the government's basic policy on May 9. Namely, it made two points concerning industrial plant exports to China: the government would consider commercial banks instead of JEXIM for financing them, and until it reached a conclusion, it had no intention of allowing the export of Nichibo's vinylon plant. To follow up, Foreign Minister Ohira made the first postwar visit to Taiwan by an incumbent foreign minister in July. The ROC government buried the hatchet and lifted its ban on purchases from Japan, and thus Japan–ROC relations returned to normal.

Ikeda considered the "Yoshida letter (1964)" as giving the ROC government a cooling-off period. In fact, at the end of May, Ikeda summoned Okazaki, a key player in promoting LT Trade, to inform him of the existence of the "Yoshida letter (1964)." At that time, Ikeda revealed his innermost thoughts to Okazaki: he would "give face" to the ROC government in fiscal year 1964 but intended to allow JEXIM financing the following fiscal year. About the same time, Nichibo's president Hara Kichihei remembered later, Ikeda also made a similar pledge to him (Soeya 1995). Generally speaking, Ikeda had a certain degree of enthusiasm about expanding Japan–China trade, and so he considered the ROC government's opposition to be excessive.

Although he won a third term in the LDP presidential election in July, Ikeda's physical condition deteriorated and he passed the reins of administration to Sato Eisaku in November. In this way, the handling of Japan–China relations and Japan–ROC relations after the "Yoshida letter (1964)" came to be entrusted to the Sato administration.

3 Japan–China relations under the Sato administration

"Operation S" and China

The Sato cabinet was formed on November 9, 1964, after Ikeda had resigned owing to illness. Having sought to win the LDP presidential election that July, Sato had already been studying policy ideas. The exemplary project was "Operation S," taking the first letter from Sato's family name. "Operation S" began as a proposal by Kusuda Minoru, the *Sankei Shimbun* reporter covering Sato. The operation got started in January 1964 by newspaper reporters such as Senda Hisashi, with Aichi Kiichi of the Sato faction serving as a coordinator (Kusuda 2001).

"Operation S" initially ranked China policy alongside the Okinawa issue as "the most important diplomatic policies" for the incoming Sato administration. Its short-term position was for deepening Japan–China contacts in every possible field and "confidently advancing economic cooperation with Communist China on the basis of JEXIM financing." Furthermore, as its future direction, it noted that, "anticipating that the day Communist China will join international society is near … we will proceed with preparations so that Japan can play a bridging role in the improvement and normalization of U.S.–China relations" (Inoue 2010, p. 306). It was a markedly more positive stance toward China than Ikeda's China policy, which had been forced to make a course correction after relations with the ROC government soured.

Furthermore, in May 1964, Sato, then director-general of the Hokkaido Development Agency in the Ikeda cabinet, met with Nan Hanchen, who was visiting Japan as leader of a Chinese economic friendship delegation; Sato made an appearance at Nan's farewell party, too. In the meeting, Sato reportedly questioned the efficacy of the policy of separating politics and economics, and Nan was left with a strong impression of Sato's proactive posture on China. Even after Sato lost in the July LDP presidential election, China continued to eye him as Ikeda's successor. Then, during a visit to China in September by Kuno Chuji, Sato's go-between with China, an agreement was reached for Sato and Zhou Enlai to meet in Rangoon,

Burma in November. At that time, however, Ikeda's physical condition worsened and the political situation grew tense, so the meeting never took place (Tagawa 1983).

These facts give a true indication of how much importance Sato attached to relations with China. However, Sato's thinking differed slightly from Ikeda's "two Chinas" policy, which sought to normalize relations with China over the medium- to long-term while seeking, in the short-term, China's joining the UN while protecting the ROC government's UN seat. The first discussion report of "Operation S" was compiled in early May and presented to Sato right before his meeting with Nan Hanchen. Sato reportedly praised the treatment of the Okinawa issue as "extremely good," whereas he remarked of the China issue, "it is a little too early for the two Chinas policy" and "just having the ROC government as the legitimate government is fine" (Senda 1987, p. 31).

The final policy declaration that "Operation S" ultimately presented went no further than "to deepen the contacts between Japan and China in each and every possible field." Yet, to decide that Sato retreated on his position on China would be hasty, because the declaration also deferred mentioning the reversion of Okinawa. Sato's positive position toward China also contained domestic political considerations in an attempt to soften his lingering "right wing" image ahead of the LDP presidential election. At the same time, however, the important thing was that he neither made "two Chinas" a premise for his China diplomacy nor the intended solution. This became apparent in Sato's approach to the issue of Chinese representation in the UN.

Sato and the issue of China's UN representation

We can understand Sato's basic thinking from his exchange of opinions on the China issue with Secretary of State Rusk during his January 1965 visit to the United States. Sato honestly showed deep concern about the steadily growing number of countries supporting China's UN membership and the dwindling support for the ROC government. If that trend were to continue, Sato stated, it would become difficult for the Japanese government to control the pressure of domestic demands to recognize China, a situation that he would prefer to put off as long as possible. He then asked Rusk whether there was any possibility that, in the future, China and the ROC government would recognize each other's existence and continuation as a state (Ikeda 2004).

Sato's fundamental position was to defend the ROC government's UN seat, a position similar to that of Japanese administrations up to that point. However, Sato held the realistic outlook that, so long as China and the ROC government both did not yield on "one China," the ROC government would be expelled from the UN were China to join. The fact that the ROC government boldly moved to sever relations with France when it normalized diplomatic relations with China in January 1964 undoubtedly influenced this judgment. As already mentioned, MOFA at the time had also arrived at the same conclusion. However, this did not mean that Sato supported the ROC government's claim to "one China" any more than China's.

The only logical solution, as Sato posed to Rusk, was for China and the ROC government both to mutually recognize each other's existence. One can say that Sato's posture on China, which looked positive for Beijing at first, was premised on the realistic position of considering the ROC government a legitimate government. However, at the same time, Sato's pro-Taiwan stance did not deny the significance of a certain degree of improvement of relations with China.

The realistic position on the issue of Chinese representation in the UN at the time was to support resolutions designating the issue "an important question," first passed in 1961. At the time the Sato administration was inaugurated, the Canadian government, which had aligned itself with the Ikeda administration on the "two Chinas" policy, tried to promote a "one China, one Taiwan" plan at the UN centered on a draft resolution on the "self-determination of the people of [Taiwan]." However, Sato interpreted this as being unchanged from the de facto "two Chinas" policy, as it would ultimately mean China's joining the UN and the expulsion of the ROC government, as well as bring about growing pressure within Japan to recognize China.

Thus, the Sato administration decided to co-sponsor the resolution designating the issue of China's UN representation "an important question" together with the United States and Australia at the 1965 UNGA. It was four years since the same General Assembly resolution was first passed in 1961. After that, the same resolution would be proposed every year and passed until 1970. It was not a safe position, looking from the domestic political situation in which the pro-Taiwan group was the mainstream within the Sato administration. Also, from the start it was not possible for Sato to strike out to actively draw Japan and China closer together in the East Asian environment with the Vietnam War intensifying and China plunging into the confusion of the Cultural Revolution.

Stagnant Japan–China relations

On November 16, 1964, right after the formation of the Sato cabinet, a contract was drawn up to export Hitachi Zosen's cargo ships to China. A condition of executing the contract was to furnish JEXIM financing by February 15, 1965 (later extended to March 31). Sato was undecided (Inoue 2010). This did not mean that he rejected JEXIM financing, but he was unable to ignore the hardline position of the ROC government and the "Yoshida letter (1964)." However, he had no bright ideas. Eventually, Sato decided against the use of JEXIM at the end of March 1965, believing that endlessly putting off a decision would instead invite misunderstanding from China and the ROC government. The Japanese government then issued its view on March 30 that the export of the cargo ships should be carried out speedily, but that domestic financing issues were under consideration as a separate matter. Thus, the Hitachi Zosen contract became invalid on March 31 and the Nichibo plant contract, too, expired on April 30.

At that moment, the United States began to move toward full-scale war in Vietnam, triggered by the August 1964 Gulf of Tonkin incident in which North

Vietnam allegedly attacked a U.S. destroyer with torpedoes. Bombing of the North commenced in 1965, and the full-scale insertion of land forces began with the Danang landing by the Marines in March. In such an international environment, the Japanese government had to emphasize relations with the United States, centered on the Japan–U.S. security treaty, and so it lost the option to prioritize consideration for China, which was supporting North Vietnam.

Viewing the same situation from the Chinese side, it meant that the Sato administration was hostile toward China. According to the Chinese view, since Sato sought to strengthen Japan's dependence on the United States to penetrate into the Republic of China and Southeast Asia, he took a hostile policy toward China, which was an impediment to that scheme (Rin 1997). Having given up on the Sato administration, China stopped the ongoing commercial talks with Japan on as many as 40 cases of industrial plants. Then, Chinese criticism of Sato suddenly grew harsher with respect to his administration's diplomacy of the latter half of the 1960s. Also, in April 1965 the Sato administration concluded negotiations and reached an agreement on Japan–ROC yen loans, an issue that had been pending since the ROC government made the request of the Ikeda administration in 1962. This, too, became material for China to attack Sato.

As Japan–China relations steadily worsened, China plunged into the confusion of the Cultural Revolution beginning in 1966. Those in power were denounced repeatedly by revolutionary rebels and Red Guards touting Mao Zedong thought. President Liu Shaoqi, who became Mao's biggest target in the power struggle, was placed under house arrest and died of unnatural causes in November 1969. Even in such chaos of the Cultural Revolution, China successfully conducted a hydrogen bomb test in June 1967 and in parallel was pouring its energy into ballistic missile development.

From the start of his time as prime minister, Sato was concerned about China's nuclear development and showed a desire to have an honest conversation with the United States about Japanese nuclear arms (Nakajima 2006). However, Japanese nuclear arms were far from being a realistic option for Japan, and in the end it underscored the importance of the Japan–U.S. security alliance. Furthermore, the United States was asking Sato, who was concentrating his energies on Okinawa reversion, that Japan share the security burden. Ahead of his trip to the United States scheduled for November 1967, Sato planned visits to Southeast Asia and Oceania, then decided to start off with a visit to the Republic of China. Thus, Sato visited the ROC (September 7–9); Burma, Malaysia, Singapore, Thailand, and Laos (September 20–29); and Indonesia, Australia, New Zealand, the Philippines, and South Vietnam (October 8–21).

At first, MOFA had planned to tack an ROC visit on at the end of the October circuit. Ultimately, however, Sato is said to have decided to visit the Republic of China separately, ahead of visiting Southeast Asia and Oceania, in reaction to strong ROC government pressure through the LDP's pro-Taiwan group, and also in light of the impact that favoring the ROC government would have on the negotiations for Okinawa reversion (Inoue 2010). Coincidently, Yoshida Shigeru died on

October 20 while Sato was in the Philippines. Sato rushed home on October 21, just four hours into his visit to South Vietnam. After ending his unprecedented grand tour of Southeast Asia and Oceania, Sato became fully engaged on the reversion of Okinawa. By chance, Yoshida's death coincided with one juncture of Sato's diplomacy.

Restructuring Friendship Trade and LT Trade

Stagnating Japan–China relations had a large impact on Japan–China trade, too. The growing divide between the Japanese and Chinese communist parties in the spring of 1966 naturally forced the restructuring of Friendship Trade, in which the JCP's influence was at play. Miyamoto Kenji, who became JCP secretary general in 1958, had come up with his own justifications for opposing peaceful coexistence and for the "united front" struggle against the United States. The JCP was stuck with a dilemma when the United States and the Soviet Union began walking toward a degree of coexistence after wrapping up the 1962 Cuban Missile Crisis while at the same time the Sino-Soviet split widened. This dilemma unavoidably forced the Miyamoto JCP to choose an "independent" line. In that process, the JCP first split decisively with the CPSU in 1964, then also cut ties with the CCP in March 1966.

Once the JCP and CCP began confrontational relations, China excluded the JCP as well as the JCP-influenced JCTPA from Friendship Trade. The JCTPA, which had demonstrated a strong presence since the 1950s, lost its Japan–China trade privileges and was forced to disband in October 1966 under pressure from many friendship trading companies that obeyed China. The JCTPA could no longer be expected to play a role in Friendship Trade and so thereafter JAPIT would carry on this important responsibility, according to the minutes of the JAPIT–CCPIT meeting held in September in Beijing. The agreement documents and the joint statement concerning Friendship Trade that JAPIT and CCPIT concluded in February and March 1967, respectively, contained the following conditions for Friendship Trade explicitly in writing: the firm adherence to the three political principles, the three trade principles, and the principle of the inseparability of politics and economics, as well as struggle against the "four enemies"—American imperialists, Japanese reactionaries, Soviet modern revisionists, and Japanese revisionists (JCP revisionist elements). As the timing was in the middle of the Cultural Revolution, incidents such as the following occurred repeatedly: about 300 friendship trading companies, at China's instructions, mobilized employees to demonstrate against Sato's September 1967 visit to Taiwan, and they had to undergo half a month of lectures on *Quotations from Chairman Mao Zedong* at the Canton Trade Fair, the site of commercial talks (Soeya 1995).

The transformation of LT Trade began after the issuance of the "Yoshida letter (1964)," notably after Sato indicated that he would be bound by the letter. Japan's LT Trade office (Takasaki office) delegation that was visiting China in September 1965 to negotiate the 1966 trade agreement was told that negotiating exports of industrial plant and cargo vessels was not possible so long as the "Yoshida letter (1964)" remained in effect. Furthermore, the "Memorandum on Japan–China Comprehensive Trade" that had been signed in 1962 was set to expire in November 1967. Right then, the Chinese side issued a warning to the Takasaki office that Sato's September visit to the Republic of China must not be viewed lightly. In contrast with Friendship Trade, this was the first time for China to put forward explicit political demands using the LT Trade channel. In the end, negotiations to extend LT Trade were not held in 1967 when China was in the throes of the Cultural Revolution.

However, a small delegation visited China in February 1968 at the invitation of Zhou Enlai. As a result, a political talks communiqué and trade terms were signed on March 6. The political talks communiqué stipulated that "the hostile policy toward China being promoted by American imperialism and the Japanese authorities" was the cause of the impediments that existed between Japan and China, and it affirmed the principle of the inseparability of politics and economics and the three political principles as the political basis for Japan–China trade. The trade terms also mentioned those two sets of principles and announced efforts to eliminate the impediments caused by the "Yoshida letter (1964)." Thus, LT Trade was transformed into "Memorandum Trade" on a yearly basis and continued thereafter in 1969 and 1970 in the same way, accompanied by the signing of a political talks communiqué and trade terms (Soeya 1995).

Reversion of Okinawa and the "Taiwan clause"

As previously stated, Prime Minister Sato early in his tenure adopted the reversion of Okinawa as his own important diplomatic task. He raised the matter on his 1965 trip to the United States, his first as prime minister; during his visit to Okinawa that August, he declared: "So long as Okinawa does not return to its homeland, Japan's postwar period will never be over." The reversion could not happen if the security of the Far East, and more specifically, America's Far East strategy, were ignored. And so, Japan's shared responsibility for security in Asia came to be questioned, and the Taiwan issue along with the Korean peninsula were highlighted.

At the same time, however, the issue of nuclear weapons in Okinawa after reversion was an important one from Japan's unique domestic situation. After nearly two months of overseas travel to the ROC, Southeast Asia, and Oceania, and after successfully managing the state funeral for Yoshida, Sato went to the United States in November 1967 and held a summit meeting with President Johnson. Their joint statement included an agreement on the period for Okinawa reversion of "within a few years" and simultaneously established agreement on the reversion of the Ogasawara (Bonin) Islands. Responding to a Diet question in December concerning the method of Ogasawara reversion, Sato referenced the three non-nuclear principles for the first time: "Japan shall neither possess nor manufacture nuclear weapons, nor shall it permit their introduction into Japanese territory."

Here, the reversion of Okinawa predicated on the removal of all nuclear weapons and equivalent application of the Japan–U.S. security treaty (*kaku nuki, hondo nami*) became Japan's clear, established policy. However, from the standpoint of U.S. military strategy, even if the United States were to withdraw all nuclear weapons from Okinawa at once, it would not yield on the issue of re-introducing them in a time of crisis. Thus, Japan and the United States came to coordinate their widely divergent positions under the U.S. policy of neither confirming nor denying the presence of nuclear weapons. Then, the Japanese side came up with an ingenious idea: paragraph eight of the joint statement by Prime Minister Sato and President Richard M. Nixon in November 1969, namely a clause that firmly promised the reversion of Okinawa "without prejudice to the position of the United States Government with respect to the prior consultation system under the Treaty of Mutual Cooperation and Security." The United States could interpret it to indicate prior consultation on the issue of introducing nuclear weapons in a time of crisis (Kuriyama 2010).

Sato and Nixon were supposed to have exchanged a secret agreement that the subject of this prior consultation included the introduction of nuclear weapons to, or their passage through, Okinawa, according to Wakaizumi Kei, Sato's secret emissary in secret negotiations with Henry Kissinger (Wakaizumi 1994). The Democratic Party of Japan (DPJ), after taking power in 2009, established an experts committee concerning Japanese postwar diplomatic "secret agreements," which concluded in its report that it could not rule out the possibility that this kind of "secret agreement" had existed, and suggested that MOFA had not been involved (Kitaoka et al. 2010). Kuriyama Takakazu recollects that there was just paragraph eight of the Sato–Nixon joint statement, and even if there were a "secret agreement," it was not all that substantial and was only, in a certain sense, a document to persuade the U.S. military (Kuriyama 2010).

One more large pending issue in Japan–U.S. negotiations on Okinawa reversion was how to declare Japan's role in the security of Taiwan and the Korean peninsula post-reversion. What Japan consistently requested of the United States in the course of negotiations was to leave a gap when referencing South Korea and Taiwan out of consideration for relations with China. The result is paragraph four of the 1969 Sato–Nixon joint statement: Sato stated, as his understanding, that "the security of the Republic of Korea was essential to Japan's own security" and that "the maintenance of peace and security in the Taiwan area was also a most important factor for the security of Japan." These declarations are known as the "Korea clause" and the "Taiwan clause," respectively.

In this way, the Okinawa Reversion Agreement was signed in June 1971. The Diet then ratified the agreement and passed a resolution on the three non-nuclear principles as a set in November. Administration of Okinawa, including the Senkaku Islands, reverted to Japan in May 1972. During this time, China rolled out a large campaign on the "revival of Japanese militarism," partly because the Sato administration had started to advocate autonomous self-defense after just having agreed to the Taiwan clause with the United States. Nevertheless, in the midst of all of this, the United States and China were secretly moving toward rapprochement, as will be discussed in the next chapter. At the time, the Nixon administration was even envisioning the scenario of withdrawing U.S. forces from Taiwan, thereby diminishing the importance of the Taiwan issue in U.S.–China relations all at once.

Cited and referenced materials

Chin Chohin [Chen Zhaobin], 2000, *Sengonihon no chugokuseisaku* [Japan's Postwar China Policy], University of Tokyo Press.

Cho Gun [Chang Chun] (Furuya Keiji, tr.), 1980, *Nikka, fuun no 70 nen* [Japan and the Republic of China: 70 Years of Troubled Times], Sankei Shimbun Publications.

Furukawa Mantaro, 1988, *Nitchu sengokankeishi, Kaitei-zoho shinsoban* [History of Japan–China Postwar Relations (New Revised and Expanded Edition)], Hara Shobo.

Iizuka Hisako, 2011, "'Kaku' ni miru chuin kankei [China–India Relations: Through a Nuclear Lens]," in Soeya Yoshihide, ed., *Genzai chugokugaiko no 60 nen* [Sixty Years of Modern China's Diplomacy], Keio University Press.

Ikeda Naotaka, 2004, *Nichibei kankei to "futatsu no chugoku"* [Japan–U.S. Relations and "Two Chinas"], Bokutakusha.

Inoue Masaya, 2007, "Kokuren chugoku daihyoken mondai to Ikeda gaiko [The Chinese Representation Issue in the United Nations and the Ikeda Administration's Diplomacy]," in *Kobe hogakuzasshi* [Kobe Law Journal], Vol. 57, No. 1.

Inoue Masaya, 2010, *Nitchu kokkoseijoka no seijishi* [Political History of the Normalization of Japan–China Diplomatic Relations], University of Nagoya Press.

Japan–China Economic Association, ed., 1975, *Nitchu oboegaki no 11 nen* [Eleven Years of Japan–China Memoranda], Japan–China Economic Association.

Kitaoka Shinichi et al., 2010, *Iwayuru 'mitsuyaku' mondai ni kansuru yushikisyaiinkai hokokusho* [Experts Committee Report on the So-Called "Secret Agreements" Issue], Ministry of Foreign Affairs of Japan.

Kuriyama Takakazu, 2010, *Gaiko shogenroku: Okinawahenkan, nitchu kokkoseijoka, nichibei "mitsuyaku"* [Diplomacy Testimonial: Reversion of Okinawa, Japan–China Diplomatic Normalization, and Japan–U.S. "Secret Agreements"], Iwanami Shoten.

Kusuda Minoru, 2001, *Kusuda Minoru nikki* [Diary of Kusuda Minoru], Chuokoron Shinsha.

Nakajima Shingo, 2006, *Sengonihon no boeiseisaku* [Postwar Japan's Defense Policy], Keio University Press.

Nakashima Takuma, 2012, *Okinawahenkan to Nichibeianpo taisei* [Reversion of Okinawa and the Japan–U.S. Security Arrangements], Yuhikaku Publishing.

O Setsuhyo [Wang Xueping], ed., 2013, *Sengo nitchukankei to Ryo Shoshi* [Liao Chengzhi and Postwar Japan–China Relations], Keio University Press.

Rin Daisho [Lin Daizhao] (Watanabe Hideo, tr.), 1997, *Sengo chunichi kankeishi* [A History of Postwar China–Japan Relations], Kashiwashobo.

Sankei Shimbunsha, 1977, *Sho Kaiseki hiroku 15* [The Secret Records of Chiang Kai-shek, Vol. 15], Sankei Shimbun Publications.

Senda Hisashi, 1987, *Satonaikaku kaiso* [Reflections on the Sato Cabinet], Chuokoron-Sha.

Shimizu Urara, 2009, "Nikkakankei saikochiku heno mosaku to sono kiketsu [Groping towards Rebuilding Japan–ROC Relations and its Consequences]," in Kawashima Shin, Shimizu Urara, Matsuda Yasuhiro, Philip Yang, eds., *Nittai kankeishi 1945–2008* [A History of Japan–Taiwan Relations 1945–2008], University of Tokyo Press.

Soeya Yoshihide, 1995, *Nihongaiko to chugoku: 1945–1972* [Japanese Diplomacy and China 1945–1972], Keio Tsushin.

Soeya Yoshihide, 2005, *Nihon no "midorupawa" gaiko* [Japan's "Middle Power" Diplomacy], Chikumashobo.

Tagawa Seiichi, 1983, *Nitchukoryu to jiminto ryoshutachi* [Japan–China Exchanges and the Bosses of the LDP], Yomiuri Shimbun.

Wakaizumi Kei, 1994, *Tasaku nakarishio shinzemu to hossu* [The Best Course Available], Bungeishunju.

3

JAPAN–CHINA RELATIONS OF THE 1970s

International politics and restructuring of Japan–China relations

FIGURE 3.1 Prime Minister Tanaka Kakuei (on right) and Premier Zhou Enlai make a toast after signing the Joint Communiqué of the Government of Japan and the Government of the People's Republic of China. Chief Cabinet Secretary Nikaido Susumu is in the center (September 29, 1972, Beijing).

Source: ©The Mainichi Newspapers/Jiji Press Photo.

Japan–China relations of the 1970s developed amid the breathtaking changes in the international politics of U.S.–China–USSR relations. The three major powers each made the Japan–China relationship an important part of their global strategies. However, the idea or premise of engaging in the same level of strategic game with the three major powers did not exist in Japanese diplomacy. Japan's diplomacy toward China in the 1970s came to embrace the objective of providing stability to China, over the course of moving from Japan–China diplomatic normalization to the start of ODA to China.

1 Japan and China in the shifting international environment

Nixon/Kissinger diplomacy

Japan–China relations grew and developed rapidly in the 1970s—from the early period of normalization of relations, through the conclusion of the Treaty of Peace and Friendship, to the start of Japanese ODA to China. Until this point, the two countries had independently forged various quasi-governmental and private ties despite international political constraints, ties that strongly influenced the process of bilateral negotiations and the substance of specific agreements. As the 1970s began, however, the biggest factor driving the revision of postwar Japan–China relations was a transformation of the international political system caused by U.S.–China rapprochement. The Nixon administration's new diplomacy since 1969 eased the U.S.–China confrontation, under which the Japanese government had been forced to conclude the Sino-Japanese Peace Treaty with the ROC government in 1952.

Before taking office, President Nixon hinted that he would work to improve ties with China and appeared willing to open a new era of negotiation with the Soviet Union. This was in the context of growing doubts about U.S. leadership and position in the world, with the country stuck in the drawn-out quagmire of the Vietnam War. Economically, the dollar-standard international monetary system was growing unstable, as excessive Cold War interventions based on the policy of containment were simultaneously causing the U.S. trade deficit to expand and provoking a massive outflow of dollars abroad. At home, too, public opposition to the Vietnam War, while in sync with the global anti-American movement, reached a high-water mark; the Cold War consensus in U.S. politics was crumbling.

Then, President Nixon invited Harvard University political scientist Henry Kissinger to be his special assistant for national security affairs (national security advisor), and they began groping for a new global strategy to build a "structure of peace" that would stabilize major power relations and break the country free from the containment policy that had brought about the relative decline of U.S. position and national power. The "Nixon/Kissinger diplomacy" to implement this new strategy moved forward simultaneously on rapprochement with China, building détente with the USSR, and withdrawing from the Vietnam War.

This diplomacy tried to use the "swing position" strategically in U.S.–China–USSR relations, given the Sino-Soviet split, which had evolved into armed conflict in border zones in the late 1960s. First, Nixon and Kissinger embarked on rapprochement with

China in a period when it faced a heightened risk of a limited Soviet aerial bombardment. At the same time, they started constructing détente relations with the Soviet Union by accelerating the U.S.–USSR Strategic Arms Limitation Talks (SALT) under way at the time. Then, they sought to remove the Vietnam War from the Cold War context and achieve "peace with honor" by transforming the Cold War into a world of traditional balance-of-power diplomacy among the great powers.

As described below, U.S.–China rapprochement came about after repeated indirect and secretive high-level contacts between the two countries that used third parties, leading to President Nixon's dramatic television announcement in July 1971 (the "Nixon shock"), and culminating in Nixon's visit to China and the conclusion of the "Shanghai Communiqué" in February 1972. Afterwards, President Nixon visited Moscow that May, concluded the SALT Treaty, and opened the path for the U.S.–USSR détente of the 1970s. In this way, the Nixon administration prepared the conditions for the "Vietnamization" of the Vietnam War and concluded it with the January 1973 Paris Peace Accords.

The Nixon doctrine and Asia

The Vietnam War was the biggest factor motivating the Nixon administration to embark on revising its global strategy. It follows that withdrawal from Vietnam was the most important task for Nixon/Kissinger diplomacy. And yet at the same time, the administration had to avoid having the withdrawal lead to a drop in U.S. leadership in the world. Revising U.S.–China–USSR relations then became the strategic objective, but naturally enough that also caused significant turbulence in U.S. relations with Asian allies.

The first step was the remarks that President Nixon made at an informal press conference in Guam in July 1969, calling on Asian countries to take more responsibility for their own military defense, except for a nuclear threat (the Guam Doctrine). The new policy later became known as the "Nixon Doctrine" after it was formalized in three points in a February 1970 foreign policy report to Congress. It made clear that the United States would keep all of its treaty commitments and provide the shield against the nuclear threat, but following these two points, that it expected Asian countries would bear responsibility for the first line of defense against all other military aggression.

The new line for Asia policy shocked South Korea and Japan. South Korea especially was shaken by the Nixon administration's plans to draw down troops stationed in South Korea. This U.S. diplomacy, which sought rapprochement with China as it touted the Nixon Doctrine, meant moving forward with U.S. troop withdrawals not just from South Korea, but also from Taiwan, in principle, and recognizing China as a trustworthy partner in the balance-of-power game. The Park Chung-hee administration, confronting the North Korean threat, felt a deeper sense of isolation and danger. In addition to pursuing the construction of the highly authoritarian Yushin system, it attempted to start clandestine nuclear development and made an internal study of defense cooperation with Japan (Soeya 2005).

The exemplary case for the application of the new Nixon Doctrine policy line to Japan was the so-called "Korea clause"—the November 1969 joint statement by President Nixon and Prime Minister Sato Eisaku stipulated that "the security of the Republic of Korea was essential to Japan's own security." Prime Minister Sato was pushing ahead on negotiations for the reversion of Okinawa at the time; the two leaders agreed to start those negotiations in that very Sato-Nixon Joint Statement. From the U.S. perspective, Okinawa reversion and the Korea clause were both in keeping with the new Asia policy based on the Nixon Doctrine.

However, Japan had a different interpretation. Put simply, the reversion of Okinawa was the product of a type of independent diplomacy of the Sato administration; the Korea clause was a concession to the United States to achieve Okinawa reversion. Japanese domestic politics and public opinion both emphasized détente, the trend of the times, and refused a more active defense policy. The exception was a group of advocates for an "independent self-defense." For instance, Nakasone Yasuhiro, who in January 1970 became director-general of the Japan Defense Agency (JDA), saw the Nixon administration's new diplomacy as a good opportunity for Japan to advance an independent self-defense. However, Nakasone's ideas reached an impasse in the face of an overwhelmingly pacifist environment domestically.

U.S.–China rapprochement

U.S.–China rapprochement was the core factor determining the success of the aforementioned Nixon/Kissinger diplomacy. Seeing opportunity in the succession of large-scale armed clashes on the Sino-Soviet border that occurred in the spring and summer of 1969, its first year in office, the Nixon administration took the first step toward the forthcoming U.S.–China rapprochement. Amid the growing possibility of Soviet air bombing against Chinese military facilities, the United States in August 1969 conveyed a message to China through the Pakistani channel that it "should not be party to any arrangements designed to isolate China." After that, U.S. and Chinese leaders, using backchannels in Pakistan and Romania (with which both countries had diplomatic ties), secretly reached an understanding regarding Kissinger's top secret trip to China in July 1971.

The main purpose of Kissinger's visit was to lay the groundwork for President Nixon to visit China. Over the span of two days, Kissinger and Chinese Premier Zhou Enlai engaged in high-level strategic talks that touched on the overall international climate and not just the bilateral issues. Kissinger firmly believed then that Chinese leaders understood President Nixon's strategic thinking on seeking to conclude the Vietnam War and reducing the U.S. military presence in Asia, including Taiwan and South Korea. This was the moment that Kissinger placed trust in China as a partner who could play balance-of-power diplomacy among great powers. Thus, one could say it was the birth of the de facto U.S.–China strategic relationship.

Following on Kissinger's top secret visit July 9–11, President Nixon disclosed the fact of Kissinger's trip and plans for his own visit to China in an electrifying televised announcement on July 15. This so-called "Nixon shock" literally stunned the world, nowhere more so than Japan, which was greatly taken aback. As you read in previous chapters of this book, there were active contacts between Japan and China even though intergovernmental ties were nonexistent. So, there was a conceit within the Japanese government that Japan itself ought to be the bridge between China and the United States.

The backlash in Japan against the "Nixon shock" played some role in the surge of pro-China sentiment domestically. Meanwhile, President Nixon visited China in February 1972, and the U.S. and Chinese leaders issued the "Shanghai Communiqué" on February 27. Along with proposing "concrete consultations to further the normalization of relations between the two countries," it affirmed the U.S. government's ultimate objective of the "withdrawal of all U.S. forces and military installations from Taiwan." In this way, a fundamental shift occurred in the U.S.–China relationship, which had dictated the shape of postwar Japan–China relations. Then after that, the Nixon administration rolled out its diplomacy for U.S.–USSR détente and for ending the Vietnam War.

Here, we would like to review the differences between U.S.–China rapprochement and the normalization of diplomatic relations, which materialized in the latter stages of the 1970s. Normalization was consequent upon putting formal intergovernmental relations in order, such as the opening of mutual embassies and the severance of diplomatic ties between the United States and Taiwan, but U.S.–China rapprochement was just agreeing to the general framework and basic rules. It was a strategic move to fundamentally alter the international political structure literally with a handshake by the U.S. and Chinese leaders. Furthermore, for the United States, rapprochement with China was compatible with U.S.–USSR détente, but at the time of U.S.–China diplomatic normalization, U.S.–USSR relations had reverted back to confrontation dubbed the "new Cold War," and thus a U.S.–China strategic partnership against the common Soviet enemy took shape.

China's strategy and Japan

In China, too, a full-scale examination of the international situation began in 1969, the year the Nixon administration started. Well known is the "International Situation Study Group" of the Four Marshals—Chen Yi, Ye Jianying, Xu Xiangqian, and Nie Rongzhen—that had made progress as the Sino-Soviet border conflict intensified. However, the policy direction within the ranks of China's leadership was not unified: Lin Biao, for instance, stressed preparations against a full-blown armed invasion from the Soviet Union while opposing "American imperialism." In addition, the 9th CCP National Congress held in April 1969—13 years since the last one in 1956—only adopted the party platform specifying the overthrow of "American imperialism"; a decision on rapprochement with the United States was not easy domestically (Masuda 2011).

In the final analysis, China's decision to take the plunge toward rapprochement with the United States should be viewed as a result of a comprehensive strategic judgment. Clearly, at the broadest level, the worsening Sino-Soviet split was important. At the same time, however, it was clear that a China with the USSR as its main adversary could not assist with the Nixon administration's policy of détente with the USSR. In fact, when the opportunity for U.S.–USSR détente grew after U.S.–China rapprochement, it spawned uncertainty in U.S.–China relations (Ogata 1992). Regardless, the reduction of threat that would accompany the Vietnam War's conclusion and the U.S. withdrawal from Asia, and Taiwan issue developments in the context of eventual diplomatic normalization that were expected to follow rapprochement were extremely important for China.

In April 1971, along with orchestrating "ping-pong diplomacy"—inviting the U.S. table tennis team that was participating at the World Table Tennis Championships in Nagoya to visit China—China conveyed a message to the United States via the Pakistani backchannel that it was prepared to accept a presidential special envoy or the president himself. Then, Zhou Enlai unveiled the "Eight Principles for the United States" at the CCP Politburo meeting in May. These principles clarified China's position at talks with the United States: if the United States would not honor China's fundamental principles of a U.S. troop withdrawal from Taiwan and that Taiwan was Chinese territory, normalization would have to be put off for the time being, although they could establish liaison offices in each other's capital (Mori 2006).

U.S.–China negotiations largely proceeded according to each country's strategic thinking between Kissinger's top secret trip to China in July 1971 and Nixon's China visit in February 1972. Then, in this timeframe, China joined the United Nations. At the UNGA meeting in autumn 1970, though a resolution was adopted titled "Representation of China in the United Nations," designating the representation of China as an important question requiring a two-thirds majority for approval, the Albanian resolution that recognized PRC representation garnered the majority of votes. The United States put up the last resistance at the UNGA in autumn 1971, countering with a resolution designating the expulsion of Taiwan an important question, but the proposal failed to pass and the Albanian resolution was adopted by an overwhelming majority. And so, China gaining UN membership was a development that had been foreseen by both the United States and China, which were groping toward strategic cooperation.

For China, normalization of diplomatic ties with Japan was nothing more than an effort to place Japan within the big picture framework depicted above. One might call the explicit strategic nature focusing on power politics its special trait. In extreme contrast, the special characteristic of Japan's diplomacy for dealing with Japan–China normalization was that of seeking to extricate itself from such logic of power politics.

Divided image of Japan

In fact, postwar Japanese diplomacy based on the "Yoshida Line"—with its two pillars of the postwar constitution and the Japan–U.S. Security Treaty—had already fallen from the stage of power politics. Curiously enough, however, in his talks with Nixon and Kissinger, Zhou Enlai was seriously concerned about the possibility that Japan, on its own, would fill the military vacuum left in Asia after a U.S. withdrawal. The concern China held about a "revival of Japanese militarism," provoked by the Japanese aspiration for an "independent self-defense" as a response to the Nixon Doctrine, was probably very real.

Indeed, U.S. and Chinese leadership shared that sort of an understanding of Japan, a point that became clear when Kissinger met Zhou during his top secret visit in July 1971. At the July 11 talks, Zhou mentioned that Japan had "expansionist tendencies" and appeared quite alarmed by Japan's Fourth Defense Buildup Plan. Kissinger agreed with Zhou, saying that those fears would become real if Japan possessed its own military power and nuclear weapons, and he stated that the Japan–U.S. Security Treaty was acting as a brake on such tendencies. This is the first instance of U.S. and Chinese leadership sharing the "cork in the bottle" argument for the Japan–U.S. Security Treaty, so far as can be confirmed in the records currently available (Mori and Mori 2001; Soeya 2003).

Similar conversations on Japan were repeated when Kissinger returned to China after the "Nixon shock" in October 1971 and again during Nixon's visit to China in February 1972. In various conversations with Zhou, Kissinger expressed greater trust in China, saying "China by tradition has a universal outlook but Japan has had a tribal outlook." Nixon said he hoped that "the situation is changed permanently away from the militarism that has characterized Japanese government in the past," although "we cannot guarantee it," and he went so far as to say "the U.S. will use its influence with Japan … to discourage policies which would be detrimental to China," i.e., Japan pursuing a military build-up (Mori and Mori 2001; Soeya 2003).

Nevertheless, the reality was that Japan's security role in Northeast Asia had increased, as demonstrated by the "Korea clause" and "Taiwan clause," mentioned previously. Further, the United States kept requesting Japan to increase its burden-sharing under the Japan–U.S. security relationship in the 1970s. Though détente was a means for the United States to reduce its geostrategic burden, it did not mean an end to U.S.–Soviet confrontation nor a decline in the importance of the Japan–U.S. security relationship. There was also some logic inherent in détente that an expanded role for Japan in the security of Asia made a reduction of the U.S. role possible.

It is interesting that even China later began to welcome an expanded security role for Japan. From China's perspective, détente centered on U.S.–China rapprochement provided the necessary international environment for the post-Cultural Revolution modernization path, and made possible the effective development of anti-hegemony diplomacy toward the Soviet Union. Following this line of reasoning, China supported Japan's position on the Northern Territories and began to argue that a certain degree of strengthening of Japan's military power was to be expected. In this way, the image of Japan viewed by the United States and China was fundamentally divided and convoluted.

Japan tries out a more diversified diplomacy

Whereas many in the outside world viewed Japan's autonomy (*shutaisei*) debate as evoking the specter of militarism, the reality was that Japanese diplomacy had been emphasizing a more diversified diplomacy rather than unilateralism in its pursuit of an "independent" foreign policy. Moreover, U.S.–China rapprochement was the very thing that provided postwar Japanese diplomacy its greatest opportunity to turn toward diversification. Japanese diplomatic officials actually experienced a great sense of freedom because of U.S.–China rapprochement, and later began experimenting with "expanding diplomatic horizons" with respect to other areas throughout the 1970s, while upholding the importance of the Japan–U.S. relationship (Iokibe 2010).

It is probably no coincidence that the early test case for diversified diplomacy was the normalization of relations with North Vietnam, which was closely linked to U.S.–China rapprochement. Both countries' diplomatic officials in Hong Kong and Paris initiated contacts in early 1971. North Vietnam conveyed its interest in establishing a commercial representative office in Tokyo to MOFA using the Hong Kong channel in June. The Japanese government made no immediate moves out of consideration toward the United States and South Vietnam, but the winds shifted after the July "Nixon shock." By November, it sounded out the North Vietnamese government on a plan to dispatch MOFA personnel to Hanoi (Wakatsuki 2006).

The agenda Japan proposed offered an exchange of resident trade office liaisons and economic exchange in general but ultimately envisioned the normalization of diplomatic relations. The agenda showed a desire for a post-Vietnam era of diplomacy toward Southeast Asia, something that should be called the kernel for the "Fukuda Doctrine" (1977), which set forth the goal of providing support for the integration of the Southeast Asia region after the Vietnam War. Thus, Miyake Wasuke, chief of MOFA's Southeast Asia First Section, made a top secret visit to Hanoi in February 1972. Then, when the Vietnam War ended with the conclusion of the Paris Peace Accords on January 28, 1973, the two sides issued an "Exchange of Notes Regarding the Establishment of Diplomatic Relations Between Japan and the Democratic Republic of Vietnam" on September 21, 1973 and established diplomatic relations.

Meanwhile, Japan established diplomatic relations with Mongolia in February 1972 and made efforts to improve ties with the Soviet Union. The USSR, also anxious about U.S.–China rapprochement, tried out a new approach to Japan, too. Consequently, Soviet Foreign Minister Andrei Gromyko visited Japan in January 1972, and with Foreign Minister Fukuda Takeo, restarted the Regular Japanese-Soviet Foreign Ministerial Consultations after a five-year gap. They agreed to start negotiations to conclude a Japan–USSR peace treaty, have reciprocal visits by leaders, and hold the foreign ministerial consultations annually. Clearly, the USSR's intention was to divert Japan's approach to China.

On the other hand, the Japanese government treated improved ties with the USSR as a means to expand the scope of Japanese diplomacy in a multipolar world, and actively moved to seek progress on the Northern Territories issue at the same time. Foreign Minister Ohira Masayoshi, who accomplished diplomatic normalization with China in September 1972, visited the Soviet Union in October. Prime Minister Tanaka Kakuei's visit to the Soviet Union and the summit with General Secretary Leonid Ilyich Brezhnev took place in October 1973, the first Japan–Soviet summit in 17 years since former Prime Minister Hatoyama Ichiro reopened ties with his 1956 visit to the Soviet Union. With the "Japanese-Soviet Joint Communiqué" of October 10, which noted "the settlement of unresolved problems left over since World War II and the conclusion of a peace treaty," Japan–Soviet relations also entered a new phase.

2 Japan–China diplomatic normalization

Sato administration gropes for approach to China

At 10:30 p.m. on July 15, 1971, President Nixon made a dramatic televised announcement disclosing Kissinger's top secret trip to China and plans for his own visit there that would take place at an appropriate time before May 1972. It was after 10 p.m. that Secretary of State William Rogers called Japanese Ambassador to the United States Ushiba Nobuhiko with the news. The shock felt by Japan's statesmen and bureaucrats was enormous. Various criticisms were heard: "The United States selfishly does whatever it wants"; "It doesn't even want to try and do something for Japan, not a bit"; "It's gone ahead and done it" (Hattori 2011, pp. 37–39). These tended to overshadow the idea of calmly trying to discern the strategic thinking of the United States and China.

The Japanese government's push to normalize relations with China began at that moment. And yet, the Sato administration had hardly had any leeway to develop an active China policy in the latter half of the 1960s when China was in the turmoil of the Cultural Revolution and the Vietnam War was intensifying. Even so, one probably cannot explain the Sato administration's efforts to seek a path to better relations with China without the resentment against the "Nixon shock." Although Foreign Minister Fukuda hinted at clandestine efforts, comparing them to "a duck's webbed feet" (paddling forward under the water), China had no intention from the start of moving ahead on normalization negotiations with the Sato administration.

The most important of the moves on an approach to China under the Sato administration is what is called the Hori letter, a letter for Zhou Enlai from LDP Secretary General Hori Shigeru that he entrusted to Tokyo Governor Minobe Ryokichi. The Hori letter, which Minobe handed to Zhou on his November 1971 trip to China, stated that "The People's Republic of China is the government that represents China, and Taiwan is the territory of the Chinese people." Zhou, who took this to mean "two Chinas," made the contents public, clearly indicating that he had no intention of dealing with the Sato administration (Ogata 1992).

At the same time, the issue of Chinese representation in the UN was another troubling the Sato administration. The United States was advancing preparations to submit a resolution designating the expulsion of Taiwan an important question ahead of the UNGA in the autumn of 1971, and it was making stronger appeals to the Japanese government to become a co-sponsor. Even as he recognized the resolution would be defeated at the UN, Sato ultimately decided to be a co-sponsor out of a sense of obligation to Taiwan. Many within the ruling party and MOFA, too, opposed jettisoning Taiwan so easily.

Even so, Sato had not yet discarded his own hopes to embark on Japan–China normalization. At the lower house budget committee right after Nixon's February 1972 visit to China, Sato expressed his view that Taiwan belonged to the People's Republic of China, going beyond the existing official government view that argued Taiwan's legal position was unsettled. The situation devolved into confusion following Foreign Minister Fukuda's rejection of Sato's statement, and ended up with the March 6 "unified view" of the Japanese government that, although it was "not in a position to comment on the affiliation of Taiwan," it "could fully understand the People's Republic of China's claim that 'Taiwan is the territory of the People's Republic of China'" (Inoue 2010, p. 484).

Start of the Tanaka administration and preparing to negotiate with China

As soon as the reversion of Okinawa occurred in May 1972—achieving the Sato administration's long-sought goal—the fight for a successor intensified between Fukuda Takeo, whom Sato supported, and Tanaka Kakuei. The issue of Japan–China normalization determined the outcome of the LDP presidential election held on July 5. In contrast to Fukuda, who appeared unenthusiastic about normalization while showing consideration for Taiwan, the pro-China group of Ohira Masayoshi, Miki Takeo, and Nakasone Yasuhiro all got to work on Tanaka. Meeting on July 2, Tanaka, Ohira, and Miki concluded a policy pact agreeing to undertake negotiations with China on diplomatic normalization. In the presidential election contested by those three men and Fukuda, there was no result in the first round of voting, and in the run-off voting, Tanaka garnered 282 votes to beat Fukuda, who took only 190.

Forming his cabinet on July 7, Tanaka spoke of hastening Japan–China normalization, true to the agreement of the policy pact. For his foreign minister, Tanaka installed Ohira, who was the leader of the pro-China group, setting the stage for close cooperation between the two. Tanaka had begun convening a study group on China issues with Hashimoto Hiroshi, chief of MOFA's China Section, right before the "Nixon shock." Ohira, too, who had time to spare at the end of Sato's administration, often consulted with Hashimoto on China matters. Right after being made foreign minister in Tanaka's cabinet, Ohira directed Hashimoto to prepare for a visit to China (Hattori 2011).

All of the legal issues associated with Japan–China normalization, including the draft of the bilateral joint statement, Hashimoto entrusted to Kuriyama Takakazu, chief of the Treaties Division. For the Treaties Bureau, the fundamental issues were Japan's response to what China called "the three principles for the restoration of relations" and the compatibility of Japan–China normalization with the San Francisco system (Kuriyama 2010). The "three principles" were the last three of five conditions appearing in the joint communiqué issued by China and the first Komeito delegation to China on July 2, 1971: (1) There is only one China, and the Government of the People's Republic of China is the sole legal government representing the Chinese people; (2) Taiwan is a province of China, an inalienable part of Chinese territory, and the Taiwan question is purely China's internal affair; and (3) The "Taiwan–Japan Treaty" is illegal and invalid and must be abrogated.

After switching diplomatic recognition from the Republic of China in Taiwan to the People's Republic of China, the first point posed no major problem. The obstacles were points two and three, which lay at the heart of the Taiwan issue for the Japanese government. The Japanese government anticipated that these two conditions would complicate the process of negotiations with China. In the end, final resolution was put off until Tanaka's visit to China in September 1972, and Kuriyama recollected there was "maybe a touch of unease, or more than a touch of unease" concerning the status of negotiations at the end of August (Kuriyama 2010, p. 122).

Compatibility with the San Francisco system, to put it simply, was the issue at the root of Japan's postwar diplomacy, that is, to achieve Japan–China normalization of relations without harming the Japan–U.S. Security Treaty system. On this point, the Japanese government's position did not waiver. In talks with President Nixon in Honolulu on August 31 and September 1, 1972, Tanaka and Ohira confirmed they were aiming for Japan–China diplomatic normalization that would not damage the Japan–U.S. security system. It was not unusual for Japan to be concerned, considering how relentlessly China had attacked the Japan–U.S. security system up to that point. But as discussed above, the United States and China, as they advanced toward rapprochement, had already made the Japan–U.S. Security Treaty system part of their own broad strategic plans.

Business community's pro-China tilt and the "Takeiri Memo"

As the Japan–China normalization process developed, the role that nongovernmental actors played was not insignificant. Notably, the Japan–China trade channels that had been organized in the 1960s were up and running, and Japan's domestic environment was prepared for normalizing relations with China (Soeya 1995). "Zhou's Four Principles" created the first development; Zhou Enlai laid these out in April 1970 to the Memorandum Trade delegation visiting China headed by Matsumura Kenzo. The gist was that China would not trade with businesses that had deep ties to Taiwan, South Korea, or the United States. Many of the friendship trading companies and businesses already engaged in trade with China announced their acceptance on the spot. Later, as the conditions were loosened in practice, all of the four big trading companies—Mitsubishi Shoji, Mitsui Bussan, Marubeni, and ITOCHU—also participated in Japan–China trade after accepting "Zhou's Four Principles" in June 1972.

Concurrently, JAPIT, which managed Friendship Trade, was in constant contact with Zhou and moving forward on plans for big business leaders from Kansai and

Tokyo to visit China. As a result, the plan for a visit by Kansai business leaders was settled in May 1971, preceding the "Nixon shock," and the top seven executives from Kansai's five major economic organizations visited China in September as planned. Tokyo business leaders, who somewhat delayed forming an agreement, finally visited China in November after deciding to form the "Tokyo Businessmen China Visit Group," with each going in a personal capacity. The Japanese business community's pro-China tilt became decisive and was a factor in generating a China boom in Japan domestically.

Amid this progress that Japanese private sector actors made on shaping the environment for normalizing relations with China, Japan's opposition parties actively sought out contacts with China. China chose the Komeito from among them to be the key conduit for government-to-government negotiations. The most important one of all was the visit to China by Komeito Chairman Takeiri Yoshikatsu toward the end of July 1972. Takeiri had talks with Zhou for three consecutive days and brought back, in the form of his own hand-written memo, a record of the conversation that included China's eight articles for a draft joint communiqué and a proposal for a "secret agreement" regarding Taiwan (Ishii et al. 2003). This is the so-called "Takeiri Memo."

To a remarkable degree, the "Takeiri Memo" laid to rest the concerns that Japan had held until then. First, Zhou Enlai clearly stated that China would not touch on the Japan–U.S. Security Treaty or the "Nixon–Sato Joint Statement" of 1969. When the Vietnam War ended, went Zhou's reasoning, the U.S. military would withdraw from Taiwan, the Taiwan issue would be resolved over time, and the Japan–U.S. Security Treaty would lose its effectiveness against China. Further, he made clear that it was Mao Zedong's intention to waive the right to claim reparations. He appeared intent on establishing Japan–China normalization that would be announced by a joint declaration or communiqué when Tanaka and Ohira visited China. After seeing the "Takeiri Memo," Tanaka and Ohira started to think the future for negotiations looked bright.

From Japan's viewpoint, there remained problems to fix, such as legal interpretation language. But Kuriyama, who set about drawing up Japan's draft of the Japan–China Joint Communiqué, had a tangled mess of information that had been brought through various channels. The "Takeiri Memo" alone was the only material that offered China's intentions, he noted reflecting back (Kuriyama 2010). However, prospects for resolving the Taiwan issue were hardly visible. Zhou had proposed a secret agreement that included the clause, "Taiwan is a territory of the People's Republic of China, and the liberation of Taiwan is China's internal affair" (Ishii et al. 2003, p. 119). However, Japan's position was to not accept the secret agreement.

Negotiated agreement in Beijing

Prime Minister Tanaka's party arrived in Beijing on September 25, 1972, even without prospects for reaching agreement on several points of difference, including the Taiwan issue. Tanaka and Zhou held talks on four successive days (September

25–28); at the same time, Ohira and Foreign Minister Ji Pengfei met four times for foreign ministry talks, including the unofficial first session. The negotiations hit an impasse several times, but the agenda of pending issues was agreed to as below, and so Tanaka, Ohira, Zhou, and Ji signed the "Joint Communiqué of the Government of Japan and the Government of the People's Republic of China" on September 29.

BOX 3.1 TANAKA'S VISIT TO CHINA AND CHINA'S DOMESTIC CAMPAIGN

At the time of Japan–China diplomatic normalization in 1972, it was only natural for the Chinese people to feel opposed to Prime Minister Tanaka's visit to China since Japan's aggression remained fresh in the memories of many Chinese, but also because of the government's campaign denouncing the "revival of Japanese militarism." And so, after Tanaka's visit was arranged, the Chinese government under the direction of Premier Zhou Enlai rolled out a campaign to persuade and educate the people in mid-August 1972.

CCP executives held lectures throughout China on normalizing relations with Japan and the meaning of renouncing reparations from Japan, as well as analysis of the international situation and Mao Zedong's strategy, and they reported the people's views back to CCP headquarters. An "internal directive concerning the Foreign Ministry's treatment of the Tanaka visit to China" was prepared, with Zhou's involvement, at the beginning of September, and it was distributed as a CCP central directive to all subsidiary CCP organizations throughout the country. The following is a summary of the points highlighted in this document, obtained by Hu Ming.

As the international situation tilts in China's favor, Prime Minister Tanaka is actively seeking to improve relations and end policies hostile toward China. To invite Prime Minister Tanaka is in accord with the interests of both peoples, who hope for friendship between China and Japan. The visit is advantageous in our struggles against U.S.–USSR hegemony, especially against Soviet revisionism; against a revival of Japanese militarism; and for the liberation of Taiwan. As for renouncing war reparations, Taiwan already renounced them; China could draw Japan closer by being more broad-minded than Chiang Kai-shek. Furthermore it is important not to add to the burden of the Japanese people (Ko 2012).

This explanation reflected the fundamental principle that China established in the 1950s for its policies toward Japan, the distinction between the Japanese people and a group of militarists. In that sense, it is very interesting that the Chinese representatives who visited Japan for cultural and sporting exchanges frequently held debriefing sessions as a part of this internal campaign. As they introduced the daily lives of Japanese citizens, they all spoke enthusiastically of being given a big welcome in Japan and of the Japanese people's strong feelings of friendship for China.

The two sides exchanged joint communiqué drafts and explanations at the first foreign ministry talks on September 25. The termination of the state of war and the Taiwan issue were the disagreements that surfaced immediately. Concerning the former, the Japanese government's legal position was that the Japan–ROC Peace Treaty had already put an end to the state of war with "China"; China objected to this stance. Finally, a compromise was reached at the final foreign ministry talks held late at night on September 27—the preamble of the joint communiqué mentioned "[t]he realization of the aspiration of the two peoples for the termination of the state of war and the normalization of relations between Japan and China" and the first article declared that "[t]he abnormal state of affairs that has hitherto existed between Japan and the People's Republic of China is terminated on the date on which this Joint Communiqué is issued." "[They] really thought of something clever," Kuriyama says of this linkage that China proposed (Kuriyama 2010, p. 131).

Regarding the Taiwan issue, the joint communiqué touched on the "three principles" in the preamble and in Article 3 of the text they compromised:

> The Government of the People's Republic of China reiterates that Taiwan is an inalienable part of the territory of the People's Republic of China. The Government of Japan fully understands and respects this stand of the Government of the People's Republic of China, and it firmly maintains its stand under Article 8 of the Potsdam Proclamation.

Article 8 of the Potsdam Declaration calls for the implementation of the Cairo Declaration, which had stipulated that Japan must restore Taiwan to the Republic of China. This means that Japan would take the position of "one China" and not support Taiwanese independence, although Japan did not necessarily recognize Taiwan as China's territory, according to Kuriyama, who had written up said idea as material for negotiations. Kuriyama recalled that Zhou Enlai understood this reasoning (Kuriyama 2010).

Taking account of all the above, Foreign Minister Ohira made the following statement regarding the Japan–ROC Peace Treaty, which China insisted was illegal, at a press conference after the signing of the joint communiqué: "It is the Government of Japan's view that, as a result of the normalization of Japan–China diplomatic relations, the [Japan–ROC] Peace Treaty had lost its *raison d'etre* and is recognized as ended." Furthermore, on the topic of "renouncing the right to war reparations," which the Japanese position held the Japan–ROC Peace Treaty had already addressed, China responded by compromising, dropping the term "right" and using the expression "renounces its demands for war reparations."

In the meantime, an "anti-hegemony" clause, which later would become a big sticking point in peace treaty negotiations, was listed as Article 7 of the Japan–China Joint Communiqué without any dispute between Japan and China. That article leads off with the sentence, "The normalization of relations between Japan and China is not directed against any third country." The interesting thing is, Japan suggested this sentence for the preamble in the second round of foreign ministers' talks on September 26.

Foreign Minister Ji Pengfei proposed that it should be included in the anti-hegemony clause, and Ohira responded that he had "no particular objections."

Actually, Ohira, who sat in on the first round of summit talks between Tanaka and Zhou Enlai held on September 25, had said that there were two issues attendant on the normalization of Japan–China relations: the Japan–ROC Peace Treaty was the first, and

> [t]he second point is relations with third countries. In particular, the Japan–U.S. relationship is critically important to Japan's existence…. In other words, our country wishes to realize Japan–China diplomatic normalization in a manner that would not harm our relations with the United States.
>
> *(Ishii et al. 2003, p. 54)*

This means that there is a high probability that Japan was thinking of its relationship with the United States when it first proposed the third country clause. The "third country" reference was changed by Ji Pengfei's proposal to mean, in fact, relations with the Soviet Union, and Japan had no qualms about it. This might be called corroborating evidence for Japanese diplomacy's attempts to distance itself from the dynamic of U.S.–China–USSR relations of the time.

Cutting Japan–ROC ties and "Japanese formula"

The Japanese government recognized the PRC government as "the sole legal Government of China" in Article 2 of the Japan–China Joint Communiqué. It followed that the ROC government (hereafter Taiwan) was no longer the legal government representing China. Foreign Minister Ohira said as much in the press conference following the signing of the joint communiqué when he expressed that the Japan–ROC Peace Treaty had ended pursuant to Japan–China normalization of state relations. However, at the same time, clearly the Japanese government did not agree fully with China's position that Taiwan was an inalienable part of its proper territory. It was self-evident that Taiwan was under different political governance than the mainland, and in fact, there were deep ties between Japan and Taiwan in the areas of trade, investment, tourism, and culture.

And yet, in the context of the international trend of many countries establishing diplomatic relations with the PRC government—not just U.S.–China rapprochement and Japan–China normalization—it was now evident that there was something odd in the argument that Taiwan was the legal government representing the whole of China including the mainland. For Taiwan, the severing of diplomatic relations was a problem of face more than anything. Late in the night of September 29, 1972, the day the Japan–China Joint Communiqué was issued, Taiwan unilaterally declared that diplomatic relations with Japan were now over, thus unequivocally indicating its basic stance.

However, even as the Taiwanese government's foreign minister pointed out that "the Japanese Government shall assume full responsibility for the rupture" in the statement breaking off relations, he declared that "[w]ith all those Japanese people who are opposed to communism for the cause of democracy, the Government of the Republic of China will continue to maintain friendship." The Japanese government felt relieved by this last sentence, because, even though cutting diplomatic ties was preordained, it had been concerned about the possibility of retaliation or harm befalling Japan–Taiwan relations, which had been substantial until then.

The "farewell diplomacy"—from when the Tanaka cabinet began to move on normalization with China until the severing of relations with Taiwan—was a heartbreaking process for both Japan and Taiwan. Charged as the Japanese government's special envoy with that responsibility, fraught with difficulties, was Shiina Etsusaburo, who had accomplished Japan–ROK normalization in 1965 as foreign minister in the Sato cabinet. Shiina visited Taiwan on September 17, 1972, carrying Prime Minister Tanaka's handwritten letter addressed to Chiang Kai-shek. The letter's content was revised at least five times, and in the process, underwent a metamorphosis from a diplomatic document into something of an extremely Oriental tenor that "would show every sign of courtesy" (Hattori 2011, p. 106). In talks with Executive Yuan President (Premier) Chiang Ching-kuo, Shiina tried to thread the needle with the cunning posture of expressing his opinion that Japan and Taiwan would be able to continue "status quo relations," including diplomacy (Nakae 2008).

Actually, the Taiwanese government had determined as soon as the Tanaka cabinet was formed that Japan–China normalization was inevitable, so it began considering plans for how to continue working-level relations or for influencing the Japanese people. Japan had worried whether Taiwan would welcome special envoy Shiina, but Premier Chiang laid out his thoughts at an Executive Yuan meeting in late August that "should there be talk of Japan formally sending a special envoy, we would be unable to refuse seeing him," even as he continued to state the principle that "there would be absolutely no understanding, nor room for discussion, concerning any act harmful to the Republic of China's interests" (Kawashima 2011, p. 207).

In this way, Japan's Interchange Association in Taipei and Taiwan's Association of East Asian Relations in Tokyo were established as early as December 1, 1972 through the "farewell diplomacy" that honored courtesy, thereby constructing an arrangement to continue working-level relations on a nongovernmental basis even after cutting ties. This system was dubbed the "Japanese formula" and became the model for U.S.–Taiwan relations when U.S.–China normalization was established in the late stages of the 1970s.

Japan–China working agreements

In the September 1972 Japan–China Joint Communiqué, the two sides agreed to enter negotiations for the purpose of concluding agreements on trade, maritime shipping, civil aviation, fisheries, and other matters. To follow up, a delegation of high-level bureaucrats from the foreign, trade, finance, agriculture, and transport ministries, led by Deputy Vice Minister of Foreign Affairs Togo Fumihiko, visited China in November and started working-level consultations toward concluding the agreements. Consequently, the Japan–China Trade Agreement (January 5, 1974), the Japan–China Air Transport Agreement (April 20, 1974), the Japan–China Shipping Agreement (November 13, 1974), and the Japan–China Fisheries Agreement (August 15, 1975) were concluded. These agreements covered a variety of working relations, but politically, one must pay attention to the Japan–China Air Transport Agreement and the Japan–China Fisheries Agreement.

At the time, the Japan–China Air Transport Agreement was the most politically contentious of the four main working agreements between Japan and China (Shimizu 2009). China refused to have Taiwan's airplanes use Narita Airport, and it urged the Japanese government to express its position on the ranking of air routes with Taiwan. The Japanese government tried to defuse the issue by asking China Airlines not to fly its flag and to change its corporate name, but naturally Taiwan complained. And so, the Japan–China Air Transport Agreement was ultimately set up only after Foreign Minister Ohira issued remarks that Japan "did not recognize the flag symbol on China Airlines planes as a national flag, nor recognize 'China Airlines Corporation (Taiwan)' as a flag carrier." Taiwan immediately shut down the air routes with Japan. But, taking into account Foreign Minister Miyazawa Kiichi's refutation of Ohira's remarks in early July 1975, Taiwan agreed to restore the air routes, using Haneda Airport, after exchanging the "Japan–Taiwan Agreement on the Maintenance of Civil Aviation Business" on July 9.

Concerning the Japan–China Fisheries Agreement, the issue of territorial waters was avoided—in contrast to the difficulties the Senkaku Islands issue caused during the negotiations of the new Fisheries Agreement that was concluded in 1997. The Senkaku Islands were excluded from the area in the 1974 Agreement, which fixed the southern limit of the area applicable under the Agreement at 27 degrees north latitude. At the time of normalization of Japan–China relations, China's position to avoid touching on the issue of sovereignty over the Senkaku Islands coincided with Japan's policy line of not making the Senkaku Islands into a matter of dispute while not recognizing the existence of a territorial problem.

Senkaku Islands case surfaces suddenly

The first time that China publicly asserted its right of territorial sovereignty over the Senkaku Islands was in a December 1971 foreign ministry statement. Previously, China had even acknowledged in the *People's Daily* in January 1953 that the Senkaku Islands were a part of Okinawa. The 1971 statement declared, "The Diaoyu-dao [the Chinese name for Uotsuri-shima, the largest of the Senkaku islands] and other islands have been China's territory since ancient times ... They were islands appertaining to China's Taiwan but not to ... [what] is now known as Okinawa" (Hosaka and Togo 2012, p. 123). Premised on this new Chinese claim, Zhou Enlai expressed the position that he would not touch on the Senkakus in the process of negotiating Japan–China normalization. In the July 28, 1972 talks with Takeiri Yoshikatsu, Zhou stated that "historians are making it an issue because of the oil problem," but that "there is no need to place too much importance on this issue." To the question, "What are your thoughts on the Senkaku Islands?" that Tanaka Kakuei posed in the September 27 summit, Zhou responded, "I do not want to talk about it this time. It is not good to discuss this now" (Ishii et al. 2003, pp. 20, 68).

The reason that the Chinese government asserted its right of territorial sovereignty for the first time in history was because, immediately before this, Taiwan started making similar claims and set out to survey the ocean floor in the surrounding area in collaboration with U.S. companies (Anami 2012). In the end, the U.S. government put a stop to these moves by U.S. and Taiwanese private companies. However, China's territorial claims over the Senkaku Islands that began as a combination of natural resource problems and the Taiwan issue came to have its own gravitational force within China's foreign policy to Japan, as they passed through the "shelving" argument that Deng Xiaoping made at a press conference in Tokyo in 1978 and unilateral measure of including the Senkaku Islands within its definition of territorial waters in its Law on the Territorial Sea in 1992.

On the Japanese side, MOFA, in a document dated July 10, 1972 titled "Agenda Topics Between Japan and China," had clearly stated that "From our government's standpoint, these islands are our nation's territory—this is a fact, with no room for debate. And so, it is our position not to consider discussing the territorial sovereignty of these islands with any country's government." On top of that, the Japanese government consistently took a measured response so as to not rile China with the Senkaku Islands case, as was shown in the Japan–China Fisheries Agreement discussed above.

Perhaps this can be interpreted as "putting it to the side" without touching on the Senkakus for the purpose of stable development of Japan–China relations rather than as recognizing that a problem exists and "shelving" it. One could also say it is essentially an example of the low profile characteristic of Japan's diplomacy regarding traditional security issues concerning such matters as territory.

3 Expansion of Japan–China relations

U.S.–China normalization and collapse of détente

The Nixon administration's policy of détente provoked criticism at home from the right. The concept of "Nixon/Kissinger diplomacy," which recognized the Soviet Union as a partner in the traditional balance-of-power game and was oriented toward coexistence, did not feel right to the Cold War hawks who took confrontation with the Soviet Union seriously. As the policy of détente lost cohesion after President Nixon resigned in August 1974 over the Watergate controversy, Soviet actions that seemed to go against the course of détente began to stand out, such as its growing intervention in the Angolan Civil War. This sparked a debate on the merits of détente policy within the United States, which became a major focal point of conflict in the process of diplomatic normalization with China pursued by the Jimmy Carter administration, which began in 1977.

This conflict surfaced between National Security Advisor Zbigniew Brzezinski, who attempted to impart the strategic significance of Soviet containment to the normalization of relations with China, and Secretary of State Cyrus Vance, who tried to advance diplomatic normalization with China while at the same time maintaining the path to détente with the USSR. Needless to say, China welcomed the Brzezinski policy line and the course of events for U.S.–China strategic cooperation was defined: Brzezinski's May 1978 visit to China was an important turning point for ironing out the logic of joint opposition to the USSR. The U.S.–China Joint Communiqué was concluded in December 1978 and normalization of U.S.–China diplomatic relations came into being in January 1979.

U.S.–China diplomatic normalization alienated the USSR and (the Socialist Republic of) Vietnam. Vietnam felt a growing sense of betrayal from Chinese cooperation with America's Vietnam policy as they pursued rapprochement in the early 1970s. Vietnam toppled Saigon in 1975 and unified the country the following year. The rift between Vietnam and China widened, until China completely stopped assistance to Vietnam in July 1978. At the time, U.S.–Vietnam normalization talks were proceeding, but President Carter decided to halt these negotiations as if to reflect China's inclinations. In this context, Vietnam joined the Soviet bloc's assistance organization, COMECON (Council for Mutual Economic Assistance), in June 1978 and concluded the USSR–Vietnam Treaty of Friendship and Cooperation that November.

With China as its biggest backer, the Pol Pot regime in Cambodia gained control of Phnom Penh in 1975 and engaged repeatedly in military clashes in the border zone with its neighbor, Vietnam. The two countries severed relations in December 1977. Isolated by U.S.–China normalization and drawing closer to the USSR, Vietnam invaded Cambodia in December 1978 and established the Heng Samrin government in January 1979. The West, including Japan and the United States, denounced Vietnam and imposed sanctions. Thereupon China, which had only just normalized diplomatic relations with the United States, invaded Vietnam in February as "punishment".

And thus détente, whose path was cleared by U.S.–China rapprochement, was once again shaken by the tight linkages between the situation in Indochina and the U.S.–China relationship. Furthermore, when the USSR invaded Afghanistan in December 1979, the United States led the West in imposing sanctions, such as the boycott of the Moscow Olympics held the following year. At this point, détente collapsed completely. It meant the start of a rather desirable international environment for China, which had been ill at ease with the Nixon administration's strategy of trying to actively use the "swing position" in the Sino-Soviet split to U.S. advantage. Thus, as the 1980s began, China took the U.S.–USSR confrontation as given and oriented itself on a more independent diplomatic line.

"Anti-hegemony" tussle

In Article 8 of the September 29, 1972 joint communiqué opening diplomatic relations, Japan and China "agreed that, with a view to solidifying and developing the relations of peace and friendship between the two countries, the two Governments will enter into negotiations for the purpose of concluding a treaty of peace and friendship." Peace treaty negotiations developed, influenced by the international politics described earlier, U.S.–China diplomatic normalization and the collapse of détente. What determined the outcome of these negotiations was China's strategy of a national anti-hegemony policy clearly directed against the Soviet Union. China went so far as to incorporate the term "anti-hegemony" in its new constitution, revised in January 1975. Vice Foreign Minister Han Nianlong went to Japan in November 1974, and at his overture, preparatory negotiations for the Japan–China Treaty of Peace and Friendship began at the working level. The anti-hegemony clause was already in China's treaty draft at that point, but initially that fact was concealed.

Right after the first preparatory negotiations, Prime Minister Tanaka resigned on November 26 owing to financial problems. The following month, Miki Takeo became the next prime minister; Miyazawa Kiichi took office as the next foreign minister. Media reporting immediately after the second working-level talks in January 1975 made clear that "anti-hegemony" was becoming a key point of dispute. This was an important principle for Chinese diplomacy, and China firmly asserted that it was already stated in the 1972 Japan–China Joint Communiqué. However, the Japanese government, seeking to advance negotiations with the USSR with a view toward a Japan–USSR peace treaty, showed it disapproved of the anti-hegemony clause, which obviously implied confrontation with the USSR.

The "Omori Memo" is a record of the negotiations over the Japan–China Treaty of Peace and Friendship drafted by Omori Seiichi, the director of MOFA's Treaty Bureau at the time. According to this memo, the Miki cabinet, which wanted to conclude negotiations, showed China a draft compromise in November 1975 that included the anti-hegemony clause (Nagano 2003). The draft tried to neutralize the anti-Soviet nature of the anti-hegemony clause, based on "Miyazawa's Four Principles" that Foreign Minister Miyazawa raised in talks with Foreign Minister Qiao Guanhua at the UNGA in September of that year. And yet, it meant Japan conceded the point of actually including an anti-hegemony clause in the peace treaty.

The "Miyazawa's Four Principles" outline included the following points: to oppose hegemony anywhere in the world, not just in the Asia-Pacific; opposing hegemony is not directed against any specific third country; and it does not imply Japan–China joint action. In reaction, China stubbornly stuck to its position that, if Japan were to ignore the essence of China's Soviet strategy, then there would be no need to conclude a peace treaty and China would just emphasize the 1972 joint communiqué. In the meantime, Foreign Minister Gromyko, who came to Japan in

January 1976 for the Japanese-Soviet Foreign Ministerial Consultations, expressed dissatisfaction with the Japan–China negotiations, and thus left Japan with a strong warning. By happenstance, Zhou Enlai in January and Mao Zedong in September died and the Chinese situation became uncertain. The Miki cabinet did not make any moves.

Within the LDP, efforts to depose Miki were growing, and he resigned; Fukuda Takeo became prime minister in December 1976. In China, Deng Xiaoping was rehabilitated in July 1977, becoming the CCP vice general secretary, vice premier, and vice chairman of the Central Military Commission (CMC). As is discussed later, Japan's economic importance to China grew after this, as the Deng-led economic construction line became entrenched. Japan began to feel that China had turned positive about concluding a peace treaty at the end of 1977. "Finally the time was ripe for negotiations" between Japan and China, Prime Minister Fukuda remarked rather specifically in his January 1978 policy speech to the Diet (Nagano 1983).

Conclusion of Japan–China Treaty of Peace and Friendship and Deng Xiaoping's visit to Japan

The Komeito played an important role in the course of negotiations for the Japan–China Treaty of Peace and Friendship, similar to the time of normalization. At China's invitation, Secretary General Yano Junya led a Komeito delegation there in March 1978. When the delegation conveyed Fukuda's forward-looking intent to conclude a peace treaty to China, Liao Chengzhi, chairman of the Sino-Japanese Friendship Society, raised the Chinese side's "view on four points." These showed consideration for the Japanese side's original position, stating that the Japan–China Treaty of Peace and Friendship was not aimed against any third country and did not mean joint action by Japan and China. In response, Prime Minister Fukuda undertook extensive consultations with the relevant Japanese leaders regarding such topics as the basic policy for Japan–China negotiations.

Fukuda then set out to win over the LDP. However, an incident happened in April that complicated his efforts to persuade the anti-China/pro-Taiwan group: a group of up to 200 fishing vessels suddenly appeared around the Senkaku Islands, dozens of them repeatedly violating Japanese territorial waters. Actually, it appears that there were interests in China that objected to Deng Xiaoping's diplomacy toward Japan. This may be viewed as one example of an internal power struggle in China sowing confusion in its diplomacy with Japan (Takahara 2011). China ultimately wrapped up the matter by characterizing the incident as spontaneous, even as it reiterated its claim that the Senkaku Islands were Chinese territory. After returning home from his May summit in Washington D.C., Fukuda secured an agreement at the May 26 LDP executive council meeting to open treaty negotiations with China.

Thus the working-level negotiations on the Japan–China Treaty of Peace and Friendship were held in Beijing July 21–August 8, 1978. However, negotiations hit an impasse over the third country clause. In preparing for negotiations, Japan had consolidated its position to insert the third country clause before the anti-hegemony clause in that paragraph to read: "This Treaty is not aimed against any designated third country." In actuality, "designated third country" indicated the USSR; the Chinese side strongly objected. At that point, MOFA, reacting to the report of the negotiation proceedings, showed China a new formulation. Deputy Vice Minister Takashima Masuo had originally drafted this new formulation as "Takashima's private plan"; Owada Hisashi, temporarily detailed as a secretary to Prime Minister Fukuda, added the finishing touches (Nagano 1983).

Final settlement of the matter was delayed until Foreign Minister Sonoda Sunao's trip to China on August 8. Then, China agreed to the Japanese formulation based on "Takashima's private plan" at foreign ministerial talks on August 9. That is how Article 4 of the Japan–China Treaty of Peace and Friendship, signed by the two foreign ministers on August 12, came to read: "The present Treaty shall not affect the position of either Contracting Party regarding its relations with third countries." Concerning the anti-hegemony clause, Article 2 states: "The Contracting Parties declare that neither of them should seek hegemony in the Asia-Pacific region or in any other region and that each is opposed to efforts by any other country or group of countries to establish such hegemony." Although the Japanese position was taken into account, the result also can be interpreted favorably from China's viewpoint: the significance of anti-hegemony was further emphasized by separating Article 7 of the Japan–China Joint Communiqué into the third country and anti-hegemony clauses (Rin Gyoko 2003).

Thus, Japan gained form with the third country clause while China got the substance with the anti-hegemony clause. This case, as with Japan–China diplomatic normalization, accentuates "the extreme difference in the fundamentals of each country's diplomacy" (Mori 2006, p. 90). The Japan–China Treaty of Peace and Friendship was ratified by overwhelming majorities by the Diet's lower house on October 16 and by the upper house on October 18. Then, Deng Xiaoping visited Japan on October 22. His meetings with Prime Minister Fukuda and Emperor Hirohito went smoothly. Deng skillfully stage-managed his Japan diplomacy, such as by extolling the technology of Japan's bullet train, in order to garner Japanese cooperation for China's economic construction policy line.

China's modernization path and Japan

The Third Plenary Session (Third Plenum) of the 11th CCP Central Committee of December 1978 is generally known as the starting point of China's policy of reform and opening. And yet, there are no records showing that the words "reform and opening" were used there; the first time they appear in the *People's Daily* was May 1984 and they are mentioned in the *Selected Works of Deng Xiaoping* in March 1986. In brief, one could say that the Third Plenum was a turning point in the sense that Deng's supremacy was established in the ideological split between Deng and Hua Guofeng, and that the Deng-led policy of reform and opening, while being buffeted by power struggles in the leadership ranks, was entrenched at the start of the 1980s (Takahara 2011).

On the other hand, the basic policy line of "post-Cultural Revolution" China— to walk the path of emphasizing the economy with the goal of "Four Moderniza- tions" in the fields of industry, agriculture, national defense, and science and technology—became clear after the October 1976 arrest of the "Gang of Four," who sought to seize power by following the policy line of the Cultural Revolution. In that sense, one could say that even the diplomatic line of Hua, who made the bold decision for the arrest, was fundamentally to emphasize the economy. However, the new policy line of advancing the "Four Modernizations" with the pillars of foreign trade and importing advanced technology from foreign countries contained a logical contradiction in the domestic political context that could not help clashing with Mao Zedong's line, which had been emphasizing class struggle until then.

At that point, the leadership ranks centered around Hua Guofeng sought to construct a theory for the modernization path while staying consistent with Mao's diplomatic line, the "one-line" strategy that could be said to be part of the anti- hegemony united front diplomacy. That is to say, foreign economic relations were defined as a means for reinforcing China's anti-Soviet strategy (Yu 2011). For the Chinese leadership ranks in a period of transition after the deaths of Zhou and Mao, it was a rather necessary adjustment and not something that Deng would have opposed. However, Deng's thought contained a "de-Maoization" vector that emphasized studying actual conditions and "seeking truth from facts," and this became the backdrop for the ideological battle with Hua, who was unable to deviate from Mao's line.

Japan–China negotiations for the peace treaty and long-term trade agreement, which proceeded at the same time as U.S.–China diplomatic normalization, evolved in the above-mentioned context of China's policy shift toward the "Four Mod- ernizations." China's objective was to take advantage of the international environ- ment in order to make progress on modernizing China's economy and opening to foreign countries.

Thus, the long-term trade agreement negotiations with Japan developed as China started out on its modernization path, which was closely linked with a trans- ition of Chinese politics and diplomacy. For China, this was the period of transition to the reform and opening line that would be in full swing in the 1980s; through this process, the basic policy of Japan's China diplomacy was shaped to support China's stability by assisting in its economic construction.

Japan–China long-term trade agreement and start of ODA to China

Exactly one month after the Japan–China Joint Communiqué established normaliza- tion of relations, what would become the final Memorandum Trade Agreement was signed in Beijing on October 29, 1972. This was the end of Memorandum Trade (including the LT Trade flows of the 1960s), and the mission of the Memorandum

Trade offices along with it. But then, as if to continue their work, the Japan–China Economic Association (JCEA) was established in November; the new chairman was Inayama Yoshihiro, chairman of Nippon Steel who had been actively involved in trade with China since the 1950s. The Japan Federation of Economic Organizations (Keidanren) proposed a bilateral "Economic Cooperation Committee" method to China around this time, in an attempt to get involved in resource diplomacy. However, China rejected this committee concept in September 1973, and acknowledged the JCEA, with its "old friends" who had supported Japan–China trade in the 1960s, as the main track for Japan–China trade (Soeya 1998).

After that, the JCEA became the core organization for concluding negotiations on long-term trade agreements, while it maintained close cooperative relations with MITI and Keidanren. Japan's primary import from China after diplomatic normalization was crude oil, which comprised 33 percent of the total value of imports from China in 1975. And so, in 1975 Japan and China agreed to make arrangements to stabilize crude oil imports and began negotiations to conclude the long-term trade agreement. Meanwhile, the turmoil surrounding the "Gang of Four" in China occurred at the same time as the successive deaths of Mao and Zhou, and negotiations floundered.

The Hua Guofeng regime was established at the end of 1976, negotiations got back on track when Deng Xiaoping was rehabilitated in 1977, and the Japan–China Long-Term Trade Agreement was concluded in February 1978. The agreement had an eight-year effective period (from 1978 to 1985) and set the value of Japanese and Chinese exports at around $10 billion each by 1985, stating that Japan would export technology, manufacturing plant, and construction materials and equipment, and China would export crude oil, coking coal, and steam coal.

Thereafter, in the process of establishing Deng's leadership authority ahead of the Third Plenum in December 1978, China began to study the possibility of borrowing from abroad for its economic construction. At the time, Japanese business leaders kept up their pressure, urging Beijing to accept the idea of official assistance. Deng revealed that China was prepared to accept government loans from Japan in talks with Democratic Party Chairman Sasaki Ryosaku at the end of November 1978. Bilateral working-level contacts soon made progress and Vice Premier Gu Mu formally requested government loans from the Japanese government on his September 1979 trip to Japan (Jo 2011).

China's lack of capital became obvious upon the start of full-scale economic construction that accompanied the establishment of Deng Xiaoping's policy line. Notably, Japan suffered a shock from the suspension of some contracts in February 1979, such as for the Shanghai Baoshan Steel Plant Project, as well as the discontinuation of contracts for the Baoshan Steel Plant's second phase of construction and for petrochemical plants in January 1981. On his visit to China in December 1979, Prime Minister Ohira Masayoshi pledged to provide about 500 billion yen in government funds in fiscal year 1979 for six construction projects such as ports, rail, and hydropower—Japanese ODA to China had started. In this way, the main objective of Japan's China diplomacy was established: to promote China's stability by assisting with its modernization path, a stance also supported by a sense of guilt for its war of aggression.

Cited and referenced materials

Anami Yusuke, 2012, "Senryakuteki gokeikankei no mosaku to higashishinakai mondai 2006–2008 nen [Groping for a Strategic, Mutually Beneficial Relationship and the East China Sea Issue, 2006–2008]," in Takahara Akio, Hattori Ryuji, eds., *Nitchu kankeishi 1972–2012 I: Seiji* [A History of Japan–China Relations 1972–2012, Vol. I: Politics], University of Tokyo Press.

Hattori Ryuji, 2011, *Nitchu kokkoseijoka* [Japan–China Diplomatic Normalization], Chuokoron-Shinsha.

Hosaka Masayasu, Togo Kazuhiko, 2012, *Nihon no Ryodomondai* [Japan's Territorial Problem], Kadokawa.

Inoue Masaya, 2010, *Nitchu kokkoseijoka no seijishi* [Political History of the Japan–China Diplomatic Normalization], University of Nagoya Press.

Iokibe Makoto, ed., 2010, *Sengonihon gaikoshi, Dai 3 pan* [The Diplomatic History of Postwar Japan, 3rd ed.], Yuhikaku Publishing.

Ishii Akira, 2003, "Nikka heiwajoyaku teiketsu kara Nitchu kokkokaifuku he [From Conclusion of the Japan–Taiwan Peace Treaty to Revival of Japan–China Diplomatic Relations]," in Ishii Akira, Zhu Jianrong, Soeya Yoshihide, Lin Xiaoguang, eds., *Kiroku to kosho: Nitchu kokkoseijoka, Nitchu heiwayukojoyaku teiketsukosho* [Records and Historical Analysis: Negotiations for Japan–China Diplomatic Normalization and Conclusion of the Japan–China Treaty of Peace and Friendship], Iwanami Shoten.

Ishii Akira, Zhu Jianrong, Soeya Yoshihide, Lin Xiaoguang, eds., 2003, *Kiroku to kosho: Nitchu kokkoseijoka, Nitchu heiwayukojoyaku teiketsukosho* [Records and Historical Analysis: Negotiations for Japan–China Diplomatic Normalization and Conclusion of the Japan–China Treaty of Peace and Friendship], Iwanami Shoten.

Jo Kenfun [Xu Xianfen], 2011, *Nihon no taichu ODA gaiko* [Japan's ODA Diplomacy to China], Keiso Shobo.

Jo Shogen [Suh Seung-won], 2004, *Nihon no keizaigaiko to chugoku* [Japan's Economic Diplomacy and China], Keio University Press.

Kawashima Shin, 2011, "Chukaminkoku gaikotoan ni miru 'wakare no gaiko (Nikka danko)' ['Farewell Diplomacy (Cutting of Japan–Taiwan Ties)' in the Diplomatic Materials of the Republic of China]," in Kamo Tomoki, Iida Masafumi, Jimbo Ken, eds., *Chugoku kaikakukaiho heno tenkan* [China's Shift to Reform and Opening], Keio University Press.

Ko Mei [Hu Ming], 2012, "Tanaka hochu niokeru chugoku no kokuminkyoiku kyanpen [The Persuasion Campaign in China for Tanaka's Visit to China]," in *Kokusai kokyoseisaku kenkyu* [International Public Policy Research], Osaka University, Vol. 16, No. 2, March.

Kuriyama Takakazu, 2010, *Gaiko shogenroku: Okinawahenkan, nitchu kokkoseijoka, nichibei "mitsuyaku"* [Diplomacy Testimonial: Reversion of Okinawa, Japan–China Diplomatic Normalization, and Japan–U.S. "Secret Agreements"], Iwanami Shoten.

Masuda Masayuki, 2011, "Chugokuseiji to beichuwakai [Chinese Politics and U.S.–China Rapprochement]," in Kamo Tomoki, Iida Masafumi, Jimbo Ken, eds., *Chugoku kaikakukaiho heno tenkan* [China's Shift to Reform and Opening], Keio University Press.

Matsuda Yasuhiro, 2011, "Beichu kokkoseijoka ni taisuru taiwan no naibu seisakukettei [Taiwan's Internal Decisions Regarding U.S.–China Diplomatic Normalization]," in

Kamo Tomoki, Iida Masafumi, Jimbo Ken, eds., *Chugoku kaikakukaiho heno tenkan* [China's Shift to Reform and Opening], Keio University Press.

Mori Kazuko, 2006, *Nitchu kankei* [Japan–China Relations], Iwanami Shoten.

Mori Kazuko (Mori Kozaburo, tr.) 2001, *Nikuson hochu kimitsu kaidanroku* [Secret Memoranda of Conversations from Nixon's Visit to China], University of Nagoya Press.

Nagano Nobutoshi, 1983, *Tenno to Toshohei no akushu* [The Handshake Between the Emperor and Deng Xiaoping], Gyosei Mondai Kenkyujo.

Nagano Nobutoshi, 2003, "Nitchu heiwayukojoyaku sukupu no shinso [The Truth of the Japan–China Treaty of Peace and Friendship Scoop]," in Ishii Akira, Zhu Jianrong, Soeya Yoshihide, Lin Xiaoguang, eds., *Kiroku to kosho: Nitchu kokkoseijoka, Nitchu heiwayukojoyaku teiketsukosho* [Records and Historical Analysis: Negotiations for Japan–China Diplomatic Normalization and Conclusion of the Japan–China Treaty of Peace and Friendship], Iwanami Shoten.

Nakae Yosuke, 2008, *Nitchu gaiko no shogen* [A Testimonial of Japan–China Diplomacy], Sohtensha Shuppan.

Ogata Sadako (Soeya Yoshihide, tr.), 1992, *Sengo nitchu, beichu kankei* [Japan–U.S./Sino-U.S. Postwar Relations], University of Tokyo Press.

Rin Daisho [Lin Daizhao] (Watanabe Hideo, tr.), 1997, *Sengo chunichi kankeishi* [A History of Postwar China–Japan Relations], Kashiwa Shobo.

Rin Gyoko [Lin Xiaoguang] (Masuo Chisako, tr.), 2003, "1970 nendai no chunichi kankei [China–Japan Relations of the 1970s]," in Ishii Akira, Zhu Jianrong, Soeya Yoshihide, Lin Xiaoguang, eds., *Kiroku to kosho: Nitchu kokkoseijoka, Nitchu heiwayukojoyaku teiketsukosho* [Records and Historical Analysis: Negotiations for Japan–China Diplomatic Normalization and Conclusion of the Japan–China Treaty of Peace and Friendship], Iwanami Shoten.

Shimizu Urara, 2009, "Nikkadanko to 72 nentaisei no keisei [The Severance of Japan–Taiwan Relations and the Formation of the '72 System]," in Kawashima Shin, Shimizu Urara, Matsuda Yasuhiro, Philip Yang, eds., *Nittai kankeishi 1945–2008* [A History of Japan–Taiwan Relations 1945–2008], University of Tokyo Press.

Soeya Yoshihide, 1995, *Nihongaiko to chugoku: 1945–1972* [Japanese Diplomacy and China 1945–1972], Keio Tsushin.

Soeya Yoshihide, 1998, *Japan's Economic Diplomacy with China, 1945–1978*, Oxford: Clarendon Press.

Soeya Yoshihide, 2003, "Beichuwakai kara Nitchu kokkoseijoka he [From U.S.–China Rapprochement to Japan–China Diplomatic Normalization]," in Ishii Akira, Zhu Jianrong, Soeya Yoshihide, Lin Xiaoguang, eds., *Kiroku to kosho: Nitchu kokkoseijoka, Nitchu heiwayukojoyaku teiketsukosho* [Records and Historical Analysis: Negotiations for Japan–China Diplomatic Normalization and Conclusion of the Japan–China Treaty of Peace and Friendship], Iwanami Shoten.

Soeya Yoshihide, 2005, "Taicyu gaiko no nikkanhikaku [Comparing the Diplomacy to China of Japan and South Korea]," in Ohata Hideki, Moon Chung-In, eds., *Nikkan kokusaiseijigaku no shinchihei* [New Horizons for Japan–ROK International Political Studies], Keio University Press.

Takahara Akio, 2011, "Gendai chugokushi niokeru 1978 nenno kakkisei nitsuite [On the 1978 Watershed in Modern Chinese History]," in Kamo Tomoki, Iida Masafumi, Jimbo Ken, eds., *Chugoku kaikakukaiho heno tenkan* [China's Shift to Reform and Opening], Keio University Press.

Tanaka Akihiko, 1991, *Nitchu kankei 1945–1990* [Japan–China Relations 1945–1990], University of Tokyo Press.

Wakatsuki Hidekazu, 2006, *"Zenhoigaiko" no jidai* [The Era of "Omni-Directional Diplomacy"], Nihon Keizai Hyouronsha.

Yu Binko [Yu Minhao], 2011, "Chugoku no taigaikaiho rosen to nihon, 1976–1982 [China's Policy of External Opening and Japan, 1976–1982]," in Soeya Yoshihide, ed., *Genzai chugokugaiko no 60 nen* [Sixty Years of Modern China's Diplomacy], Keio University Press.

4

JAPAN–CHINA RELATIONS OF THE 1980s

Greater development and appearance of problems

FIGURE 4.1 Chinese Communist Party General Secretary Hu Yaobang (center) receives thunderous applause during his speech before a plenary session of the House of Representatives of the Japanese Diet (November 25, 1983, Tokyo).

Source: ©Jiji Press.

Except for a few political incidents, Japan–China relations largely proceeded apace in the 1980s until the Tiananmen Incident of 1989. The expansion of economic exchange formed the basis for developing the relationship. Driving this expansion were the development of Japan's economy and the acceleration of overseas expansion by Japanese corporations after the Plaza Accord, as well as the start of China's reform and opening. Favorable political ties were symbolized by the close relationship between Prime Minister Nakasone and General Secretary Hu Yaobang.

Japan was full of dynamism in the 1980s, having overcome the two oil crises of the 1970s. In China, the Cultural Revolution was over and economic development was acknowledged as the primary task of the party and state. Economic reform and opening gradually made progress under Deng Xiaoping's leadership, though forces of opposition did exist. While the United States strove to build up arms against the Soviet Union and the Soviet Union, although late, grappled with economic reform, there was a meeting of the minds between Japan and China: Japan sought to expand its markets and natural resource suppliers and China needed economic cooperation. Such a harmony of interests contributed to the most favorable bilateral relations that had ever existed.

It is true that history issues, such as textbooks and the Yasukuni Shrine visit, and the Taiwan issue related to the Kokaryo court decision made waves in Japan–China relations during this period. Also within China there arose a sense of distrust toward reform and opening as well as a wariness toward Japan as it built up its national power. But then again, each people's image of the other country was basically favorable, owing to such developments as General Secretary Hu's invitation for 3,000 Japanese youths to visit China, and the Japanese television drama *Oshin* being a big hit in China.

1 Industrial plant contract troubles and start of ODA to China

After Mao Zedong's death, the Hua Guofeng administration in China declared the Cultural Revolution over and unveiled a policy to promote economic development by introducing facilities and technology from advanced industrialized countries of the West. It was the overseas Chinese diaspora and Japan that China counted on as important partners. However, when these unrealistic large-scale development plans failed, China implemented policies of adjustment at Chen Yun's initiative, and before long, it discontinued industrial plant contracts with Japanese corporations. The Japanese government proposed providing ODA to China, an offer that China, which lacked foreign exchange, accepted. Japanese ODA became a powerful support to the early stages of China's economic development through its reform and opening.

Expansion of Japan–China economic exchange and Chen Yun's adjustment policy

It was not the first time for China to import large-scale industrial plant from advanced industrialized countries of the West. Chemical fiber, chemical fertilizer, and other industrial plants were introduced in 1972 in the midst of the Cultural Revolution because it was judged that introducing advanced facilities from abroad was indispensable for expanding the production needed to improve the people's daily lives (Chin Kinka 2007). The construction of ten large steel complexes, nine large non-ferrous metal complexes, eight large coal complexes, ten large oil and gas fields, and 30 large power plants by 1985 were included in the "Outline of the Ten-Year Plan for Developing the National Economy (1976–1985)" that had been adopted in March 1978. This impatient development policy that sought a "new (great) leap forward" for the national economy by introducing large-scale industrial plant in large volume from abroad lacked an objective basis and was divorced from reality, and it later came to be ridiculed as the "Western leap forward."

Of all the West's advanced industrialized countries, Japan was the one China relied on. Deng Xiaoping went to Japan in October 1978 (Showa 53) in order to exchange the instruments of ratification of the Japan–China Peace and Friendship Treaty. In addition to meeting the Emperor and other dignitaries during his eight-day stay, Deng visited the advanced factories of such firms as Nissan, Nippon Steel, and Matsushita, rode the *Shinkansen* (bullet train) to Kyoto, then visited Nara and Osaka. In Kyoto and Nara, when told that the culture there was all learned from China, Deng responded that "[n]ow the positions are reversed" and "[n]ow we must learn from you" (Pei 2002). For Deng Liqun (who, because of his tendency for conservative thinking, later switched sides to criticize Deng Xiaoping's policies), a month-long inspection tour of Japan in 1978 was his first time to see actual capitalism, and he said he was enlightened by the advanced management of Japanese corporations (Deng 2006). For China, which just ended the Cultural Revolution, the closest advanced industrialized country was Japan, and so it chose to study Japan as one model of development.

Meanwhile, having experienced the oil crises, Japan was now enjoying stable economic growth and was focused on China as a new market and a supplier of energy resources. Also, some of the businessmen and politicians who had been making efforts to develop Japan–China ties long before diplomatic normalization also wished to contribute to China's industrialization out of a sense of atonement for the war (Okada 2008). The Japan–China Long-Term Trade Agreement had already been concluded in February 1978, and it was agreed that Japan would export construction materials and equipment along with technology and industrial plant, and import crude oil and coal from China. A bilateral protocol was signed that May concerning the construction of the Shanghai Baoshan Iron and Steel Complex through the extensive cooperation of Nippon Steel. This project kicked off a series of negotiations over high-value projects; the aggregate value of contracts concluded in 1978 and 1979 reached $7.99 billion.

Mao Zedong, Hua Guofeng, and also Deng Xiaoping tended to aim for quick growth of the economy; the one to put a stop to that was Chen Yun, a proponent of balanced development. Chen came to lead economic policy following the Third Plenum of the 11th CCP Central Committee in December 1978. He was tapped in March 1979 to head the State Council's Financial and Economic Commission, newly established as the main policy decision-making organ on the economy; his deputy was Li Xiannian. As his guiding principle for economic management, Chen adopted the eight-character guideline: *tiao zheng, gai ge, zheng dun, ti gao* (adjustment, reform, consolidation, and improvement). The key point was prohibiting excessive investment and imports so as to promote balanced development in accordance with the actual situation. Crude oil was expected to earn foreign exchange as an export product; since oil production remained sluggish, the "Western leap forward" came under criticism for expanding contradictions in the economy because it had been advanced without regard to national conditions or national power (Okada 2008). China had suggested already in February 1979 that it wanted to suspend implementing all contracts for the types of industrial plants contracted since December 1978, such as those related to the Shanghai Baoshan Iron and Steel Complex.

Hua Guofeng held on to power even after the Third Plenum, but he was losing his actual authority bit by bit, starting with the economy. In March 1980, Zhao Ziyang became responsible for overseeing the economy as director of the CCPCC's Leading Small Group on Finance and Economics. Then, China implemented a contractionary policy at the end of 1980 under the rubric of adjustment, and it gave notice at the start of 1981 that it would be discontinuing industrial plant contracts, including for the second phase construction of the Baoshan complex. From the late 1970s to the early 1980s, policies of adjustment were accorded a higher priority ranking than reform and opening. Consequently, a distinct cycle appeared in the management of China's planned economy, in which the accounting year was the same as the calendar year: "easing" in midyear and "tightening" at the end/beginning of the year. The influence of this cycle was evident in the contractionary policy that led to the suspension of industrial plant contracts, an event that spilled over into Japan–China economic relations.

Japan's policy for ODA to China

At the same time, there was great interest in China in learning from overseas experiences: 529 groups and 3,213 people were sent on overseas inspection tours between January and November 1978. The use of foreign capital also came to be studied in response to the suggestion of some leaders, including Vice Premier Gu Mu who was in charge of external economic exchange. China at the time was troubled by a lack of foreign exchange, and there was a growing number of people inside and outside the country saying that it should boldly introduce foreign capital. China's posture gradually softened toward the proposal to consider taking loans from foreign governments, made by JCEA Chairman Inayama Yoshihiro. China officially requested economic cooperation from Japan in September 1979 (Kazankai 2008b; Okada 2008).

Japan responded rapidly to this request. The first yen loan projects were announced during Prime Minister Ohira Masayoshi's visit to China in December 1979. There were six projects (seven, counting the later commodity loan) providing a total of 330.9 billion yen through fiscal year 1983: two ports (Shijiusuo Port Construction Project, Qinhuangdao Port Expansion Project), three rail lines

(Yanzhou–Shijiusuo Railway Construction Project, Beijing–Qinhuangdao Railway Expansion Project, and Guangzhou–Hengyang Railway Expansion Project), and one hydropower plant (Wuqiangxi Hydroelectric Power Plant Construction Project). In addition to those projects, construction began on a grant aid project, a modern hospital that became a symbol of Japan–China friendship (Tanaka 1991).

A major goal of Japan's economic cooperation with China was to support China's stable development through its modernization policy line, thereby seeking for China to develop and maintain cooperative relations with the Western world (Tanaka 1991). At the time it started ODA, Japan was also working to diversify its sources of imported energy resources, having gone through the two oil crises of the 1970s.

BOX 4.1 JAPAN–CHINA JOINT OIL DEVELOPMENT IN THE BOHAI

One issue symbolizing cooperation and competition in Japan–China relations is the development of maritime resources. Right after China began to claim sovereignty over the Senkaku Islands, which it calls the Diaoyu Islands, Zhou Enlai said that "historians raised it as a problem due to the oil issue."[1] Japan and China continue their long dispute over how to demarcate the East China Sea exclusive economic zones (EEZs). Even though an agreement was finally reached in 2008 concerning the joint development of the East China Sea, they have been unable to move toward implementing the hard-reached agreement regardless of Japan's strong wishes because of strong domestic opposition in China.

However, there is an important historical fact concerning joint development that is hardly known now. A protocol concerning the research and development of oil and natural gas in the Bohai was concluded at the time of Prime Minister Ohira's trip to China. Pursuant to this, the Japan–China Oil Development Corporation and the Chengbei Oil Corporation were established in 1980, and they carried out exploration, development, and production. Japan even imported a portion of this crude oil, but in the end, the production volume and price of the crude oil as well as the exchange rate all fell below the initial expected values, and so the Japanese side pulled out in 2000 (Takamizawa 2007).

Afterwards, the China National Offshore Oil Corporation continued operations in the sectors that the Japanese side had abandoned, and it developed Bohai into the second highest producing oil field after Daqing, in part because of the subsequent spike in oil prices. Joint development undertaken with the U.S. firm Phillips Corporation after Japan left also contributed to this result. If Japan–China joint development in Bohai had succeeded, subsequent relations between Japan and China over East China Sea resource development would have taken a rather different course.

1 *The Record of the Second Meeting between Takeiri Yoshikatsu and Zhou Enlai*, document released by the Ministry of Foreign Affairs, www.ioc.u-tokyo.ac.jp/~worldjpn/.

The value of the industrial plant contracts that China announced at the beginning of 1981 to be discontinued amounted to $3 billion, out of a total $7.99 billion contracted between 1978 and 1979; the sum associated with Japanese corporations reached half of that amount or $1.57 billion. While there were strong complaints and criticisms from the Japanese side, there were some who argued from a big picture perspective that now was the time to decide on government reparations to China, which had waived war reparations. In the end, since the purpose of economic cooperation to China was to assist in its stable development, Japan decided at the end of 1981 that, aside from switching a portion of ODA yen loans to a commodity loan that was then used for industrial plant construction, it would provide a total of 300 billion yen in additional JEXIM soft loans (financing with lenient lending conditions) and private loans.

Furthermore, Ohira unveiled a three-point policy at the time of starting cooperation with China. Namely, Japan (1) would not undertake military cooperation with China; (2) would consider the balance with the countries of the Association of Southeast Asian Nations (ASEAN); and (3) would not make Japan–China relations exclusive. The third point specifically came to mean that ODA to China was untied aid in principle (a method in which the supplier of materials was not limited to Japan), out of consideration for Europe and America, which were worried that Japan would monopolize Chinese markets. Prime Minister Ohira at a press conference after the summit meeting also said the following: "There are concerns that, by increasing the degree of our cooperation, Japan and China will form a bloc, but there are no intentions whatsoever to conspire against third countries. I would like them not to have any groundless concerns" (Okada 2008, p. 136). The Ohira cabinet had set forth a concept of pan-Pacific solidarity, with rising

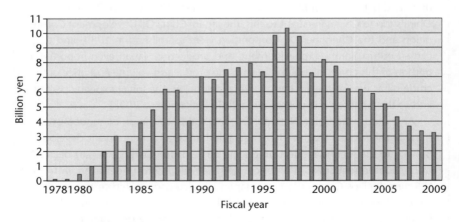

FIGURE 4.2 Trends in technical cooperation to China.

Source: JICA "Outline of JICA's Activities in China," October 2010, p. 7.

Note
Actual expenditure basis.

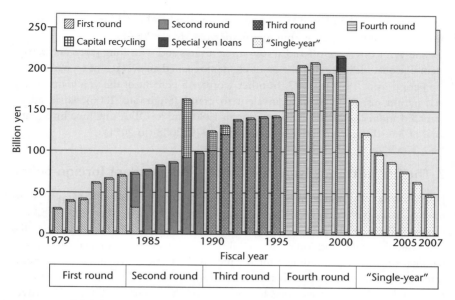

FIGURE 4.3 ODA loan commitments to China by fiscal year.

Source: JICA "Outline of JICA's Activities in China," October 2010, p. 8.

Notes
The amount of the loan agreement signed on April 30, 1980 is counted in fiscal year 1979 for the sake of expedience.
In FY2001, Japan changed its ODA lending to China from a multi-year "round" to "single-year" system; the last such agreement was signed in FY2007.

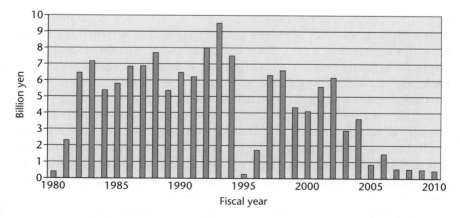

FIGURE 4.4 Trends in grant aid to China (JICA's portion).

Source: JICA "Outline of JICA's Activities in China," October 2010, p. 9.

Note
Grant Agreement basis.

protectionism in the United States being one cause; helping China to open itself to modernization was taken within that framework (Mori 2006).

The yen loans were offered at low interest rates and with long grace and repayment periods, meaning that the grant element reached an average of 65 percent for the period from 1979 to 1997. In other words, 65 percent of the yen loans during that period essentially were equivalent to grants (Sugimoto 2006). Japan added grant aid and technical assistance starting in 1980, and its ODA to China hit a grand total of 3.6 trillion yen between fiscal years 1979–2008 (Jo 2011).

2 The first textbook issue and China's independent foreign policy

Japan–China relations appeared set for smooth sailing after the industrial plant contract troubles were resolved. Zhao Ziyang went to Japan in May–June 1982 and proposed three principles for good bilateral relations: peace and friendship, equality and mutual benefit, and long-term stability. There were movements in the international situation surrounding China, which had set out on its path to modernization: harsh economic frictions between Japan and the United States, China's dispute over the U.S. export of weapons to Taiwan, and the USSR's call for an improvement in Sino-Soviet relations. In this context, China chose to develop stable relations with Japan.

Nonetheless, the textbook issue erupted soon after Zhao Ziyang had gone to Japan. China's leadership was sketching out a new diplomatic strategy; how it understood the key for managing relations with Japan, the up-and-coming major power, was reflected in this dispute.

Textbook issue

Japan–China relations of the 1980s were largely favorable, but in addition to the trade imbalance, the seeds of the disputes over the history, security, and Taiwan issues that would grow in the 1990s were already visible. The first textbook issue was set off by Japanese reports in June 1982 that, in an authorization of history textbooks, the Japanese Ministry of Education had the expression "invasion of Northern China" in one company's textbook rewritten to "advance in Northern China." In actuality, the reporting was mistaken—there were no textbooks that changed "invasion of Northern China" to "advance in Northern China" because of authorization that year. As the issue grew bigger, however, it became clear that the Ministry of Education for many years had put forward its "opinion for improvement" about the term "invasion," and that there was a textbook that had rewritten "invasion of Southeast Asia" to "advance into Southeast Asia."

On the Chinese side, first the *Xinhua News Agency* published the story as it was reported in Japan without comment, several days later just one article criticizing the news ran in the *People's Daily* on June 30, and then silence continued until mid-July. However, reporting restarted in the *People's Daily* after July 20. The backlash of Japanese popular opinion against the Ministry of Education for beautifying

Japan's aggression and distorting history was the subject of reporting through July 23. After July 24, the subject of reporting shifted to China's criticism of Japan. On July 26, Xiao Xiangqian, director of the First Asia Bureau of China's Ministry of Foreign Affairs (MFA), lodged an official protest with Watanabe Koji, a minister at the Japanese embassy. Moreover, triggered by a commentator's essay in the *People's Liberation Army Daily* on August 2, the tenor of the argument expanded further: the textbook issue became an indication of the counter current within Japan that schemed to revive militarism (Kazankai 2008a, Documents 68 and 69).

It is now clear that it was Hu Qiaomu, the most powerful ideologue at the time, who directed China's campaign criticizing Japan (Eto 2012). Hu directed his secretary on July 23 to tell Zhao Ziyang and Deng Liqun to have every newspaper issue commentaries and all organizations such as the Sino-Japanese Friendship Association issue statements saying that Japan's history of aggression in China was falsified in textbooks authorized by the Japanese Ministry of Education—the earlier the better, preferably in the next day's papers. At the same time, the MFA also needed to take measures, the specifics of which he left up to them. The August 2 *People's Liberation Army Daily* commentator's essay, too, was actually penned by Hu Qiaomu.

Deng Xiaoping did not overlook this incident, either. In a July 29 meeting bringing together the leaders of the foreign affairs and propaganda departments, Deng instructed them not to compromise on China's interpretation of the history of Japanese aggression against China. He directed them to issue an editorial on August 15, a rebuttal of the Japanese argument that China was interfering in an internal matter, that would state: amid the long history of friendship between Japan and China, there was an unfortunate period in which Japan invaded China, and that China would not allow the distortion of that history (Eto 2012). There is no doubt that China's position hardened considerably because of these instructions.

Actually, the *People's Daily* carried out one more instance of criticizing Japan during this period (Eto 2012). On July 22, the day before Hu Qiaomu had ordered the campaign criticizing Japan, Radio Peking criticized the wording "both countries" that it said had been used in a formal meeting with Taiwanese authorities by a visiting LDP delegation headed by Ezaki Masumi, chair of the LDP's Special Committee for International Economic Measures. The next day, the *People's Daily* ran that article next to one on the textbook issue. The LDP emphasized that the delegation to Taiwan was purely an economic mission. However, the Taiwanese side propagandized that this was a breakthrough, smashing China's united front operations aimed at isolating Taiwan.

Actually, there were quite a few Japanese who complained that China's protest over the textbooks was an interference in domestic affairs. The government stated repeatedly that its understanding of the war, as expressed in the Japan–China Joint Communiqué and the Treaty of Peace and Friendship, had not changed one bit and explained Japan's system for authorizing textbooks. Yet, China would not accept this justification by any means, saying the Japanese government was shirking its responsibilities.

In the latter part of August, the government issued the "Statement by Chief Cabinet Secretary Miyazawa Kiichi on History Textbooks," declaring that "[f]rom the perspective of building friendship and goodwill with neighboring [Asian] countries, Japan will pay due attention to these criticisms and make corrections at the Government's responsibility," and to that end, that it would revise the guidelines for textbook authorization after discussions in the Textbook Authorization and Research Council (Kazankai 2008a, Document 70). Based on the council's report issued in November, the government added the so-called "neighboring countries clause" as a guideline for textbook authorization: "due consideration shall be given, from a standpoint of international understanding and cooperation, to the treatment of modern and contemporary historical events between [Japan and] neighboring Asian countries."

What factors led to Japan making concessions? Undoubtedly there was a basic judgment about the importance of friendly and cooperative relations between Japan and China, both politically and economically. When Prime Minister Suzuki Zenko visited China at the end of September to coincide with the tenth anniversary of the normalization of Japan–China diplomatic relations, he stated that the issues that Japan and China must cooperate on and tackle together did not end in Asia, that both countries must actively contribute to global peace and stability, and he appealed to the importance of friendship and cooperation (Kazankai 2008a, Document 78). One might also mention that Chinese criticism of the revival of militarism was so far off the mark that, in Japan, feelings of bewilderment exceeded the desire to lash back, and that domestic popular opinion was strongly critical of the Ministry of Education's opinion for improvement on "invasion/aggression" that had become public. Furthermore, promoting friendship and cooperation formed the general framework of Japan's China policy, partly from a sense of atonement for the war, partly from the difference in stages of development.

China finally accepted Japan's views on September 8, in the middle of the 12th CCP National Congress. Hu Yaobang had already indicated his stance to attach great importance to Japan, however, in the political report that he read at the opening ceremony of the Congress on September 1.

China's shift to independent foreign policy

At the start of the 1980s, China's wariness of the Soviet Union was undiminished and its tendency to view relations with Japan from a strategic viewpoint remained unchanged and strong. Wu Xiuquan, deputy chief of the PLA General Staff, went so far as to tell visiting Dietman Nakasone Yasuhiro in April 1980 that raising defense expenditures to as much as 2 percent of GNP probably would not have a negative impact on the Japanese economy (Kazankai 2008b). However, China clearly indicated its turn toward an "independent foreign policy" at the 12th CCP National Congress in September 1982, and it began to grope about to improve relations with the Soviets before long. It even called its policy "omnidirectional diplomacy," the same phrase the Fukuda cabinet had coined.

A main objective of China's independent foreign policy was adjusting the sense of distance with the United States. The biggest issue at the time for China in U.S.–China relations was U.S. arms exports to Taiwan. President Ronald Reagan, who took the stage in 1981, was well-known for being pro-Taiwan. At the end of 1981, he decided on the export of fighter jet parts as well as air force services to Taiwan, sparking a violent backlash from China. At the end of intense negotiations, the U.S.–China Joint Communiqué was issued in August 1982 (Second Shanghai Communiqué), and the problem was resolved for the time being. But, China's sense of distrust remained strong and most of the paragraph concerning U.S.–China relations in Hu Yaobang's report at the 12th CCP National Congress was devoted to expressing displeasure toward the United States on the Taiwan issue. He also scathingly criticized superpower hegemony in this report, stressing that China "would never rely on any major country or bloc of nations." As a fellow member of the Third World, China also targeted this expression of independence from the superpowers to appeal to the solidarity of developing countries.

Meanwhile, easing border tensions and improving relations with the Soviet Union were important tasks for Deng Xiaoping, who had prioritized economic construction over construction of national defense. In March 1982, in the very middle of the U.S.–China argument over the Taiwan issue, CPSU General Secretary Brezhnev gave a speech in Tashkent acknowledging China's sovereignty over Taiwan and he called for a discussion on improving Sino-Soviet relations. In Hu Yaobang's report to the Party Congress, China indicated that "there is a possibility for the relations of China and the Soviet Union to move toward normalization if [the USSR] were to take actual steps to remove the threat to our country's security," citing three cases: the Soviet's placement of a large army on the Sino-Soviet and Sino-Mongolian borders, its support of Vietnam's invasion of Cambodia, and its invasion of Afghanistan.

Hu Yaobang's report addressed China's relations with Japan before its relations with the United States or the Soviet Union. While it did mention the danger of a group of Japanese conspiring to revive militarism, its main point was to stress the benefits of developing relations according to the three principles of peace and friendship, equality and mutual benefit, and long-term stability. In summary, for China—a developing country, aiming for unification with Taiwan—improving ties with the Soviets emerged as a diplomatic strategic objective when it recognized there were limits to the honeymoon with the United States. Then, it was a natural choice for China to pick Japan as its top partner for cooperation in order to achieve its primary task of promoting modernization under increasingly complex conditions.

Japan became a major economic power, driving the "flying geese" pattern of Asia's development, even as it was troubled by trade frictions with the United States. Having assessed that Japan would become a major political power (Tanaka 1991), China strongly feared the possibility that Japan's perception of history or its Taiwan policy might change. That is why China decided to lash out thoroughly at any words or actions that could be viewed as the buds—whether real or not—for "the falsification of the history of aggression and the beautification of militarism by

Japan's Ministry of Education" (*People's Daily* editorial 8/15/1982) and any attempts to restore relations with Taiwan.

3 Wide-ranging development of Japan–China relations

Japan pursued wide-ranging development of its relations with China, a developing country that had adopted a modernization path and embarked on reform and opening of its economy. The fact that China was socialist was not necessarily an obstacle at the time. Those who had experienced the war were still in leadership positions in Japanese society in the 1980s, and a sense of atoning for the war remained strong. China strongly desired to harness Japan's economic vitality for its own modernization, even as it held a certain sense of wariness of Japan becoming a major political power. Mutual exchanges broadened beyond just the political and economic to include cultural and social aspects, too.

Politics

In Japan, the Nakasone cabinet, which lasted from November 1982 until November 1987, increased Japan's presence in the international community on the basis of political stability and economic development. Prime Minister Nakasone made *sengo seiji no sokessan* ("the final settlement of postwar political accounts") his guiding principle, the first point of which sought Japan's participation in a global solidarity on security issues (Wakatsuki 2012). During his visit to the United States in January 1983, Nakasone called Japan–U.S. relations a "community with a common destiny" and the Japanese islands an "unsinkable aircraft carrier" in the strategy against the USSR, in addition to deciding to increase defense spending and furnish weapons technology to the United States. President Reagan proposed that they call each other by their first names; on the basis of this "Ron–Yasu" relationship of trust between the leaders, both sides aimed to develop Japan–U.S. relations overall, despite intensifying trade frictions. Meanwhile, Nakasone also worked hard to develop relations with Asian countries. He chose South Korea as his first overseas destination in January 1983, where he offered greetings in the Korean language. In addition, he toured Southeast Asia for 11 days from the end of April 1983 and asserted that Japan would uphold its peace constitution, its exclusively defense-oriented security policy, and the three non-nuclear principles, and that it refused to become a major military power. He gained the understanding and support of the leaders, including General Haji Muhammad Soeharto in Indonesia and President Ferdinand E. Marcos of the Philippines.

Even with respect to China, Nakasone thought that Japan–China relations were second in importance only to Japan–U.S. relations, and so he built a close relationship with General Secretary Hu Yaobang. When Hu visited Japan in November 1983, Nakasone gained Hu's agreement on his proposals to add a fourth principle of "mutual trust" to the three principles for Japan–China relations that Zhao Ziyang had proposed when he visited Japan the year before (peace and friendship, equality and mutual benefit, and long-term stability) and to establish a Japan–China Friendship Committee for the 21st Century made up of private sector members as a channel for frank and honest discussion (Nakasone 2004). Moreover, Nakasone said in the summit meeting, "You are truly candid. You could be my older brother," to which Hu responded, "No, no, we are friends ... I want us to be friends until the last day that I live" (Hattori Ryuji 2012, p. 171). While he was in Japan, Hu gave speeches to the National Diet and to a gathering of young people at NHK Hall, and announced an invitation for 3,000 Japanese youths to visit China for one week the following autumn. At the time that visit took place, the president of the All-China Youth Federation, the host organization, was Hu Jintao, who later became the general secretary of the CCP.

Actually, two months before Hu Yaobang's trip to Japan, JSP Chairman Ishibashi Masashi visited China in September–October, where he scathingly criticized the Nakasone cabinet in meetings with Hu and Chinese leaders for impetuously walking the road to becoming a military power by aligning itself with the U.S. global strategy. However, Hu and the others made no response (Hattori Ryuji 2012). While somewhat uneasy about Japan's move toward becoming a political power, and although China was beginning efforts toward normalizing relations with the Soviet Union, at that point in time, there were no big changes in the relationship yet. Zhang Aiping went to Japan in July 1984 for the first time as defense minister and met with JDA Director-General Kurihara Yuko; they agreed on the need to strengthen defense exchanges. When Nakasone visited China in March 1984, Premier Zhao Ziyang expressed understanding toward the Nakasone cabinet's defense policies. Nakasone gave a speech at Peking University, where he said, "I can state here and now, without the slightest hesitation, that our nation will never allow a revival of militarism" (Tanaka 1991, p. 133).

Economy, society, culture

The "gift" that Nakasone brought on his visit to China was the second yen loan package of about 470 billion yen to be provided between fiscal years 1984 and 1989. Actually, this support held important political significance for Deng Xiaoping and Zhao Ziyang, who were advancing the policy of opening. As discussed in some detail later, strong criticism was emerging within the CCP against reforming China's planned economy and opening it up to foreign countries. The second yen loan package included such projects as expanding the port facilities of Qinhuangdao, Lianyungang, and Qingdao and the telecommunications networks of Tianjin, Shanghai, and Guangzhou. Immediately after Nakasone returned home, China publicly announced further implementation of its policy of opening with its open coastal cities policy for 14 cities: Dalian, Qinhuangdao, Tianjin, Yantai, Qingdao, Lianyungang, Nantong, Shanghai, Ningbo, Wenzhou, Fuzhou, Guangzhou, Zhanjiang, and Beihai. Both Deng and Zhao, in their meetings with Nakasone, had enthusiastically advocated that Japanese corporations expand into these regions and that the private sector pursue economic and technology cooperation. This indicated that the group promoting reform and opening within the Chinese leadership at the time were depending on Japanese cooperation for the success of its policy of opening. In 1987, as part of a financial recycling scheme based on its huge trade surplus, Japan provided China with 70 billion in yen loans and 30 billion yen in JEXIM Bank soft loans to develop Qingdao and Hainan Island.

In actuality, the volume of Japan–China trade showed a high rate of growth in 1984 and 1985 of 31.7 percent and 43.9 percent year-on-year, respectively (Hattori Kenji 1985). It was also around this time that the number of large Toyota and Nissan sedan passenger vehicles suddenly increased in Beijing, greatly changing the appearance of the city streets.

On the Chinese side, it was the further development of the policy of opening that brought about these changes. Following the designation of the 14 open coastal cities and the start of building economic and technological development zones there, the Third Plenum of the 12th CCP Central Committee adopted the "Decision on Reform of the Economic System" in October 1984. It introduced the concept that a commodity economy would replace the planned economy and declared that reform in cities would advance to a new stage. The Pearl River Delta, Yangtze River Delta, and Minnan Delta zones were designated as open deltas in 1985, and the policy of opening expanded as if from a point into a plane (Hattori Kenji 1995).

On the Japanese side, easing trade frictions with the United States had become the nation's task. Japanese corporate investment overseas was fueled by the stronger yen/weaker dollar from the Plaza Accord of September 1985.

Japanese trade and investment with China both slumped in 1986, in part because China reacted to the growth in demand in 1984–85 by switching to a contractionary economic policy. However, trade and investment both showed large gains in 1988, partly because the Japan–China Investment Protection Agreement was concluded, and also because Zhao Ziyang announced an economic development strategy for the coastal regions (coastal development strategy) and the designation of Hainan Province in its entirety as a special economic zone (SEZ) (after Hainan Island was made independent from Guangdong Province). The brakes were applied to economic exchange after that, however, because of Chinese tightening once again as well as the impact of the 1989 Tiananmen Incident.

Japan's influence on the Chinese economy did not stop at quantity, as it were. Nippon Steel, in accordance with Inayama Yoshihiro's strong wish, furnished technology to the Shanghai Baoshan Iron and Steel Complex that built the foundation critical to Baoshan's growth into a global iron and steel company (Chin Kinka 2007). China attached importance to the Japan–China Forum for Exchange of Economic Knowledge, which began in 1981 and continues to this day, actively using it as a venue for receiving advice from public and private sector experts, especially in the early period of reform and opening. Conversations with Japanese friends appear frequently in Deng Xiaoping's statements recorded in the *Selected Works of Deng Xiaoping*. Deng obviously gleaned various ideas from them, such as setting a target of quadrupling gross domestic product (GDP). Japan's economic assistance to China included more than just yen loans targeting social infrastructure. It implemented grant aid cooperation projects that anticipated China's needs, such as the Japan–China Friendship Hospital, Japan–China Youth Exchange Centers, and Japan–China Friendship Environmental Protection Centers. Furthermore, public- and private-sector agricultural technical assistance contributed to improving China's agricultural output in terms of both quality and quantity; the amount of rice production reportedly increased over two million tons after Hara Shoichi taught wet-rice cultivation techniques as a volunteer.

The fields of society and culture also were important facets of the exchanges that made progress in the 1980s. "Friendship city" partnerships already existed in the 1970s between the local governments: the cities of Kobe and Tianjin, Yokohama and Shanghai, Osaka and Shanghai, Tokyo and Beijing, and Niigata and Harbin. In the 1980s, this was not limited just to cities, as 23 Japanese prefectures and 20 Chinese provinces concluded friendship relations.

On the cultural front, following the "panda boom" of the 1970s (Ienaga 2011), Japan got caught up in a "Silk Road boom" in the 1980s sparked by the popular NHK Tokushu documentary series *Silk Road*. In China, Japanese movies like *Kimi yo Fundo no Kawa o Watare*, *Sandakan Hachiban Shokan Bokyo*, and *Ogin-sama* were shown at the end of the 1970s, and stars like Takakura Ken and Nakano Ryoko became famous overnight. In the 1980s, many Japanese dramas were broadcast on Chinese television and gained popularity: the "Red series" with performances by Utsui Ken and Yamaguchi Momoe; the NHK historical drama *Oshin*; shows based on sports themes, such as *Judo Icchokusen* and *Sain wa V*; and the anime *Ikkyu-san* (Ryu 2006; Tamakoshi 2012). You could say it was in the 1980s that Japanese production—in cultural, not just economic, terms—penetrated Chinese society and held a position of comparative advantage over foreign countries. From automobiles and household appliances to sweets and TV dramas, great quantities of high quality and high functionality Japanese products flooded into China. It was the era of the rising image in China of Japan as a modern advanced country.

The number of Japanese tourists and students on school trips visiting China also increased in the 1980s. A train accident occurred in the Shanghai suburbs in 1988, killing 27 Japanese students from Kochi Gakugei High School on a class trip (Tsuboi 2012). Meanwhile, orphans and wives left behind in China after the war as well as their families increasingly visited or returned home to Japan (Okubo 2006). Also, Prime Minister Nakasone's 1983 Plan to Accept 100,000 International Students promoted the acceptance of Chinese exchange students (Makino 2012). Furthermore, after China enacted the Law on the Control of the Exit and Entry of Citizens in 1986, leaving the country for private reasons was permitted and so the number of language and vocational students from China in Japan rapidly increased (Chin 2012).

Thus, Japan–China relations of the 1980s basically transitioned smoothly because of such factors as the close relations between the leaders, agreement on security interests, enthusiasm toward economic exchange, and a rising degree of goodwill owing to the expansion of cultural and social exchanges. Especially in the 1983–84 period with the reciprocal visits by leaders and the visit to China by 3,000 Japanese youths, it was said that Japan–China relations were at their best in history (Tanaka 1991).

4 Criticism of policy of opening and the latent Japan factor

The fact that Japan–China relations enjoyed wide-ranging development in the 1980s does not mean that, aside from the history textbook issue of 1982, examined above, there was no discord between them. In addition to the sense of wariness toward the newly powerful Japan, one may posit other causes for dispute on the Chinese side, such as the existence of conflicting opinions on the substance of reform and opening and a power struggle within the leadership, which at times influenced China's Japan policy and its relations with Japan.

Politics of reform and opening and linkage to relations with Japan

In 1980s China, criticism of the gradually deepening policies of reform and opening at times grew powerful and surfaced. On those occasions, it was natural, in a sense, that China's domestic politics influenced its relations with Japan, as Japan was at the time China's greatest partner in its opening up to foreign countries. For instance, we already touched on the linkage of the introduction of Japanese capital and technology to industrial plant contract troubles caused by the policies of adjustment as well as to the scaling up of the open coastal cities policy.

After the Cultural Revolution, there were various views on reform and opening even among the leadership who had been rehabilitated. Despite agreeing to the partial introduction of the market economy, CCP Vice Chairman Chen Yun, who could boast of a party career and reputation rivaling Deng Xiaoping, stood in the position of upholding the planned economy and preached the theory of the bird-cage economy: the bird of the market economy must always and forever remain locked away in the cage of the plan. Chen was also cautious about opening up to foreign countries and generally had a negative attitude regarding the introduction of foreign capital; not once had he made an inspection tour of an SEZ, let alone a capitalist country. Deng Liqun, who agreed with Chen Yun, went on an inspection tour to Japan in 1978 and was enlightened by the advanced state of Japanese enterprises, yet he pursued a movement against spiritual pollution beginning in the autumn of 1983 as the director of the Central Propaganda Department. That movement targeted the expansion of the policy of opening to foreign countries at the time, symbolized by the SEZs. That is, corruption and money worship, criticizing socialism and valuing liberal thought (so-called "bourgeois liberalization" tendencies), and idolizing Western culture were some of the phenomena said to be the manifestation of spiritual pollution, much of which was blamed on the influx of Western capitalist culture.

In reaction to the intensifying criticism, Deng Xiaoping carried out the first southern inspection tour in 1984 around the Chinese New Year, visiting such places as the SEZs in Shenzhen, Zhuhai, and Xiamen, and the Baoshan Iron and

Steel Complex in Shanghai. He was accompanied by Vice Premier Wang Zhen, who was also the honorary chairman of the Sino-Japanese Friendship Association. Deng indicated his support for the zones and further opening of the economy by proclaiming that "SEZs are good"; he was emulating Mao Zedong, who said "People's communes are good" when he inspected the countryside during the Great Leap Forward. The further opening of 14 coastal port cities, which was decided that spring, was linked to the introduction of Japanese capital and technology, as was previously stated. At the Baoshan Iron and Steel Complex, Deng wrote: "we must master new technology and techniques, be good at learning, and be even better at innovating" (Deng 1993, p. 51).

Criticism that exports from the SEZs were inadequate grew, however, when a surge in imports caused the trade deficit to expand beginning in the latter half of 1984. China communicated its complaints regarding the broad excess of Japan's exports and inadequate investment at the Japan–China ministerial meeting in the summer of 1985. Around this time, reports appeared that Japan was exporting defective automobiles to China (Tanaka 1991). Suspicions that Japan may have foisted defective goods on China had already arisen at the end of the 1970s. As one example, at the time of the construction of the Baoshan complex, a pile driver imported from Japan was damaged, and even Deng Xiaoping protested that Japan was trying to trick China, offloading unusable second-hand goods on it (Kazankai 2008b). It was established, however, that the Chinese side actually caused the damage, but that fact was neither made public nor communicated to Japan at the time (Chin Kinka 2007).

The reasons why such confusion arose on the Chinese side were not simple, but most likely the overall lack of mutual trust lay at the root of the problems. It is thought that aspects of psychology were at work, particularly on the Chinese side, of guarding against, and at times trying to restrain, Japan, a capitalist, advanced industrial country full of self-confidence in its development. For instance, university student protest activities opposing the "revival of Japanese militarism" and "Japanese economic aggression" took place in Beijing, Xian, Chengdu, and other cities between September and October 1985.

Wariness of Japan

The protesting university students took issue with Prime Minister Nakasone Yasuhiro's visit to the Yasukuni Shrine, purporting that it was a "revival of militarism." The Yasukuni Shrine's enshrinement of Class A war criminals in 1978 was reported the following year, reigniting the domestic debate in Japan. Prime ministerial visits continued even after that, but Nakasone's official visit to the Yasukuni Shrine that happened on August 15, 1985 received a shower of criticism from the MFA spokesman, from the *People's Daily*, the CCP's mouthpiece, and even from some political leaders, saying that it hurt the feelings of the peoples of Asian countries that had suffered greatly from Japanese militarism.

The second history textbook issue erupted in 1986: in July the Japanese government had high school history textbooks that had gone through authorization rewritten in reaction to South Korean and Chinese protests the month before. Nakasone did not visit the Yasukuni Shrine that August because he judged it could breed misunderstanding and mistrust regarding reflections on the war and result in hurting the feelings of the peoples in neighboring Asian countries, and also because of fears it would undermine (the pro-Japan) Hu Yaobang's domestic standing (Nakasone 2004; Yabuki 2004). However, Hu Yaobang was ultimately forced to resign at the beginning of 1987, triggered by student protests that arose in a number of cities at the end of 1986. His soft response to "bourgeois liberalization" tendencies was primarily blamed, but his invitation to 3,000 Japanese youths without the party center's decision also constituted a part of the criticism against Hu (Zheng 2005). Unlike the "Ron-Yasu" relationship with President Reagan, the leaders' exchange between Nakasone and Hu, who was not actually the highest leader, was linked to China's domestic politics and so it did not always contribute to the stability of bilateral relations.

When the Nakasone cabinet decided at the end of December 1986 to abolish the 1 percent of GNP limit on defense expenditures, Deng Xiaoping showed a sense of wariness, stating, "the Chinese people are sensitive, particularly the young students" (Tanaka 1991, p. 154).

Following that, when the Osaka High Court issued its decision in February 1987 recognizing that the ownership of a student dormitory in Kyoto named Kokaryo was "Taiwanese," the Chinese government protested rigorously and demanded that the Japanese government take effective measures immediately. The Japanese government responded that it was unable to intervene under the principle of the separation of powers between the executive and judicial branches. China was not persuaded; Deng Xiaoping himself complained that Nakasone ought to be able to resolve the issue, commenting that the tendency to revive militarism was apparent in Japan among some politically influential people, albeit "a very small number." That June, Deng reiterated his remarks on the breaking of the defense spending limit and on the Kokaryo issue to Komeito Secretary General Yano Junya. Deng added that no other country in the world was as indebted to China as Japan, yet China did not demand war reparations at the time of diplomatic normalization, and so Japan should make greater contributions to help China's development (Tanaka 1991; Kojima 2012).

A high-level MOFA official responded to this by commenting that Deng was like "a man above the clouds," and that his viewpoint was not necessarily representative of the entire Chinese leadership. China reacted harshly to these remarks, in part because of misunderstanding over the expression "man above the clouds": in Japanese it means a high official of the imperial court who has removed himself from the day-to-day world, but in Chinese it means a "senile old man."

As seen above, several persistent issues made their appearance in the 1980s, but regardless, Japan–China relations achieved development in many aspects. The expansion of economic exchange was remarkable: trade with Japan comprised over one-fifth of China's total trade value and China became Japan's number four source of imports and seventh largest export market. The trade imbalance also disappeared. Prime Minister Takeshita Noboru, a member of the former Tanaka faction whom

Nakasone designated as his successor, visited China in August 1988 and promised the third yen loan package of 810 billion yen, for which Deng Xiaoping expressed his "heartfelt thanks."

One can give the following factors as reasons why Japan–China relations basically developed favorably: China's policy of reform and opening was developed through repeated trial and error; Japan's economic involvement in China grew; many Japanese held feelings of guilt and a sense of atonement for past aggression in China; each country's national image of the other improved because of the information reported by television and other media; and favorable Japan–U.S.–China relations were maintained amid the continuation of the Cold War structure (Tanaka 1991). However, the catalyst for changing such factors arrived in 1989.

5 June Fourth (the Second Tiananmen Square) Incident

In the Tiananmen Incident (also called the June Fourth Incident and the Second Tiananmen Square Incident), the CCP mobilized the PLA at dawn on June 4, 1989 to forcibly suppress a pro-democracy movement by university students and citizens. There were over 200 dead (over 200 civilians and dozens of soldiers and police) and about 10,000 injured (over 3,000 civilians and over 6,000 soldiers and police), according to the announcement by Chinese authorities (Chen et al. 1999). This event, transmitted worldwide by television in real time, fueled criticism of the Chinese government mainly in a stunned North America and Europe, and worsened China's image for the many people who had held a favorable opinion of the country until that point. The situation was similar in Japan, too. Seeing a conspiracy of foreign enemies for "peaceful evolution" (i.e., regime change) lurking in the background of this incident, the Chinese authorities began to warn against idolizing the West and to strengthen patriotic education.

It does not mean that the CCP had not been grappling with political reform. It had adopted bold political reform plans at the 13th CCP National Congress in 1987 including such measures as the separation of party and government, establishment of a civil service system, and preparations for a consultation system for interest groups and the CCP. Just several months before, South Korea issued a declaration of democracy and Taiwan lifted martial law measures. The People Power Revolution that overthrew the Marcos administration took place the previous year in the Philippines and *glasnost* (openness of information) was beginning under the leadership of General Secretary Mikhail Gorbachev in the Soviet Union. Implementation of political reform policies was lagging in China, however, owing to the backlash of forces within the CCP who feared "relativizing" the CCP's absolute authority and who tried to preserve vested interests. Meanwhile, inflation rose in 1988, owing in part to the failure of price reforms. At that point, contractionary fiscal and monetary policies that State Council Premier Li Peng, Vice Premier Yao Yilin, and others had insisted be taken were enacted by command economy methods. The result was to push the most overheated economic situation since the founding of the country suddenly into recession.

And so, against the backdrop of dissatisfaction with such management of the economy and sparked by the April 1989 death of Hu Yaobang who had been sympathetic to political reform, a movement of intellectuals and university students began a protest against corruption and the delay of political reform. The CCP's response was chaotic, and the movement spread to ordinary citizens and regional university students, too. The media, which had gathered from all over the world to cover Gorbachev's historic visit to China in May, came to see the democracy movement filling the streets of Beijing right before its eyes. But eventually hardliners who insisted on upholding dictatorship won the power struggle within the party center; Zhao Ziyang, who had shown understanding toward the students' actions, was blamed for his soft response and lost power.

For those who emphasized the CCP's monopoly on political power and ideology, opening up to foreign countries was clearly having a negative influence on politics. They saw their struggle as one against "bourgeois liberalization" tendencies that seek to revise the one-party dictatorship and that invariably are part of opening to foreign countries. After Jiang Zemin was installed as general secretary by agreement of Deng Xiaoping, Chen Yun, and the old revolutionaries after the Tiananmen Incident, guarding against "peaceful evolution" became one of the major themes of the new leadership. Deng simultaneously called for the continuation of reform and opening, but there were many who disagreed. They branded reform and opening the introduction and development of capitalism, and claims spread that the primary danger of peaceful evolution would come from the economic domain (CCP Shenzhen Municipal Committee Propaganda Department 1992). Rumors spread that recollectivization of the means of production would take place in farming villages, and stories began to appear of farmers who cut down young trees and sold off their cows and agricultural tools. The Politburo did deliberate on "Regulations on Agricultural Cooperatives" in mid-1990 that aimed at recollectivization; though that was rejected, "Regulations on Assessment of Workers," which revived ideological and political achievement in workers' rating standards, was in fact passed in an executive meeting of the State Council (Takahara 1992).

In 1989, the Berlin Wall came down in November, the Cold War was concluded in December, and the world order began to grow fluid. Japan was in the middle of its economic bubble at the time. China had realized Sino-Soviet rapprochement with Gorbachev's visit to China in May, but shortly afterwards it was dragged to the brink of crisis—diplomatic isolation and a reversal of reform and opening—by the shock of the Tiananmen Incident at the beginning of June. As the curtain was rising on the 1990s, perhaps quite a few people shared the premonition that the era of economic globalization would arrive after the Cold War ended. In Japan, a book published in 1987 titled *Borderless Economy: Alarm Bells for an Isolationist Japan* became a big topic of conversation (Nakatani 1987). Yet, probably nobody at the time could have predicted the sudden change in the domestic situations of both Japan and China just a few years later, or that their bilateral relationship would come to an important turning point.

Cited and referenced materials

CCP Shenzhen Municipal Committee Propaganda Department, 1992, *1992 nianchun Deng Xiaoping yu Shenzhen* [Deng Xiaoping and Shenzhen, Spring 1992], Haitian Publishing House: China.

Chen Wenbin, et al., 1999, *Zhongguo gongchandang zhizheng wushinian* [Fifty Years of the Communist Party of China in Power], Chinese Communist Party History Publishing House: China.

Chin Kinka [Chen Jinhua] (Sugimoto Takashi, tr.), 2007, *Kokuji okujutsu* [Recollections on Affairs of State], Japan–China Economic Association.

Chin Raiko, 2012, "Ikebukuro chainataun koso ni 'matta': 2008 nen [A False Start in the Concept of Ikebukuro's Chinatown (2008)]," in Sonoda Shigeto, ed., *Nitchu kankeishi 1972–2012 III: Shakai, bunka* [A History of Japan–China Relations 1972–2012, Vol. III: Society, Culture], University of Tokyo Press.

Deng Liqun, 2006, *Deng Liqun Zishu* [Deng Liqun, In My Own Words], Strong Wind Press: Hong Kong.

Deng Xiaoping, 1993, *Deng Xiaoping wenxuan disanjuan* [Selected Works of Deng Xiaoping, Vol. 3], People's Publishing House: China.

Eto Naoko, 2012, "Dai 1 ji kyokasho mondai: 1979–82 nen [The First Textbook Issue (1979–82)]," in Takahara Akio, Hattori Ryuji, eds., *Nitchu kankeishi 1972–2012 I: Seiji* [A History of Japan–China Relations 1972–2012, Vol. I: Politics], University of Tokyo Press.

Hattori Kenji, 1995, "Nitchu keizaikoryu no kimmitsuka [Japan–China Economic Exchange Growing Closer]," in Kojima Tomoyuki, ed., *Ajia jidai no nitchu kankei* [The Asian Era of Japan–China Relations], Simul Press.

Hattori Ryuji, 2012, "Nakasone, Ko Yoho kankei to rekishi mondai: 1983–86 nen [Nakasone-Hu Yaobang Relations and the History Issue (1983–86)]," in Takahara Akio, Hattori Ryuji, eds., *Nitchu kankeishi 1972–2012 I: Seiji* [A History of Japan–China Relations 1972–2012, Vol. I: Politics], University of Tokyo Press.

Ienaga Masaki, 2011, *Panda gaiko* [Panda Diplomacy], Media Factory.

Japan International Cooperation Agency, 1991, *Chugoku: Kunibetsu enjo kenkyukai hokokusho* [Country Study for Japan's Official Development Assistance to China], Japan International Cooperation Agency.

Jo Kenfun [Xu Xianfen], 2011, *Nihon no taichu ODA gaiko* [Japan's ODA Diplomacy to China], Keiso Shobo.

Kazankai, 2008a, *Nitchu kankei kihon shiryoshu 1972–2008 nen* [Collection of Basic Documents in Japan–China Relations, 1972–2008], Kazankai Foundation.

Kazankai, 2008b, *Nitchu kankei kihon shiryoshu 1972–2008 nen: nenpyo* [Collection of Basic Documents in Japan–China Relations, 1972–2008: Chronology], Kazankai Foundation.

Kojima Kazuko, 2012, "Kokaryo mondai: 1987–88 nen [The Kokaryo Dormitory Issue (1987–88)]," in Takahara Akio, Hattori Ryuji, eds., *Nitchu kankeishi 1972–2012 I: Seiji* [A History of Japan–China Relations 1972–2012, Vol. I: Politics], University of Tokyo Press.

Makino Atsushi, 2012, "Sakata tankidaigaku, heikosu: 2002 nen [The Closure of Sakata Junior College]," in Sonoda Shigeto, ed., *Nitchu kankeishi 1972–2012 III: Shakai, bunka* [A History of Japan–China Relations 1972–2012, Vol. III: Society, Culture], University of Tokyo Press.

Mori Kazuko, 2006, *Nitchu kankei* [Japan–China Relations], Iwanami Shoten.

Nakasone Yasuhiro, 2004, *Jiseiroku* [A Record of Self-Reflection], Shinchosha Publishing.

Nakatani Iwao, 1987, *Bodaresu ekonomi* [Borderless Economy], Nihon Keizai Shimbun.

Okada Minoru, 2008, *Nitchu kankei to ODA* [Japan–China Relations and ODA], Duan Press: China.

Okubo Maki, 2006, *Chugoku zanryu nihonjin* [Japanese Left Behind in China], Kobunken.

Pei Hua, ed., 2002, *Zhongri waijiao fengyunzhong de Deng Xiaoping* [Deng Xiaoping in Turbulent Times of Sino-Japanese Diplomacy], Central Party Literature Press: China.

Ryu Bunpei [Liu Wenbing], 2006, *Chugoku 10 okunin no nihoneiga netsuaishi* [A History of the Infatuation of Japanese Cinema of a Billion Chinese], Shueisha.

Sugimoto Nobuyuki, 2006, *Daichi no hoko* [Roar of the Earth], PHP Institute.

Takahara Akio, 1992, "A Head-on Collision: The Political Currents in China, Spring 1992," Discussion Paper for the Japan–U.S. Consultative Group on Policies toward the People's Republic of China, Second Meeting: Political Issues, in Tokyo, co-sponsored by the Asia Society and the Japan Institute of International Affairs, April.

Takamizawa Manabu, 2007, *Shinjidai no "nogen" furonteia* [A New Era of "Nengyuan (Energy Resources)" Frontier], Libro.

Tamakoshi Tatsumi, 2012, "Kangei, Nakano Ryoko!: 1984 nen [Welcome, Nakano Ryoko! (1984)]," in Sonoda Shigeto, ed., *Nitchu kankeishi 1972–2012 III: Shakai, bunka* [A History of Japan–China Relations 1972–2012, Vol. III: Society, Culture], University of Tokyo Press.

Tanaka Akihiko, 1991, *Nitchu kankei 1945–1990* [Japan–China Relations 1945–1990], University of Tokyo Press.

Tsuboi Yasuhiro, 2012, "Nitchu no kankokoryu to JTB [JTB and Japan–China Tourism and Exchange]," in Hattori Kenji, Marukawa Tomoo, eds., *Nitchu kankeishi 1972–2012 II: Keizai* [A History of Japan–China Relations 1972–2012, Vol. II: Economy], University of Tokyo Press.

Wakatsuki Hidekazu, 2012, *Taikoku nihon no seijishido: 1972–1989* [The Political Leadership of Major Power, Japan (1972–1989)], in *Gendainihon seijishi 4* [A History of Modern Japanese Politics, Vol. 4], Yoshikawa-kobunkan.

Yabuki Susumu, 2004, *Nitchu no kazaana* [A Breakthrough in Japan–China Relations], Bensei Publishing.

Zheng Zhongbing, ed., 2005, *Hu Yaobang nianpu ziliao changbian (xiace)* [Materials for a Chronicle of Hu Yaobang's life (preliminary draft edition) (Vol. 2)], Time International Publishing Ltd.: Hong Kong.

5

JAPAN–CHINA RELATIONS OF THE 1990s

Rise of China and increase of frictions

FIGURE 5.1 Prime Minister Obuchi Keizo (rear right) and President Jiang Zemin look on as their foreign ministers sign agreements on environmental protection and other matters (November 28, 1998, State Guest House in Moto-Akasaka, Tokyo).

Source: ©Jiji Press.

The 1989 Tiananmen Incident and the end of the Cold War together became a major turning point in Japan–China relations; the "1972 System" that had followed normalization of Japan–China relations began to change significantly. Moreover, both countries underwent a generational change, and so those people who had sustained bilateral ties left the stage and bilateral connections started to atrophy. Japan–China relations of the 1990s saw an increase in frictions, sparked by the history and Taiwan issues and entangled in the influence of domestic politics in both countries.

1 From the Tiananmen Incident to Japanese imperial visit

Policy to avoid isolating China

The Tiananmen Incident was a tremendous shock for the Japanese people. People steeped in an atmosphere of "Japan–China friendship" until that point were astonished by another face of China they saw in live news video. In the routine survey of Japan's image of China conducted by the Prime Minister's Office in October 1989 (Heisei 1), the share of those who responded "I feel close" or "I feel somewhat close" fell suddenly to 51.6 percent from 68.5 percent the year before, and the share responding "I don't feel close" or "I don't feel somewhat close" jumped from 26.4 percent to 43.1 percent. Incidentally, the Japanese people's image of China has hardly recovered since that time, falling into a long-term downward trend (Cabinet Office, various years; see Figure 6.2).

The Japanese government's position was not entirely swept up in that sentiment, however. Uno Sosuke, then prime minister, said in a press conference:

> As for this tragic situation, in which many lives were lost because of the military's use of force, [the PRC government's] actions are intolerable from a humanitarian standpoint, and it is truly regrettable.... Even if [the recent crackdown on the demonstrators] is an internal matter for China, which has a different regime, it is incompatible with the values of our country that champions the cause of democracy.
>
> *(Kazankai 2008, Document 130)*

But ahead of the G-7 Summit of the Arch scheduled for mid-July 1989, the Japanese government firmed up its policy that isolating China was undesirable. Prime Minister Uno stepped down after just over two months in office because of a scandal, and the Kaifu Toshiki administration started on August 9.

Meanwhile, criticism of China's suppression of human rights hit a peak in the United States and many Western countries. Of course, the Japanese government also took measures, such as a travel advisory and freezing ODA to China, but its response differed somewhat from that of other Western countries. Its position sought to avoid isolating China in the international community even as it harshly criticized the Chinese government's response (Tanaka 1991).

One might say that Japan's position was shaped by a sense of unease stemming from geographical proximity. At the time, illegal migrants posing as refugees, many clearly feigning political asylum from a destabilized China, swarmed by the hundreds to Kyushu. The Declaration on China issued at the G-7 Summit of the Arch was critical, but it also called on China to resume moving toward reform and opening, avoid isolation, and return to cooperative relations with the international community. Such wording reportedly was at the decision of Prime Minister Uno who, with the support of U.S. President George H. W. Bush, instructed the declaration be changed to urge China to make these efforts (Kunihiro 2004).

Path to unfreezing ODA

In keeping with such basic policies, the Japanese government decided to rescind the travel advisory to China outside of Beijing on August 18 and to rescind it completely on September 25, 1989. State Planning Commission Chairman Zou Jiahua visited Japan in January 1990 to restart the third ODA yen loan package that had been frozen following the Tiananmen Incident. This was the first vice-premier level visit to Japan since the incident. Following up, Matsuura Koichiro, director of MOFA's economic bureau, visited China for working-level negotiations. Foreign Minister Nakayama Taro expressed the government's opinion on March 2 that returning bilateral relations to the status quo prior to the incident would require efforts from both sides (Kazankai 2008, Document 134). Finance Minister Hashimoto Ryutaro indicated in April that Japan would stop providing assistance with strings attached and make its aid untied, so that it would not be thought to be rushing to lift the freeze ahead of other Western countries. Then, Deputy Foreign Minister Owada Hisashi traveled to China on July 16 to inform the Chinese side about the plan to lift the freeze on ODA in stages.

That so many powerful Diet members visited China around that time, searching for a way to mend relations, merits attention. Indeed, the following parliamentarians visited China in succession between April and September of 1990: former JDA Director-General Kato Koichi, former LDP Policy Chief Watanabe Michio, former Prime Minister Uno Sosuke, JSP Secretary-General Yamaguchi Tsuruo, former Foreign Minister Mitsuzuka Hiroshi, former Deputy Prime Minister Miyazawa Kiichi, President of the House of Representatives Sakurauchi Yoshio, former Deputy Prime Minister Kanemaru Shin, former Prime Minister Takeshita Noboru, and Education Minister Hori Kosuke. State Councillor Li Tieying visited Japan from late June until early July. In economic relations, too, Japan established the Japan–China Investment Promotion Organization in March, China established the China–Japan Investment Promotion Organization in June, a JCEA delegation visited China in September, and Nishigaki Akira, president of the Overseas Economic Cooperation Fund, visited China in October for working-level negotiations on ODA.

In this way, even though an interdependent relationship between Japan and China had not been fully established, at least a variety of official and private channels for improving relations existed in abundance and functioned effectively. The Japanese government then formally decided on November 2 to lift the freeze on the third ODA yen loan package and also decided in December to extend the Japan–China long-term trade agreement for five years. In response, Finance Minister Hashimoto visited China starting January 8, 1991, and a comprehensive mending of relations was planned. There is often a tendency to view such a diplomatic sequence by Japan as placing priority only on the economy, but it should probably be seen as a consistent Japanese policy toward China that tries to get China to participate in the international community (Jo Shogen 2004; Jo Kenfun 2011; Miyake 2012).

While this was going on, in the realm of international politics, the Gulf Crisis broke out. After the end of the Cold War, it was thought that there would be stability in the world, but in fact, we saw the spread of regional conflicts. Iraqi forces invaded Kuwait on August 2, 1990, and Iraq announced the annexation of Kuwait on August 8. In response, the UNSC that day adopted a resolution condemning Iraq and demanded its unconditional withdrawal from Kuwait. But, dissatisfied with lack of improvement in the situation, the United States cobbled together a coalition of multinational forces and commenced aerial bombing of Iraq on January 17, 1991—a chain of events known as the Gulf War. There were debates in Japan over whether this was a war of self-defense or war of aggression, whether or not Japan should dispatch the SDF, and whether or not that action would violate the constitution. In the end, Japan contributed just financial assistance, an enormous sum of $13 billion, providing neither rear area support nor medical cooperation. Viewed with suspicion by the international community, Japan did all it could to dispatch minesweepers after the war. As if it had been closely following Japan's domestic debate on the matter, China, which had been forced on the defensive after Tiananmen, frequently communicated its concerns about Japan deploying the SDF overseas, and issued a statement that Japan should handle the dispatch of minesweepers carefully (Kazankai 2008, Document 140).

Revival of high-level visits

Japan–China relations suddenly moved in a positive direction once Japan decided to lift the freeze on ODA to China. Trips to China by Japanese cabinet members flowed in succession following Finance Minister Hashimoto's January 1991 visit. Trade and Industry Minister Nakao Eiichi on March 21 and Foreign Minister Nakayama Taro on April 5 visited China, laying the groundwork for reviving high-level visits. Former prime ministers Nakasone Yasuhiro and Takeshita Noboru visited China on April 30 and May 2, respectively; Minister of Foreign Economic Relations and Trade Li Lanqing on May 8 and Foreign Minister Qian Qichen on June 25 visited Japan where, in addition to setting Prime Minister Kaifu's visit to China, they formally invited the Emperor of Japan to visit China. At this point, there were frequent visits by politicians during times of crisis between Japan and China, something that is unthinkable at the present time.

In this way, the Japanese government even took the lead internationally in helping China to avoid isolation, but as mentioned above, Japanese public opinion of China concerning its undemocratic actions kept worsening, which aroused criticism of the existing China policy. The primary target of that criticism was ODA to China. In that context, the government disclosed its basic policy for ODA, including to China, in April 1991. Then, it was June 30, 1992 when the Official Development Assistance Charter (formerly ODA outline) finally was put explicitly in writing and approved by cabinet decision. The charter specified the following four points as guiding principles, namely: (1) pursuing environmental conservation and development in tandem; (2) avoiding any use of ODA for military purposes or aggravating international conflicts; (3) paying attention to recipient countries' military expenditures, development and production of weapons of mass destruction and missiles, and arms trade, and (4) giving consideration for promoting democratization, efforts to introduce a market-led economy, and guaranteeing fundamental human rights and freedoms (Ministry of Foreign Affairs 1992).

Prime Minister Kaifu visited China August 10–13, 1991. In his meeting with Premier Li Peng, Kaifu decided to provide in a lump sum the 130 billion yen from fiscal year 1991 of the third ODA yen loan package that had been frozen. Along with highly praising Japan's efforts to mend relations between China and the West, the Chinese side promised to explore the possibility of participating in the UN reporting system covering transfers of conventional weapons, and announced its participation in the NPT, as a way to respond to the Japanese side's request (Kazankai 2008, Document 142). In a meeting with General Secretary Jiang Zemin held on August 12, Kaifu announced an invitation for Jiang to visit Japan, in addition to broadly reaffirming the same substance. As evident here, clearly China post-Tiananmen was gradually achieving a return to the international community through Japan.

In Japan, the cabinet of Miyazawa Kiichi began on November 5, 1991, replacing the Kaifu cabinet. Around this time, visits between Japan and China continued in succession. Komeito Chairman Ishida Koshiro visited China on October 7, whereas Vice Premier Zou Jiahua visited Japan on October 14, Vice Premier Tian Jiyun visited Japan on December 2 and requested that the Japanese Emperor's visit to China take place in 1992. Then, Foreign Minister Watanabe Michio visited China on January 3, 1992, during which visits to Japan by General Secretary Jiang and NPC Chairman Wan Li were settled and agreement was reached on the Emperor's visit to China within the year.

Looking at international relations, in the USSR in August 1991, a coup d'état by conservatives failed and Gorbachev stepped down as CPSU general secretary, and in December, the Soviet Union ceased to exist and Gorbachev resigned as president, too. The dissolution of the Soviet Union was also an enormous blow to China. Yet, U.S. Secretary of State James Baker's trip to China took place on November 15 and Sino-U.S. relations finally began to get back on track. In addition, China had normalized relations with Vietnam immediately before this by accepting a visit to China from Do Muoi, general secretary of the Vietnamese

Communist Party. Also, China, Taiwan, and Hong Kong at the same time attended the Asia–Pacific Economic Cooperation (APEC) summit held in Seoul starting November 12.

Southern tour talks and Jiang Zemin's visit to Japan

Over January and February 1992, Deng Xiaoping, China's most powerful leader, made an inspection tour of the south to such places as Guangdong and Shanghai, and the compilation of the informal talks that Deng reiterated on that tour became the "Southern Tour Talks (*Nanxun Jianghua*)," in which he declared an economic policy shift toward bold reform and opening. After the end of the Cold War and the dissolution of the Soviet Union, the idea of "peaceful evolution" was front and center in China, expounding the possibility of regime change caused by pressure from Western countries to democratize. Confronted with the option to strengthen its closed system or continue with reform and opening and return to the international community, by Deng's decision, China chose to strengthen its fundamentals by pursuing marketization more actively and thereby avoid walking the same path as the USSR. Deng decided that socialist China should boldly embrace marketization regardless of how the plan and the market resulted in a classification of socialism or capitalism, and that the important thing was to strengthen the CCP's leadership politically.

Relieved at China's direction, foreign enterprises suddenly increased their direct investment from this point on, becoming the catalyst for China's entry into an era of high economic growth. China's annual economic growth rate exceeded 10 percent year-over-year between 1992 and 1995 because of increased direct investment. Before long, the southern tour talks were linked to making the "socialist market economy" official at the 14th CCP National Congress in October 1992. Looking at the process from the southern tour talks to the socialist market economy, one can understand how important Japan's indirect support on the diplomatic front was, as China escaped from the international isolation it had fallen into following the Tiananmen Incident.

China's diplomacy began to move all at once after the southern tour talks, predictably starting with diplomacy toward Japan. General Secretary Jiang Zemin visited Japan April 6–10 and in his meeting with Prime Minister Miyazawa, he formally invited the Emperor to visit China. On April 7, Jiang had a meeting with the Emperor and held a memorial lecture in NHK Hall. In his lecture, Jiang spoke of how Japanese militarism had caused the Chinese people to suffer a great misfortune in the 15 or so years since the 1930s, but that postwar Japan had built prosperity by walking the path of peaceful development and thus had expanded its influence in the international community (Kazankai 2008, Document 150). NPC Chairman Wan Li also visited Japan in May and met with the Emperor. Former prime ministers Takeshita in May, Tanaka Kakuei in August, and Nakasone in September visited China and shored up the political foundations of the bilateral relationship. During this time, the Japanese government approved the Emperor's trip to China by cabinet decision on August 25.

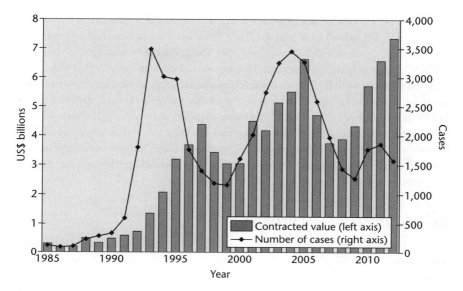

FIGURE 5.2 Japanese direct investment in China (1985–2012).

Source: Chinese Ministry of Commerce, CEIC Data.

Chinese diplomacy's greatest accomplishment during this period was the normalization of diplomatic relations with South Korea on August 24, 1992. Consequently, Taiwan and North Korea broke off diplomatic relations, and bilateral ties remained strained for a long time afterwards because of misunderstandings that arose in the course of severing ties. This was a large diplomatic victory from China's perspective, but undeniably its relations with North Korea became rather complicated. The issue of North Korea's suspected nuclear program sprang up right after this, so one might say that the dissolution of the USSR and friendly relations between China and South Korea drove North Korea to seek direct talks with the United States.

However, the fact is that China's diplomacy still had many challenges. Christopher Patten assumed office as the last governor of Hong Kong in July 1992, and moved proactively on measures to foster democracy in Hong Kong after its reversion. President Bush approved the sale of 150 F-16 fighter jets to Taiwan in September, and Taiwan under President Lee Teng-hui came out with various measures on democratization and Taiwanization, one after another. France also approved the sale of Mirage fighter jets to Taiwan in October. And then Democrat William Jefferson (Bill) Clinton, who had criticized China quite strongly for its democratization and human rights problems in the presidential election campaign, was elected as the next president in November. Looking at it from this situation, one could say that Japan's China policy was certainly one or two steps ahead of other countries'.

There are a few points with this stage of Chinese diplomacy that must not be forgotten. China enacted its Law on the Territorial Sea in February 1992, stipulating that the Spratly (Nansha) and Paracel (Xisha) islands in the South China Sea as well as the Senkaku (Diaoyu) Islands in the East China Sea were its own national territory. After the end of the Cold War, China under Deng Xiaoping's leadership shifted its strategic emphasis from the continent to the seas, and switched over to a policy direction that focused on bolstering its naval forces and securing and enlarging its maritime interests. This emphasis on naval forces was plainly visible in Deng's appointment of Liu Huaqing, a career navy man, to the highest level of the party and military. China's insistence on its maritime interests and sovereignty over the Senkakus perhaps should be seen as having been developed steadily and historically. The Japanese government of course made official protests at this time, but the situation later became vague with the passage of time.

Japanese Emperor's visit to China

The visit to China by Emperor Akihito and Empress Michiko took place October 23–28, 1992, right after the conclusion of the 14th CCP National Congress, mentioned above. During the welcome banquet, President Yang Shangkun said, "It is regrettable that in modern history Sino-Japanese relations went through an unfortunate period, which meant untold sufferings for the Chinese people," and in response, the Emperor said, "In the long history of relations between our two countries, there was an unfortunate period in which my country inflicted great suffering on the people of China. About this I feel deep sadness" (Kazankai 2008, Document 156). There were no troubles or protests whatsoever in China during the visit, and all of the daily events could be finished without incident. Although the Jiang Zemin era had just begun, it was a time when Deng Xiaoping's leadership was still strong and there is no doubt that his initiative was effective.

Before the Emperor went to China, there was an argument opposing the visit in Japan (Sugiura 2012). The primary reasons for opposing a visit were that China was an undemocratic state, as seen in the Tiananmen Incident, and that China would try and use the Emperor's visit politically at home and abroad. In fact, Foreign Minister Qian Qichen recalled some time after he retired that the Emperor's visit to China was a policy to use Japan, the weakest link, in order to help return an isolated China to the international community (Sen 2006). For a former foreign minister, even one who has retired, these remarks lack courtesy, and moreover the suggestion itself is not entirely accurate. China had invited the Emperor to visit before the Tiananmen Incident happened. Even should China have had that intention after the Tiananmen Incident, it had already lost its alleged significance by the time the visit took place. When the Emperor visited China in October 1992, China had by and large already restored its relations with the industrialized countries, including Japan and the United States, and had even normalized diplomatic relations with South Korea. Furthermore, having presented the idea of the socialist market economy with the southern tour talks, China had embarked on a path wholly devoted to growth, and direct investment by foreign enterprises had been growing swiftly. In other words, by having completely changed both its domestic and foreign policies already, China had mended ties with Japan and the rest of the international community and had largely overcome its isolation.

At the imperial banquet to welcome President Hu Jintao who was visiting Japan as a state guest in 2008, Emperor Akihito said:

> The Empress and I visited your country in 1992 ... I still cherish the fond memory of the kind hospitality shown by ... the Government of the People's Republic of China ... and of the warm welcome we received from many people in the places we visited.
>
> *(Kazankai 2008, Document 260)*

Perhaps mindful of the sort of arguments discussed in the previous paragraph, Hu responded:

> In 1992, Your Majesties, the Emperor and Empress, made a visit of historic significance for China. Your visit has become a beautiful memory for both our peoples, and it will be remembered as a beautiful episode in the history of Sino-Japanese relations.
>
> *(Kazankai 2008, Document 264)*

Could it not be said that this was the moment that Hu himself essentially refuted Qian's remarks?

2 From Hosokawa/Murayama administrations to Taiwan Strait Crisis

Economic ties deepen and Japan's political situation

China's declaration of a real market economy in Deng's southern tour talks attracted the interest of the world's businessmen. One can see from Figure 5.2 how much the expected value of direct investment into the Chinese market by Japanese enterprises, notably manufacturers, increased since 1992. China had truly broken through to the era of high growth, with the annual GDP growth rate hitting 14.2 percent year-on-year in 1992, 14.0 percent in 1993, 13.1 percent in 1994, and 10.9 percent in 1995. At the same time, Japan–China trade surged, led by the secondary (manufacturing) sector (see Figure 5.3), and afterwards there was a growing interdependence in economic relations, quickly remaking the conventional North–South pattern of providing advanced technologies for natural resources.

As this was happening, Japan's politics suddenly changed. In August 1993, the LDP, which had been in power since 1955, became the opposition party and the Hosokawa Morihiro administration, a multiparty coalition, was formed. China initially appeared at a loss with the end of LDP rule, but soon it began to view the change as positive after Prime Minister Hosokawa acknowledged the Second Sino-Japanese War as a "war of aggression" and, in his policy speech at the opening of

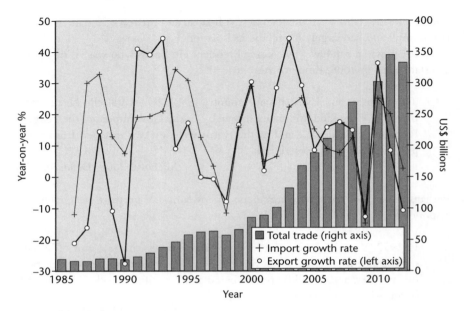

FIGURE 5.3 Japanese trade with China (1985–2012).

Source: Ministry of Finance: Trade Statistics of Japan, CEIC Data.

the 127th Diet session, expressed "profound remorse and apologies for the fact that past Japanese action, including aggression and colonial rule, caused unbearable suffering and sorrow for so many people" (Kazankai 2008, Document 164). Meeting Prime Minister Hosokawa at APEC in November, General Secretary Jiang Zemin also had high praise and invited him to visit China. So, Prime Minister Hosokawa did visit China in March 1994 and consulted on such issues as North Korea amid growing suspicions of its nuclear program at the time.

Just after this, however, Hosokawa suddenly announced his resignation at the beginning of April, and the Hata Tsutomu administration started at the end of April 1994. However, his administration immediately got off to a rocky start and also experienced a setback in relations with China after Justice Minister Nagano Shigeto remarked in early May that he thought the Nanking Incident was "a fabrication" and was pressured to step down. In the end, a coalition administration with Prime Minister Murayama Tomiichi of the JSP began on June 30, after the Hata administration had collapsed in about two months in the face of the three-party LDP–JSP–Sakigake coalition.

Nuclear testing and the Murayama statement

The Taiwan issue was what generated tensions in the Murayama administration's relations with China. At the time, as democratization measures made broad progress in Taiwan under President Lee Teng-hui, glimpses of an independence trend called "Taiwanization" of the Republic of China began to appear. After amendments to the

ROC constitution were adopted at the end of July 1994, the 1996 presidential election was to be decided by direct popular vote, which meant widening the already large gap with the process of democratization in mainland China. In reaction to this situation, frictions arose between Japan and China over the participation of senior ROC officials in the Hiroshima Asian Games scheduled to open in October. The Japanese government had issued a visa to Vice Premier Hsu Li-teh as a representative from Taiwan, but China strongly opposed this, ultimately deciding to cancel State Councillor Li Tieying's visit to Japan.

Immediately afterwards, China conducted an underground nuclear test on October 7, a follow-up to its test in June. Japan strongly protested the tests, and many in Japan seized this opportunity to criticize the provision of a fourth ODA yen loan package to China. A global debate on the Comprehensive Nuclear-Test-Ban Treaty (CTBT) was taking place at the time, and Japan, the only victim of nuclear attack, was also showing an active posture on the issue. However, China conducted another underground nuclear test on May 15, 1995. About ten days before, Prime Minister Murayama had visited China and had just shown a clear position on history issues. Furthermore, China took the drastic step of another underground nuclear test on August 17. France, too, was similarly conducting nuclear tests at the time; all were in a rush to test, anticipating the CTBT's conclusion. These developments helped to worsen China's image in the eyes of the Japanese, who had special feelings toward nuclear matters. It also resulted in further bolstering the skeptics of ODA to China (Jo Kenfun 2011).

1995 was also the 50th year after the end of the war. There was a debate in the Japanese Diet on whether or not to pass a resolution on the renunciation of war to mark this occasion. However, unable to summarize the discussion because of the frequent changes of coalition administrations and instability in the political situation, in the end, the Murayama administration indicated its intentions in the form of a statement (Yakushiji 2012).

The following is one well-known section that Prime Minister Murayama declaimed:

> During a certain period in the not too distant past, Japan, following a mistaken national policy, advanced along the road to war, only to ensnare the Japanese people in a fateful crisis, and, through its colonial rule and aggression, caused tremendous damage and suffering to the people of many countries, particularly to those of Asian nations. In the hope that no such mistake be made in the future, I regard, in a spirit of humility, these irrefutable facts of history, and express here once again my feelings of deep remorse and state my heartfelt apology. Allow me also to express my feelings of profound mourning for all victims, both at home and abroad, of that history.
>
> *(Kazankai 2008, Document 178)*

The substance was characteristic of a prime minister hailing from the JSP, but no one would have thought at the time that this statement would later become an important basic position of the government to be referenced each time history issues would arise repeatedly between Japan and the countries of Asia.

Meanwhile, China began to strengthen its education for patriotism. The CCPCC promulgated the "Outline on Implementing Patriotic Education" in August 1994 and worked out a policy stating that education associated with ethnic patriotism for youths must be thorough. The CCP developed this policy out of a growing concern for the increasingly conspicuous weak degree of awareness regarding socialism and the CCP because of the accelerating pace of marketization of the economy and opening to foreign countries since the 1992 start of the socialist market economy line. In 1995, it then tied the policy to 50 years of postwar history education, seeking to thoroughly enforce the instruction of the CCP's Anti-Japanese War in particular. The number of Anti-Japanese War-related news reports and television dramas spiked sometime around August 1995, which as a result, is thought to be connected with the deterioration of Japan's image in China.

Redefining Japan–U.S. security arrangements

The end of the Cold War and the breakup of the Soviet Union, the erstwhile enemy, as well as the communication gap between Japan and the United States in the Gulf War all weighed on both countries to reaffirm the significance of the Japan–U.S. Security Treaty. The growing seriousness of North Korea's nuclear program in 1993–94, too, was a development sufficient to make this need more keenly felt. This background gave rise to the discussion on redefining the Japan–U.S. security arrangements starting in 1994, and it was the reason for issuing the "Japan–U.S. Joint Declaration on Security—Alliance for the 21st Century" on April 17, 1996, at the summit between President Clinton and Prime Minister Hashimoto (who had taken office on January 11, 1996).

In the joint declaration, they confirmed that the Japan–U.S. alliance was the foundation for peace and stability in the Asia-Pacific region, the importance of the roughly 100,000 forward deployed U.S. military personnel in the region, as well as that they would do a review of the "Guidelines for Japan–U.S. Defense Cooperation" drafted in 1978. In addition, both countries agreed on the return of the Futenma Air Base conditional upon its relocation, because reducing the burden from bases in Okinawa had become an issue after the 1995 rape of a girl by U.S. troops in Okinawa. This relocation issue was initially a task to be worked out in the not too distant future, but as is commonly known, it remains unresolved even today.

Based on the joint declaration, the new "Guidelines for Japan–U.S. Defense Cooperation" were issued in September 1997. Bills laying the concrete legal groundwork related to the new guidelines were submitted to the Diet in 1998 and enacted in May 1999: the "Law Concerning Measures to Ensure the Peace and Security of Japan in Situations in Areas Surrounding Japan" (SIASJ Law), the amendment of the SDF Law, and the revised Acquisition and Cross-Servicing Agreement (ACSA) between Japan and the United States. The point drawing the most attention in the new guidelines was that the scope for Japan–U.S. cooperation was expanded to include rear area support even with respect to surrounding areas outside of Japanese territory, whereas the old guidelines had assumed Japan–U.S. cooperation fundamentally in emergency situations in Japan. The new guidelines' content truly strengthened the Japan–U.S. alliance, specifically the establishment of a "comprehensive mechanism" that can be seen in the "two-plus-two" meetings (comprising diplomatic and defense officials), for instance.

The biggest issue was the scope of "situations in areas surrounding Japan" (SIASJ). The new guidelines stated:

> The aim of these Guidelines is to create a solid basis for more effective and credible U.S.–Japan cooperation under normal circumstances, in case of an armed attack against Japan, and in situations in areas surrounding Japan. The Guidelines also provide a general framework and policy direction for the roles and missions of the two countries and ways of cooperation and coordination, both under normal circumstances and during contingencies.

In addition, it stipulated that the concept of SIASJ "is not geographic but situational." The SIASJ Law passed by the Diet two years later defined the concept in Article 1 as "situations that will have a serious impact on Japan's peace and security, including situations that could develop into a direct armed attack against Japan if left unaddressed." Without question, the expression is not specific.

The Taiwan situation, then in a state of heightened tensions, was the issue that sparked a big debate over SIASJ—whether or not SIASJ included the Taiwan issue, and supposing it did, that it would provoke a strong backlash from China. But, at the stage this was being debated, China was already engaged in unsparing criticism. China's international affairs experts at the time, fearing that the post-Cold War eastward expansion of the North Atlantic Treaty Organization (NATO) was a "net to encircle China" and that the new guidelines were the "NATO of the East," were vigilant against China becoming hemmed in from both sides.

Taiwan Strait Crisis

The Chinese military carried out military exercises by firing missiles in the Taiwan Strait in July 1995, a backlash against ROC President Lee Teng-hui's trip to the United States in June to give a speech at Cornell University, where he had received his Ph.D. Furthermore, the first direct presidential election in Taiwan was held in March 1996, a consequence of Lee's democratization push; ahead of the election, the Chinese military held large-scale military exercises along with conducting missile launch tests in the Taiwan Strait. It is thought that the goal was intimidation, trying to block the election of Lee or Peng Ming-min, the pro-independence candidate, but it backfired, helping to push up their votes, and as a result Lee Teng-hui was elected president with 54 percent of the vote. Meanwhile, sensing the danger, the United States quickly dispatched two aircraft carriers, the *Independence* and the

Nimitz, to the Taiwan Strait. Also, the discussion of a "China threat" heated up around the world owing to this series of crises.

What had kicked off the discussion over the new Japan–U.S. guidelines was the end of the Cold War and the Gulf War; the new guidelines had not been directly linked to the Taiwan issue at the start. However, the discussion over the new guidelines, and especially SIASJ, inevitably became deeply linked to the Taiwan issue as such serious changes in the regional situation took place (Funabashi 1997). This could have easily been imagined since the announcement of the "Japan–U.S. Joint Declaration on Security," the point of departure for the new guidelines, was made right after the Taiwan Strait crisis. Prime Minister Hashimoto expressed strong concerns about China's military exercises at the time. Yet, he had denied that there was any direct relevance between the new guidelines and the Taiwan issue to avoid antagonizing China, perhaps because he led a coalition government that included the JSP.

The Taiwan issue was also a factor in the history issue between Japan and China. With the sudden death of Chiang Ching-kuo in 1988, Vice President Lee Teng-hui was installed as president. He was a *benshengren*, a native-born Taiwanese, not a mainland-born *waishengren*, and so he became the first Taiwan-born president since the Republic of China moved to Taiwan in 1949. After his inauguration, he set about democratizing the political system monopolized by *waishengren* and promoted the "Taiwanization" of the Republic of China. He put an end to the KMT's one-party authoritarian rule, made the 1996 presidential contest a direct election by the citizens, and, as a matter of course, stood for the election and won. Meanwhile, Lee tried to end the state of civil war with the mainland in 1991, permitted the pro-independence Democratic Progressive Party (DPP) to expand its activities, and introduced elections for the Legislative Yuan and dissolved the "Eternal Parliament," the symbol of KMT authoritarianism.

During the course of this democratization, Lee, who had studied at Kyoto University, asserted that Japan's prewar colonial rule had been the basis for Taiwan's economic development. China, which claims Taiwan as part of its own territory, was furious. For China, in other words, Japan's prewar rule of Taiwan was an invasion and so Lee Teng-hui, who gave Japanese colonial rule legitimacy, is unpardonable. China criticized Lee as a "closet supporter of independence" and was deeply wary of him becoming close to Japan. Needless to say, Japanese society, which struggles for a response on the history issue, reacted favorably to what Lee said.

BOX 5.1 JAPAN–TAIWAN RELATIONS OF THE LEE TENG-HUI ERA

Taiwan entered an era of rapid democratization from 1988 to 2000 under the powerful leadership of President Lee Teng-hui. He was a KMT member, but as the first Taiwan-born president, he put an end to the rule of Taiwan by mainland-born KMT *waishengren*. This period of democratization is also expressed as the "Taiwanization of the Republic of China" based on a Taiwanese identity. Democratization enabled free debate over the period of Japanese colonial rule (1895–1945), in stark contrast to the anti-Japanese education under the *waishengren* rule until then.

Embodying this kind of trend are the May 1991 declaration ending the civil war with the mainland (abolishing the Period of Mobilization for the Suppression of Communist Rebellion Provisional Act), and the conversation between Lee and Japanese writer Shiba Ryotaro in the pages of the *Shukan Asahi* weekly magazine in April 1994. In this conversation, together with giving high praise of Japanese colonial rule, Lee argued that Taiwan had consistently been ruled by "foreign administrations," in which he also included the KMT administration. Experiencing such developments in the Jiang Zemin era, China came to strongly criticize Lee as a "closet supporter of independence."

The primary point of disagreement was, in the final analysis, how to assess the First Sino-Japanese War—Lee claimed that Japan legitimately acquired Taiwan as a colony whereas China insisted that Taiwan was China's own territory and that Japan's colonization was aggression. In other words, China has tried to designate Japan's rule of Taiwan as a history issue. This is also the part that is linked to the argument nowadays over the Senkaku Islands.

Concerning Japan–Taiwan relations of the Lee Teng-hui era, since interstate relations did not exist, venues for private sector intellectual exchanges like the Asia Open Forum held important meaning. Established by Lee and Nakajima Mineo, then a professor at Tokyo University of Foreign Studies, the Forum was held from 1989 until 2000, when Lee stepped down as president. Bringing many academics and businessmen together in Japan or Taiwan in alternate years, the Forum had a large significance for people-to-people exchanges for the two countries without diplomatic ties.

The origin of Lee's perspective on Japan is Taiwan under Japanese rule. Born in Taiwan in 1923, Lee grew up as a Japanese under the "imperialization" education of the 1930s–1940s. He entered the agricultural faculty of Kyoto University in 1943, but was called to service under the student draft. The war ended, however, and he returned to Taiwan in 1946 and transferred to National Taiwan University (NTU).

After that, Lee also faced many hardships in Taiwan, as the authoritarian KMT regime oppressed the Taiwanese people. He became active in the field of agricultural economics as an NTU professor, but changed careers and entered the world of politics beginning in the 1970s. He was discovered by Chiang Ching-kuo, was selected to be his vice president in 1984, and because of Chiang's sudden death in 1988, Lee unexpectedly became president. Lee's pro-Japan stance was welcomed in Japan, but China was deeply wary of such close historical connections.

In addition to the Taiwan issue, the issue of China's nuclear tests also came up suddenly; there was strong criticism of China's testing in Japan. In the rush to test before the UN opened the CTBT for signature in 1996, France conducted one nuclear test in January and China two, in June and July. Though the Japanese government did not respond by freezing ODA, it did decide to postpone its implementation as well as the consultations for the fourth ODA yen loan package. Also, it was confirmed that Chinese ocean survey vessels had been conducting resource exploration operations near the Japan–China median line in the East China Sea from around 1995. The Japanese government repeatedly criticized this activity and called for a halt; China's actions also became a big factor in the worsening of its image in Japan. When a Japanese political group landed on the Senkaku Islands in July 1996 and set up a lighthouse, this time it was China that asserted its sovereignty rights and strongly criticized the Japanese side.

In this way, Japan–China relations followed a downward path in 1995–96, entangled in the complexity of domestic conditions and such issues as Taiwan, the new guidelines, nuclear testing, and East China Sea resource development. Despite these many frictions, one can say that the Japanese government at the time gave special consideration to its relations with China; key members of the ruling Hashimoto administration were from the Keiseikai faction, which followed in the tradition of Tanaka Kakuei, who had accomplished normalization of Japan–China relations. Later, Prime Minister Hashimoto who visited China in September 1997 clearly stated in his meetings with Premier Li Peng and General Secretary Jiang Zemin that the new guidelines did not presuppose a situation against any specific country or region, and that he did not support "two Chinas" or Taiwanese independence (Kazankai 2008, Documents 194, 195). Meanwhile, Prime Minister Hashimoto made a private visit to Yasukuni Shrine on July 29, 1996, tacitly showing consideration for the Japan War Bereaved Families Association for which he worked as chairman. As far as we know from open sources, however, there is no question that this was the first visit by a prime minister since Prime Minister Nakasone's visit 11 years ago. Hashimoto refrained from visiting after that, perhaps because China had strong criticisms.

3 From Asian financial crisis to Jiang Zemin's visit to Japan

Reversion of Hong Kong and Asian financial crisis

Deng Xiaoping, China's most powerful man, died on February 19, 1997 at the age of 92. Though essentially he had been in retirement since his southern tour talks in 1992, one might say that his very existence was a guarantee of the policy line established since 1978, and despite some slight shifts, basically there had been no large changes in policy toward Japan, either. Deng had dreamed of seeing Hong Kong's reversion with his own eyes and crossing the border on his own feet, but he reached the end of his days a few months short, his dream left unrealized.

Though power had already been entrusted to Jiang, it was after Deng's death that the Jiang Zemin era began, both in name and essence. His first trial was the

Taiwan Strait Crisis. A secret channel for negotiations had always existed between China and Taiwan, but even this opening was shut down under pressure from hardliners, led by the military, enraged by Lee Teng-hui's visit to the United States in 1995. They beefed up military exercises for the purpose of intimidation. As stated above, however, this crisis-generated intimidation had the opposite effect, instead becoming a factor aiding Lee's election victory, and so the Taiwan Strait Crisis had the result of helping Jiang gain power over the military. Several important events that occurred in 1997 made Jiang's hold on power secure. One was the July 1 reversion of Hong Kong, another was the 15th CCP National Congress held in September. Even though Hong Kong's reversion had already been decided in 1984, the world was carefully watching the 1997 reversion ceremony. The world was interested in whether or not China would keep Hong Kong's freedom and democracy in the wake of the Tiananmen Incident, but China and especially Jiang were interested in the domestic objectives of restoring national dignity and exercising power. The 15th CCP National Congress accelerated the move toward marketization by permitting the introduction of various forms of ownership (including private ownership) even as it kept public ownership at the core.

A significant event happened between the return of Hong Kong and the 15th CCP National Congress—the Asian Financial Crisis, which erupted right after Hong Kong's reversion. Triggered by the drop in the Thai baht, the crisis spread throughout the countries of Southeast Asia and to the Republic of Korea, hitting Hong Kong before long. To counter the crisis, Japan proposed creating an Asian Monetary Fund (AMF), an Asian version of the International Monetary Fund (IMF). But the United States and China opposed the idea, perhaps worried that an AMF would reduce their influence, and so in the end, Japan prepared the New Miyazawa Initiative, a $30 billion emergency assistance mechanism named after the finance minister at the time. China did not have any financial assistance, but Premier Zhu Rongji touted the magnitude of China's role, declaring in a first-rate performance for him that China would maintain 8 percent growth, avoid devaluing the renminbi, and take decisive action on financial, administrative, and state-owned enterprise reforms. Associated with these reforms, the Guangdong International Trust and Investment Corporation (GITIC) was pushed by Zhu's order into bankruptcy in 1998. Many Japanese financial institutions had invested in GITIC and many enterprises were affected by its bad debts.

Japan passing

At its start in January 1993, the Clinton administration initially presented a hardline stance toward China starting with the issue of human rights, but in 1994 it decided to separate business from human rights as China's growth path started to get on track. Yet, the basic structure of U.S.–China relations did not improve after that because of events such as Lee Teng-hui's visit and the Taiwan Strait Crisis. However, U.S.–China relations shifted greatly from 1997 to 1998. China seemed to think at the time that it had been threatened in the Taiwan Strait Crisis and encircled by NATO's eastward expansion and the new guidelines, as previously mentioned, so that is why it considered activating big power diplomacy as an effective means to break out of this situation. It was the roll-out of this period's omnidirectional partnership diplomacy.

Jiang Zemin made a state visit to the United States October 26–November 3, 1997. The first site he visited was Pearl Harbor in Hawaii, a location that amply harkened back to the U.S.–China partnership in World War II against their common enemy, Japan. China had secretly made several concessions to make Jiang's U.S. visit happen. One was to sign the UN Human Rights Covenant A (the International Covenant on Economic, Social, and Cultural Rights) during the visit; another was to release imprisoned pro-democracy activist Wei Jingsheng on the pretext of medical treatment, in reality allowing his defection to the United States in mid-November, right after the visit.

Clinton and Jiang exchanged a joint statement that confirmed the building of a "constructive strategic partnership" at the summit held in Washington D.C. on October 29. The great debate in U.S. policy toward China between containment versus engagement had continued after the Taiwan Strait Crisis, and it resulted in the policy of engagement becoming mainstream, and on that basis, the policy's aim became establishing a "strategic partnership." In short, engagement meant that, by drawing it into the international system through repeated exchanges and negotiations, China would become a creator of the international order, not a destroyer.

President Clinton went to China June 25–July 3, 1998, the first state visit by a U.S. president since the Tiananmen Incident. In April before this trip, former Beijing University student Wang Dan, one of the leaders of the 1989 pro-democracy movement who was later imprisoned, was released for medical treatment and was allowed to defect to the United States. This was apparently linked to the preliminary preparations for Clinton's visit to China. In Shanghai, midway through his visit, Clinton announced the "three noes" in connection with the Taiwan issue: that the United States did not support "independence for Taiwan," "two Chinas or one China–one Taiwan," or Taiwan's membership "in any organization for which statehood is a requirement." At the July 27 summit meeting, the leaders also agreed to cooperate on nuclear nonproliferation and peaceful use and to not target each other with their strategic nuclear weapons. Here, too, they reaffirmed the building of a "constructive strategic partnership" premised on the U.S. policy of engagement.

Clinton's visit to China was an exceptionally long trip at nearly 10 days. This kind of strategic partnership by the two major powers at the time, the United States and China, could be called the precursor of the "G-2 era" that was hotly debated after 2010. But, the fact that Clinton did not make a stop-off in America's ally, Japan, became a big problem there. Of course, the administration was also criticized at home for such disregard for an ally. Under these circumstances that might be rendered as Japan being slighted by the U.S.–China honeymoon, the phrase "Japan passing" cropped up more frequently in Japan, a pessimistic theory that perhaps reflected the realities of the country's inability to recover from the collapse of its bubble economy and, moreover, being at the mercy of the Asian Financial Crisis.

Also, *The Rape of Nanjing* by author Iris Chang on the topic of the Nanking Incident had been published in 1997 and became a best seller in the United States, and so Japan's so-called history issues came under scrutiny around the world.

Jiang Zemin's visit to Japan

China was expanding its partnership diplomacy to all the world's major countries, not just the United States. It seems that, amid the discussion of American unipolar rule, China's strategic intent was to escape encirclement. Of course, one link of that diplomacy was Japan. President Jiang Zemin's trip to Japan to celebrate the 20th anniversary of the conclusion of the Japan–China Treaty of Peace and Friendship was originally scheduled for the early part of September 1998. China decided to postpone the visit, however, giving damage from summer flooding as the reason. There is another theory. The Hashimoto cabinet met a sudden end at the end of July, owing to the LDP's loss in the upper house election. Obuchi Keizo was hurriedly chosen as the successor. The Japanese media had an extremely low assessment of Obuchi, however, and there were many predictions that his cabinet would be short-lived. So, another interpretation is that China, fearing this, used flood damage as an excuse to postpone a visit to Japan for the time being.

Consequently, ROK President Kim Dae-jung's state visit to Japan came first (October 7–10, 1998), a fact that complicated Jiang Zemin's later visit. In the Japan–Republic of Korea Joint Declaration issued on October 8, Prime Minister Obuchi expressed "his deep remorse and heartfelt apology" concerning Japan's past colonial rule, for which President Kim expressed his appreciation, along with highly appreciating postwar Japan's orientation toward peace and development. There were reasons for including such wording in the declaration. Not once had a formal expression of "apology" (*owabi*) been used in Japan–Korea relations in the past. Also, Kim promised never to raise the matter again if it were expressed thus. Of course, there had reportedly been a fierce debate within the LDP over this.

General Secretary Jiang Zemin's state visit took place November 25–30. It was on the return from his visit to Russia and became the last trip of partnership diplomacy, which had peaked with the visit to the United States. China, having seen Japan express "apology" on Kim Dae-jung's visit, requested the same expression from Japan in talks between Foreign Minister Komura Masahiko and Foreign Minister Tang Jiaxuan, who went to Japan for prior consultations. However, the LDP General Council did not accept this request, saying that what had been expressed in the Japan–China Joint Communiqué was all that needed to be said with China. As a result, Prime Minister Obuchi conveyed an "apology" verbally during the meeting, but it was not in the joint declaration: it and the section praising postwar Japan's peace and development, the ostensible quid-pro-quo, were removed. Also, that the leaders did not sign the joint declaration was an unprecedented situation (Kokubun 2000a; Eguchi 2012).

As background to this situation, Jiang Zemin, who is said to have personally held bad memories regarding prewar Japan, made a series of very harsh remarks centered on the history issue. Jiang reiterated his remarks on the issue of Japan's understanding of history in his official meeting with Prime Minister Obuchi on November 26 and continued lecturing on history at that evening's imperial banquet, too, strongly criticizing the "militarism" of the past. Incidentally, Jiang wore a Zhongshan suit at the banquet; designated the national costume by Sun Yat-sen, it was men's formal attire in the Republic of China era. Some of the media criticized Jiang for wearing a "Mao suit" (*jinmin fuku*), but Japanese and Chinese diplomatic officials had reportedly agreed to this. Jiang strongly criticized Japan's past actions as a witness of history in his November 28 speech at Waseda University, too.

As a result of Jiang Zemin's visit to Japan, the "Japan–China Joint Declaration on Building a Partnership of Friendship and Cooperation for Peace and Development" was issued, and the two countries took a step toward a more global relationship from Japan–China relations based on "neighborly friendship," the core of bilateral relations until then. The fact that "gratitude" for Japan's economic cooperation was expressed in this joint declaration was new. And yet, the surprising thing is that Jiang's visit is remembered by history as a "failure" from this course of events. In Japan, Obuchi came to be praised for not having yielded his position to China. In China, however, while the outcome of Jiang's trip was lauded on the surface, some internally felt that Jiang should have been admonished for having let his personal emotions show.

4 Development of multilateral diplomacy and increase of frictions

Kosovo War and TMD concept

U.S.–China relations were developing stably in 1997 and 1998 with the establishment of the strategic partnership. Bilateral relations once again deteriorated in 1999, however, owing to events related to the conflict in Yugoslavia. After the Cold War ended, Yugoslavia split apart and six independent states were created, in the course of which wars broke out repeatedly. In one of them, the Republic of Serbia under President Slobodan Milošević tried to annex Kosovo, an autonomous province with many ethnic Albanians, whereupon Kosovo declared its independence. Serbia responded by attacking Kosovo and began to suppress the ethnic Albanians, and so the conflict erupted. NATO took the role of arbitrator in order to mediate the conflict at the start of 1999, but these Rambouillet peace talks ultimately broke down and NATO forces commenced aerial bombing of Serbia at the end of March. For its part, China had deep ties with Serbia.

On May 8, a NATO stealth bomber bombed what was supposed to be a military supply depot in Serbia's capital, Belgrade, but it was the Chinese embassy and the bombing killed three staff members. The bombing was a mistake, a result of using an old map, according to the excuse by U.S. forces, but China said that the United States knew what the building was and bombed it intentionally. Fearing large-scale anti-American demonstrations, the Chinese authorities mobilized students in front of the U.S. embassy in Beijing and allowed them to throw stones. This incident significantly damaged the U.S.–China relationship that had just been built up, and negotiations over indemnity for the victims became drawn out. Without question, U.S. actions like the NATO bombing were seen as threatening by China, which was criticizing "unipolar rule," insisting on multipolarity.

Just then, Japan enacted the laws associated with the new guidelines in May 1999. About that time, the Chinese media reported a series of scathing critiques by experts regarding the new guidelines bills, especially the SIASJ Law, though this was not the official view. In addition to these bills, one more topic was a point of dispute at the time between Japan and China: the issue of theater missile defense (TMD).

The United States came out with the Strategic Defense Initiative and its use of outer space in the Reagan era of the 1980s, and made some progress actualizing the concept of TMD with its focus on land-based interception in the Clinton era of the 1990s. The Japanese government, which had a positive view toward joint research of this concept, strengthened this stance after September 1998. That is because on August 31, North Korea held a test launch of its Taepodong missile, which passed through the airspace over the Japanese islands. This incident, dubbed the "Taepodong shock," was enough to force the Japanese people to reconsider the importance of security. The Japanese government bolstered its position supporting the TMD concept after this, but the Chinese side began to harbor strong concerns about such enhanced Japan–U.S. defense cooperation together with the new guidelines. Premier Zhu Rongji and Foreign Minister Tang Jiaxuan strongly criticized Japan–U.S. joint TMD development at a press conference after the NPC in March 1999. China was made to keenly feel a danger of encirclement from Japan–U.S. defense cooperation and the reality of NATO's eastward expansion because of the conflict in Kosovo (Kokubun 2000b).

ASEAN + 3

The 1990s is designated the era of the rise of regionalism. This rise was especially remarkable in the Asia-Pacific region. APEC, launched in 1989, began to hold informal summit meetings in 1993. The ASEAN Regional Forum (ARF) was established in 1994 as a venue to discuss security primarily among ASEAN members. ARF was to be held in conjunction with the pre-existing expanded ASEAN foreign ministerial and the ASEAN cabinet minister meetings. Japan had been actively engaged diplomatically, having long emphasized Southeast Asia as one pillar of its diplomacy; China, too, began strengthening its diplomatic offensive toward ASEAN in the latter half of the 1990s, whether to dispel the "China threat" theory or out of economic necessity.

Then, with the outbreak of the Asian Financial Crisis in 1997, Japan called for the creation of an AMF in place of the IMF, but the United States and China rejected the Japan-centric alternative plan, as mentioned above. However, the crisis triggered a keen sense of the need for stronger cooperation within the Asian region. Also, since 1997 was the 30th anniversary of the creation of ASEAN, the leaders of

Japan, China, and South Korea were invited to the ASEAN summit held in Kuala Lumpur, where they agreed on the importance of regional cooperation. At this point, a framework for intraregional cooperation was established under the ASEAN plus Japan, China, and South Korea (ASEAN + 3, also called 10 + 3 after ASEAN grew to ten members); it came to be called an "East Asian" framework, combining "Southeast Asian" and "Northeast Asian."

At Prime Minister Obuchi's initiative, a meeting of the leaders of Japan, China, and Korea was held separately on the sidelines at the ASEAN+3 meeting held in Manila in November 1999. Obuchi, ROK President Kim Dae-jung, and Chinese Premier Zhu Rongji participated, but it was only called a "breakfast meeting" because China preferred not to call it a formal summit meeting. It is speculated that China was somewhat hesitant toward such a framework that included South Korea out of consideration for North Korea, because Sino-DPRK relations had finally started to recover in 1999 after a rocky period following the 1992 normalization of Sino-ROK relations. China had a change of heart, becoming more positive toward the Japan–China–ROK summit, perhaps because the Inter-Korean Summit took place in 2000 with President Kim Dae-jung's visit to North Korea and because North Korea joined the ARF.

In any case, this is the start of trilateral summits—the first ever among Japan, China, and South Korea, three countries sharing a complex history—a framework that has continued to this day. Precisely because the three countries' existing bilateral relations have all concentrated on the negative legacies of the past (the Korean War, in Sino-ROK relations), such a new framework is important as evidence that they are overcoming history and starting to transition to more pragmatic, forward-looking relations.

Start of the Chen Shui-bien administration

Chen Shui-bien, the pro-independence DPP candidate, won Taiwan's presidential election in March 2000. China avoided military exercises or other threatening actions ahead of the election, as if having learned from its mistakes in 1996; Premier Zhu Rongji just made verbal threats. Nevertheless, the outcome was similar, contributing to Chen's victory. China had been wary of how Lee Teng-hui would behave, but Lee was defeated because he supported a losing candidate, Lien Chan, who divided the KMT, and so he resigned as KMT chairman. Lee later formed the Taiwan Solidarity Union in 2001, bringing together Taiwan independence seekers, but having announced his retirement from politics, his influence had waned.

China, naturally, grew more concerned about Chen Shui-bien. But Chen declared the "four noes and one without" in his May 20 inauguration speech—that he would: not declare independence; not change the name of the nation from the Republic of China to Taiwan; not include the two states doctrine in the constitution (remarks that Lee Teng-hui made in 1999 that the PRC and ROC had special state-to-state relations); not hold a national referendum on the questions of unification or independence; and not abolish the National Unification Guidelines or the

National Unification Council. The Japanese government avoided commenting directly on Taiwan's presidential election, needless to say, but within Japan, a debate began over whether the now-retired Lee Teng-hui should visit.

On April 2, just after the ROC presidential election, Prime Minister Obuchi fell ill (dying on May 14), and the Mori Yoshiro cabinet was formed on April 5. Prime Minister Obuchi had shown a firm stance toward China, such as on the occasion of Jiang Zemin's visit to Japan, but he had set out to sign a memorandum on the disposal of abandoned chemical weapons that Japanese forces left in China (concluded July 1999)—he could be firm or flexible as the situation required. It is thought that Nonaka Hiromu had also played a large role; Obuchi's chief cabinet secretary (and later, LDP secretary-general), Nonaka had built a personal relationship with Zeng Qinghong, a close associate of Jiang Zemin.

In this period, there were ever louder calls for a review of ODA in Japan's relations with China. Doubts had been raised as early as the 1989 Tiananmen Incident about providing ODA to China, which was suppressing human rights, yet there had been no resolution. Later, as China grew powerful through its economic growth, criticisms of ODA to China intensified: Why provide assistance to China, whose growth is doing so well, while Japan's own economy is suffering? Moreover, China is constantly expanding its military expenditures. The Chinese people feel no gratitude since the facts of Japanese ODA are not widely known in China. Based on such criticism and after receiving the recommendations on ODA to China made by a private advisory body to the director-general of MOFA's economic cooperation bureau, the LDP's special committee on foreign economic cooperation demanded in December 2000 that, in light of Japan's own fiscal situation and national interests, ODA be shifted to environmental protection, preservation of ecosystems, poverty assistance, and other problem areas that China itself found difficult to solve, and to provide assistance that highlighted Japan's role (Kazankai 2008, Documents 210, 211).

George W. Bush, former President Bush's eldest son, won the U.S. presidential election in November 2000. The Republican candidate, Bush was critical of President Clinton's "soft on China" policy in the election campaign, and repeatedly insisted that the United States should emphasize its allies more, denouncing the policy of engagement with China. Consequently, there was a greater possibility that the United States would emphasize Japan over China, and so China's wariness toward the United States increased.

Cited and referenced materials

Cabinet Office, Government of Japan, various years, "Gaiko ni kansuru seronchosa [Public Opinion Survey on Diplomacy]," http://survey.gov-online.go.jp/index-gai.html (last accessed December 9, 2016).

Eguchi Shingo, 2012, "Hashimoto shusho no yurashiagaiko to Ko Takumin no rainichi: 1997–98 nen [Prime Minister Hashimoto's Eurasia Diplomacy and President Jiang Zemin's Visit to Japan, 1997–98]," in Takahara Akio, Hattori Ryuji, eds., *Nitchu kankeishi 1972–2012 I: Seiji* [A History of Japan–China Relations 1972–2012, Vol. I: Politics], University of Tokyo Press.

Funabashi Yoichi, 1997, *Domei hyoryu* [Alliance Adrift], Iwanami Shoten.

Japan–United States Security Consultative Committee, 1997, *Nichibei boeikyoryoku no tameno shishin* [Joint Statement: Completion of the Review of the Guidelines for U.S.–Japan Defense Cooperation], www.mofa.go.jp/mofaj/area/usa/hosho/kyoryoku.html (last accessed December 9, 2016).

Jo Kenfun [Xu Xianfen], 2011, *Nihon no taichu ODA gaiko* [Japan's ODA Diplomacy to China], Keiso Shobo.

Jo Shogen [Suh Seung-won], 2004, *Nihon no keizaigaiko to chugoku* [Japan's Economic Diplomacy and China], Keio University Press.

Kazankai, 2008, *Nitchu kankei kihon shiryoshu 1972–2008 nen* [Collection of Basic Documents in Japan–China Relations, 1972–2008], Kazankai Foundation.

Kokubun Ryosei, 2000a, "Shiren no jidai no nitchukankei [Japan–China Relations in the Era of Difficulties]," in *hogaku kenkyu* [Journal of Law, Politics, and Sociology], Keio University Press, Vol. 73, No. 1.

Kokubun Ryosei, 2000b, "Higashiazia anzenhosho to nichibeichu [East Asian Security and the United States, Japan, and China]," in *Kokusaimondai* [International Affairs], Japan Institute of International Affairs, No. 478.

Kunihiro Michihiko, 2004, "Tenanmon jiken to arushusamitto [The Tiananmen Incident and Summit of the Arch]," *Kasumigasekikai kaiho*, August edition.

Ministry of Foreign Affairs of Japan, 1992, *Seifu kaihatsu enjo taiko (Kyu ODA taiko)* [Japan's Official Development Assistance Charter (former ODA Outline)], www.mofa.go.jp/mofaj/gaiko/oda/seisaku/taikou/sei_1_1.html (last accessed December 9, 2016).

Miyake Yasuyuki, 2012, "6.4〈Dainiji tenanmon〉jiken: 1989–91 nen [June 4 (Second Tiananmen) Incident, 1989–91]," in Takahara Akio, Hattori Ryuji, eds., *Nitchu kankeishi 1972–2012 I: Seiji* [A History of Japan–China Relations 1972–2012, Vol. I: Politics], University of Tokyo Press.

Sen Kichin [Qian Qichen] (Hamamoto Ryoichi, tr.), 2006, *Sen Kishin kaikoroku* [Memoirs of Qian Qichen], Toyo Shoin.

Sugiura Yasuyuki, 2012, "Tenno hochu: 1991–92 nen [The Emperor's Visit to China, 1991–92]," in Takahara Akio, Hattori Ryuji, eds., *Nitchu kankeishi 1972–2012 I: Seiji* [A History of Japan–China Relations 1972–2012, Vol. I: Politics], University of Tokyo Press.

Tanaka Akihiko, 1991, *Nitchu kankei 1945–1990* [Japan–China Relations 1945–1990], University of Tokyo Press.

Yakushiji Katsuyuki, ed., 2012, *Murayama Tomiichi kaikoroku* [The Memoirs of Murayama Tomoichi], Iwanami Shoten.

6

JAPAN–CHINA RELATIONS AT THE START OF THE TWENTY-FIRST CENTURY

The rocky path to a strategic mutually beneficial relationship

FIGURE 6.1 Japan's international rescue team silently pays its respects before the deceased bodies of a mother and baby that they recovered from the rubble of the Great Sichuan Earthquake (May 17, 2008, Qingchuan County, Sichuan Province).

Source: ©Xinhua/Photoshot.

At the start of the twenty-first century, China's rise became ever more apparent and China overtook Japan in terms of GDP in 2010, jumping to the world's number two position. Economically, Japan and China have deepened their interdependence as they increased the aggregate value of their bilateral trade and investment. The national image each country has of the other has worsened, however, as bilateral frictions have grown over political and security issues, notably the perception of history and the Senkakus. A mutually beneficial relationship based on common strategic interests got its start in 2006, but the path has been rocky.

1 From start of the Koizumi administration to start of the Hu Jintao administration

Safeguards issue and former President Lee Teng-hui's visit to Japan

As the curtain rose on the twenty-first century, the first issue to arise between Japan and China was a topic symbolizing a new era of bilateral relations—trade frictions. It was the China safeguards issue. Safeguards are exceptional measures to restrict imports that the General Agreement on Tariffs and Trade (GATT) allows a country to enact to protect its own products in cases where imports of particular items from another country increase rapidly. Three items were a problem this time—green onions, raw *shiitake* mushrooms, and soft rush outer covers for *tatami* mats—their imports from China were surging, and the Japanese farmers affected applied political pressure. Separately, towel imports from China were also rising rapidly and the Japanese towel industry, too, called for the imposition of safeguards. These moves by Japan were undeniably related to the upper house election scheduled for July 2001 (Heisei 13) because they were easy topics and timed to secure the rural and farm vote.

In such a context, the Japanese government decided on April 23, 2001 to enact provisional safeguards for 200 days on the three agricultural items noted above. In response, the Chinese government immediately issued a statement criticizing the move and mentioned the possibility of retaliatory measures. A debate ensued over whether or not retaliation would take place, but starting on June 22, China imposed special import tariffs on three Japanese-made items: automobiles, cellular and car phones, and air conditioners. For the Japanese government, this was the first safeguard action taken by China. At the time, China was in the final stages of negotiations with the United States on joining the World Trade Organization (WTO), and there was vehement opposition from domestic agricultural interests within China. So, it is possible that to dodge such criticisms, China used the safeguards issue that had cropped up by chance in relations with Japan (Yu 2007). In the end, the two countries held a ministerial level meeting on December 21, 2001 and decided to withdraw their various measures, so it was all wrapped up quite cleanly despite all of the speculation.

Preceding this, China formally joined the WTO on November 10. The most important factor for China's membership was U.S.–China relations; agreement had been reached between Japan and China at an early stage. The Japanese position was that actively drawing China into international organizations like the WTO would compel it to act responsibly within the international rules. Since this was fundamentally the same idea as at the time of the Tiananmen Incident, one could say that it has been the consistent stance of Japan's China diplomacy.

One more point of dispute was brought up between Japan and China at the start of the twenty-first century—the issue of a visit to Japan by former ROC President Lee Teng-hui. Having retired from politics when he stepped down from the presidency in May 2000, Lee fervently desired to visit Japan, something he was unable to do while in office even though it was his deepest relationship personally.

However, having branded Lee a "closet supporter of independence," China remained very wary of his large, authoritative influence in Taiwanese politics notwithstanding his retirement, and it applied pressure on Japan at every opportunity to block his visit. Yet, Japanese domestic opinion was highly supportive of a visit by the retired president; every newspaper ran articles suggesting unanimous agreement on this point. The *Asahi Shimbun* clarified its position in favor of a visit in an April 12, 2001 editorial; in an editorial the following day it argued that

> fearing a Chinese backlash, the government has held Mr. Lee's visa request in limbo, trying to avoid making the decision to issue one or not, a bumbling response that can only result in giving the impression that Japanese diplomacy is rather shallow.

Strongly backed by Japanese popular opinion and having promised not to engage in political activities that would excite China, former President Lee Teng-hui travelled to Kurashiki City in Okayama Prefecture April 22–26 on the pretext of receiving medical treatment for a heart ailment. Reportedly, it was Chief Cabinet Secretary Fukuda Yasuo whose leadership steered such a delicate course on the Japanese side. By coincidence, on April 23 the Japanese government announced the safeguard actions mentioned above. Responding to Japan's apparently coordinated hardline stance against it, China notified Japan on April 25 that NPC Chairman Li Peng's visit to Japan was postponed (he would visit Japan one year later in April 2002). Yet, China's decision to postpone Chairman Li's visit was made at the time of Prime Minister Mori Yoshiro's resignation and Prime Minister Koizumi Junichiro's start, so one might say the decision took that complicated Japanese political situation into consideration. Incidentally, Lee Teng-hui subsequently visited Japan in 2004, 2007, 2008, 2009, 2014, and 2015.

Start of the Koizumi administration and Yasukuni Shrine visit

The Mori Yoshiro administration started in April 2000, after the sudden illness and death of Prime Minister Obuchi Keizo; its polling numbers started low and never improved, in part because of verbal gaffes, and it lasted a little over one year. Then, beating Hashimoto Ryutaro in the April 26, 2001 LDP presidential election,

Koizumi Junichiro started his tenure as prime minister. Koizumi was able to stay in power until September 2006, almost five and a half years.

When he had launched his candidacy for LDP president, Koizumi had successfully secured the vote of the Japan War-Bereaved Families Association, traditionally a voting bloc of the Keiseikai, a major LDP faction (Yomiuri Shimbun seiji-bu 2006). He promised to visit the Yasukuni Shrine on August 15 in the event that he became prime minister, actually touting it as a pledge in the presidential election. Naturally, China was wary of Koizumi's stance on the issue and criticized him repeatedly. Perhaps to avoid the confusion on the actual day, Koizumi's Yasukuni visit was moved forward two days and occurred on August 13. In a statement, Koizumi expressed "feelings of profound remorse and sincere mourning" for Japan having caused suffering by "following a mistaken national policy … through its colonial rule and aggression" and stressed that his visit was a "vow for peace" (Kazankai 2008, Document 213). This was the first official visit to Yasukuni Shrine by a prime minister in 16 years since Prime Minister Nakasone; it was five years since Prime Minister Hashimoto's private visit.

China strongly protested. Yet, bearing in mind the changed date of the visit, the Chinese side's objections were relatively restrained and did not turn into a full-blown campaign. It is thought that both countries' diplomatic officials, having already judged they could not stop the visit itself, held talks on how to reduce the damage after the visit.

Perhaps because of such bilateral preparations and readiness, Prime Minister Koizumi made a hurried trip to Beijing on October 8, not two months after his Yasukuni visit, though it was just a day trip. Paying a rushed visit to the Museum of the War of Chinese People's Resistance Against Japanese Aggression near the Marco Polo Bridge, Koizumi expressed a "feeling of heartfelt apology and condolences for those Chinese people who were victims of aggression" (Kazankai 2008, Document 217). He again visited China to attend the APEC Leaders' Meeting on October 19 in Shanghai. Koizumi met with President Jiang Zemin on October 21 and they agreed to strengthen the relationship ahead of 2002, the 30th anniversary of the normalization of diplomatic relations. Also, at the informal Japan–China–South Korea summit held in November in Brunei, Koizumi, Zhu Rongji, and Kim Dae-jung reaffirmed they would continue and enlarge ministerial-level talks. The Yasukuni issue that had caused such a stir in Japan–China relations since the summer had quieted down momentarily through such moves seeking to improve relations.

Meanwhile, Japan was caught up domestically in a big debate over the issue of the Yasukuni Shrine. In addition to fierce arguments for and against a prime minister's visit, a robust discussion also took place concerning separating the spirits of the Class A war criminals (who had received the death sentence in the Tokyo War Trials and had been enshrined in Yasukuni some time later) as well as establishing alternative facilities. Concerning the latter point, in December the Koizumi cabinet established "The Advisory Group to Consider a Memorial Facility for Remembering the Dead and Praying for Peace" under Chief Cabinet Secretary Fukuda, and entrusted experts to debate the feasibility of a national war memorial in lieu of the

Yasukuni Shrine with the enshrined Class A war criminals. The group delivered a report on the issue exactly one year later in December 2002 that indicated the necessity of a new memorial in the conclusion, though it said the government must make the final decision.

It seemed that China was increasingly favorable toward Koziumi following his forward-looking stance seen in his Marco Polo Bridge visit, his conduct at APEC in Shanghai, and also his groping about for alternative facilities for Yasukuni. Perhaps because of this, or perhaps to boost interest in the Boao Forum for Asia in Hainan Province, the Chinese version of the Davos meeting that had not garnered as much public interest as expected, China invited Koizumi to the first annual conference in April 2002. The Japanese side, including MOFA, was unenthusiastic about the prime minister's attendance at this forum, which almost no heads of government were attending. However, Koizumi's hurried participation came about by his own decision. He delivered the keynote speech on the opening day of the forum, April 12, entitled "Asia in a New Century—Challenge and Opportunity," and along with praising China's development, he spoke of the large expectations of its challenges. Undoubtedly Koizumi's presence was greatly welcomed at the time by the Chinese side—not only Premier Zhu Rongji, who attended, but also Jiang Zemin, whose family was related to the forum's leadership (Kamo 2012).

Chinese hopes were completely undermined nine days later on April 21. Prime Minister Koizumi made a sudden visit to Yasukuni, coinciding with the annual spring festival. Diplomatic officials of both countries completely failed to anticipate the visit, and needless to say, there was nothing they could do about it. From Koizumi's perspective, he likely thought that there would be no problem if he were to again fulfill his campaign pledge to visit the Yasukuni Shrine, particularly because he had considered alternative facilities and had also paid consideration to China by participating in the Boao Forum for Asia. For its part, China felt betrayed because it apparently had expected that a shrine visit would be a one-time event for Koizumi, who had seemed forward-leaning on the Yasukuni issue. In other words, the Yasukuni issue grew more serious because of the communication gap at the time of the second visit, not because of the first visit (Yomiuri Shimbun seiji-bu 2006).

9/11 and Shenyang consulate-general incident

In the United States, Republican George W. Bush was inaugurated in January 2001. The new president, criticizing the Clinton era policy of engagement with China, called for strengthening relations with allies starting with Japan, and changed the designation of China from strategic partner to strategic competitor. It was in this context that a U.S. military surveillance aircraft (EP-3E) and a Chinese military fighter jet collided in the skies over the South China Sea on April 1. The fighter jet crashed, killing the Chinese pilot, and the U.S. surveillance plane made an emergency landing on Hainan Island. The incident led to rising tensions in U.S.–China relations over responsibility for the collision, but it also became a lucky break by opening bilateral contacts, as China and the United States, which had not had much contact since the start of the Bush administration, sat down at the negotiating table to resolve the issue.

The coordinated series of terrorist attacks on September 11, 2001 (9/11) became the catalyst to completely remake the chilly atmosphere in U.S.–China relations. Afterwards the Bush administration focused on measures to counter terrorism, and it plunged from the Afghanistan conflict into the Iraq War in 2003. Amid this state of emergency, cooperation with China, a UNSC permanent member, became important for the Bush administration; in fact, China was no longer a strategic competitor. China, too, basically began to show consideration for the U.S. position following 9/11, and U.S.–China relations settled down. After 9/11 the United States' greatest hope was for Japan and China to cooperate, although it did not signify a big about-face on the U.S. posture of emphasizing its allies. Yet, contrary to expectations, Japan–China relations became prickly over the Yasukuni issue.

This was symbolized by the May 2002 incident with North Korean defectors at the Consulate-General of Japan in Shenyang. A family of five North Koreans seeking political asylum was running into the consulate general—two had actually made it into the compound—when armed Chinese police entered the premises and arrested them. The positions of both countries were at odds: Japan said the fact that Chinese police entered the consulate general compound was a violation of the Vienna Convention, whereas China insisted that its officers, concerned for the safety of the consulate general, had entered the compound only upon the Japanese vice consul's consent. This incident was extensively covered by the Japanese media; at the time, Japan was full of sympathy for North Korean defectors because of reports of the sharp increase in the number fleeing the deteriorating economic situation there. As a result, Japan and China saw the national image of the other worsen further. In the end, the asylum-seeking family that had been arrested by Chinese public security officers was sent to Manila on May 22 and, from there, sought refuge in South Korea aboard a Korean Airlines flight the following day.

Foreign Minister Kawaguchi Yoriko and Foreign Minister Tang Jiaxuan, meeting on the sidelines of the ARF in Brunei at the end of July, reached agreement to prevent a similar incident from reoccurring. On August 28, they held intergovernmental consultations on a bilateral framework for consular cooperation. Visiting China on September 8, Minister Kawaguchi met with Jiang Zemin, and using the opportunity of the 30th anniversary of normalization of relations, they agreed on long-term stability for bilateral relations. On September 22, Prime Minister Koizumi and Premier Zhu Rongji held talks on the sidelines of the Asia-Europe Meeting (ASEM) in Copenhagen, the first summit since Koizumi's second Yasukuni visit in April. On the same day, a friendship exchange ceremony marking the 30th anniversary of the normalization of Japan–China relations was held in Beijing; President Jiang Zemin made an appearance and former Prime Minister Hashimoto Ryutaro attended from Japan. Also, Vice President Hu Jintao attended the reception celebrating the 30th anniversary of diplomatic normalization that was held at the Great Hall of the People in Beijing on September 28. The first

Japan–China Economic Partnership Consultation, a dialogue at the deputy-minister level established as an outgrowth of the safeguards issue, was held in Beijing on October 15. Talks between Koizumi and Jiang were set up for October 27 on the sidelines of the APEC Leaders' Meeting in Mexico, where Jiang requested that the Yasukuni issue be appropriately handled as a history issue. This was Jiang's last summit meeting with Japan as China's highest leader.

2 Yasukuni visit problem and anti-Japanese protests

Coming of the Hu Jintao era and "new thinking on Japan"

The 16th CCP National Congress was held November 8–14, 2002, and the highest post of general secretary of the CCPCC transferred from Jiang Zemin to Hu Jintao. Hu was appointed president, the chief executive for diplomacy within the PRC political system, however, at the NPC the following March. That is to say, Hu Jintao's diplomacy began in 2003. Nevertheless, his predecessor Jiang Zemin kept his positions as Chairman of the CCP CMC until September 2004 and as Chairman of the State CMC until March 2005—in that sense, the Hu Jintao era started in the spring of 2005. Moreover, most of the nine-member Politburo Standing Committee, the CCPCC's highest leadership, were members of Jiang's faction.

Regardless, a part of Hu's diplomacy became visible after he assumed the presidency in 2003. Starting in August, China agreed to chair the Six-Party Talks, negotiating North Korea's abandoning its nuclear development. Until then, China under Jiang Zemin had eschewed a hardline policy that would corner North Korea, but Hu assumed the Six-Party Talks' chairmanship and pressured the North to give up its nukes, almost as if accepting the U.S. request. At the time, the United States was entirely wrapped up in the Iraq War and did not have any strength to spare for Asia. Under Chen Shui-bien, Taiwan was bolstering its tilt toward independence around this time, but the Bush administration warned against this, as if out of consideration for China's inclinations. The Taiwan issue had been a top task of the Jiang Zemin era, but in the Hu Jintao era, China began moving toward a policy of maintaining the status quo and peaceful dialogue. In other words, Hu Jintao diplomacy essentially sought to take a flexible policy toward the United States.

It was similar toward Japan. Around this very time, a debate began over the direction of a new Japan policy that would be called the "new thinking (*xinsikao*)" on Japan. *People's Daily* commentator Ma Licheng published an essay in the magazine *Strategy and Management* (*Zhanlue yu Guanli*) in December 2002 entitled "New Thinking on Relations with Japan," in which he argued that since Japan had apologized several times already, China should stop dwelling on the history issue beyond that and should advance more forward-looking relations (Ba 2004). As if acting in concert, Shi Yinhong, a professor at the Renmin University of China, also wrote in *Strategy and Management* that it is the United States that China must stand up to in the future, so thinking strategically, China must downplay the history issue and switch to forward-looking relations with Japan; he proposed a "diplomatic revolution" supportive of

Japan becoming a UNSC permanent member (Ji 2004). In response to these arguments, harsh criticisms calling the authors *hanjian* (traitors to their race) appeared on the Internet and elsewhere. But the arguments became the object of great attention in both countries as one new trend appearing around the same time as the formation of a new leadership group in China.

Meanwhile, Prime Minister Koizumi made his third Yasukuni Shrine visit on January 14, 2003, and yet, perhaps because of the new thinking on Japan, Koizumi and Hu Jintao held talks, the first since Hu assumed the presidency, when both attended events celebrating the 300th anniversary of St. Petersburg's construction at the end of May 2003. Hu spoke of consideration of the history issue, but he emphasized building relations that look toward the future, without mentioning the Yasukuni issue.

At these talks, they also agreed to establish a New Japan–China Friendship Committee for the 21st Century to succeed the committee that met from 1984 to 2001. This private advisory body was expected to be a venue for intellectuals from both countries to freely debate issues the governments found difficult to discuss. The Japanese chair was Kobayashi Yotaro, chairman and chief executive officer of Fuji-Xerox Corporation, and the Chinese chair was Zheng Bijian, chairman of the China Reform Forum (former executive vice-president of the CCPCC's Party School). The committee held its first session in December 2003 and met eight times in the five years through 2008; thereafter, the membership was replaced (Kokubun 2008b).

Incidentally, in spring 2003 China suffered from the spread of an unknown infectious disease, a new strain of pneumonia (SARS: severe acute respiratory syndrome). A fierce power struggle played out between the Hu Jintao and Jiang Zemin factions over the handling and responsibility for this incident—as seen in the dismissal of Minister of Public Health Zhang Wenkang of Jiang's faction. The World Health Organization declared at the end of June that SARS had been contained, but SARS was a heavy blow for the start of the Hu Jintao administration that was supposed to be making its world debut. During all this, economic relations, including with Japan, took a big hit.

Hot economics, cold politics

Former prime ministers Murayama and Hashimoto and Chief Cabinet Secretary Fukuda Yasuo visited China in August 2003 to participate in a ceremony celebrating the 25th anniversary of the Treaty of Peace and Friendship between Japan and the People's Republic of China. It is unusual for an incumbent chief cabinet secretary to travel abroad, but Fukuda likely went because the prime minister when the treaty was concluded was his father, Fukuda Takeo. The following day (August 12), Foreign Minister Li Zhaoxing went to Japan to lay the groundwork for the official visit to Japan by Wu Bangguo, chairman of the NPC Standing Committee, starting September 4. JDA Director-General Ishiba Shigeru visited China at the start of September, planning to expand the points of contact for a security dialogue.

Attending the ASEAN + 3 meeting in Bali, Indonesia on October 7, Prime Minister Koizumi held his first summit meeting with Premier Wen Jiabao; he also held a summit meeting with Hu Jintao on the sidelines of the APEC summit held in Bangkok on October 20.

So, although the number of reciprocal visits by leaders was inadequate for the 25th anniversary of the Treaty of Peace and Friendship, at least exchanges continued at various levels, and the leaders also groped about for the possibility to make contact, borrowing the venues of international meetings. Many of the world's corporations held a growing interest in the Chinese market that was becoming institutionally more integrated into the international economic framework after China's entry into the WTO. Japanese corporations, of course, were no exception. In July 2003, Nippon Steel and Shanghai Baoshan Iron and Steel agreed to establish a joint venture company to make steel sheet for automobiles.

During this time, however, the expansion of contacts did not improve bilateral relations; in fact, many frictions were arising in Japan–China relations that were then being reproduced via the Internet, rapidly developing as a tool for communications, a situation that contributed to making the national image each country had of the other worse. As the negative effects of SARS lingered on into the summer, the image of China's public safety situation grew considerably worse, including in Japan. In June 2003, the Japanese Coast Guard stopped activists from Hong Kong and the mainland who had approached the Senkaku Islands. As if to protest this incident, nine members from Japan Youth League, a right-wing group, landed on the Senkaku Islands in August. The same month, gas shells from chemical weapons abandoned by the Imperial Japanese Army leaked at a construction site in Qiqihar, Heilongjiang Province, poisoning 29 residents. Formally acknowledging the cause, the Japanese government in October paid China 300 million yen, based on the Japan–China memorandum concerning the disposal of abandoned chemical weapons signed in July 1999.

Furthermore, an incident occurred at the end of October—Japanese exchange students performed a skit at a cultural festival at Xibei (Northwest) University in China that was deemed "lewd," a student protest broke out on campus on October 30, and the Japanese students involved were all punished. Mutual relations continued to deteriorate right from the start of 2004. In January, Chinese activists trespassed into the waters around the Senkaku Islands and managed to land in March. Furthermore, provocative actions were repeatedly directed against Japanese spectators at Japan's soccer matches at the Asian Cup held in July in Chongqing and elsewhere. At the Asian Cup finals in Beijing on August 7, too, some Chinese fans got out of control, attacking the Japanese Embassy's official vehicle; in reaction, Foreign Minister Kawaguchi lodged a protest with Chinese Ambassador to Japan Wu Dawei.

State Councillor Tang Jiaxuan, meeting with members from both countries at the first session of the New Japan–China Friendship Committee for the 21st Century in December 2003, described the phenomenon of bilateral political relations that cause cooling in contrast to their economic relations that appear active as "hot economics, cold politics" (Yomiuri Shimbun Seiji-bu 2006). This expression came to be used generally by both countries as a neologism symbolizing Japan–China relations at that time.

East China Sea resource development issue

UN ECAFE had announced that oceanographic surveys suggested the possibility of large-scale oil and natural gas undersea reserves in the East China Sea in 1968. After that, China began claiming territorial sovereignty over the Senkaku Islands (then under U.S. military administration and reverting to Japan together with Okinawa in 1972), as is commonly known. As stated earlier, China formally designated the Senkaku Islands as its own territory later, in its Law of the Territorial Sea in 1992. It was from this time that China came to attach importance to its maritime interests and expand its activities. As well as anticipating the future growth of energy demand, China naturally intended to improve its naval power as the basis of enhancing its national power. Concerning EEZs, Japan has insisted that the border should be the standard median line under international law, whereas China has insisted on its right of the natural prolongation of its continental shelf up to the Okinawa Trough.

China's marine research activities gradually grew more active after that, Japan's opposition hardened, and so in February 2001, they established a framework for mutual prior notification on such activities and agreed upon a two-month pre-notification for every survey. However, the agreement became a dead letter little by little as Chinese ocean survey vessels undertook activities violating the agreement starting several months after this. China began development of the Shirakaba natural gas field (Chinese name: Chunxiao) near the Japan–China median line in 2003, which became big news in Japan in 2004. Development construction also began near the median line at Kusunoki (Duanqiao), Kashi (Tianwaitian), and other sites apart from Shirakaba.

Minister of Economy, Trade, and Industry Nakagawa Shoichi openly requested China to provide documents on its gas fields development at a press conference in June. At the ASEAN + 3 Ministers on Energy Meeting in Manila later that month, he requested Zhang Guobao, vice chairman of the National Development and Reform Commission, to provide relevant documents, while criticizing the possibility for drilling near the median line to suck up natural gas from reserves on Japan's side. Minister Nakagawa inspected the area at the end of June, the Japanese government chartered an ocean survey vessel from Norway and conducted a survey of the same ocean area in July, and China dispatched a warship, trying to interfere with the survey. After that, construction began on a pipeline connecting Shirakaba to the mainland, and China's foreign ministry made an announcement, essentially refusing to provide Japan with documents related to the gas fields near the median line. Japan protested, needless to say. Then, a Chinese navy nuclear-powered submarine trespassed in Japanese territorial waters off the Miyako island chain in November; ordered to conduct maritime security operations, the Maritime SDF pursued the submarine. Considering that this coincided exactly with growing social issues such as the Japanese exchange students' skit and the Asian Cup soccer, Japan–China relations could be said to be at loggerheads over the Yasukuni issue during this period. The networks and relationships of trust between the leaders that could have prevented this were atrophying.

It was only natural that doubts about ODA to China were growing in Japan amid such conditions. China's rapid economic growth, the rising trend of its military expenditures, and the fact that China, itself, was providing economic assistance to other countries were at the heart of these criticisms. Prime Minister Koizumi, visiting Laos to attend the ASEAN+3 Summit in November 2004, remarked that it would be desirable for China, which had achieved such considerable economic development, to "graduate" from ODA, reportedly conveying this to Chinese Premier Wen Jiabao there. Following up on this, Foreign Minister Machimura Nobutaka also started talks with China on finishing up, later reaching agreement to end ODA to China by the 2008 Beijing Olympics.

Meanwhile, Japan issued new National Defense Program Guidelines and the next Mid-Term Defense Program in December, which both mentioned China's military modernization and the expanding scope of its maritime activities; China reacted strongly against this.

Anti-Japanese protests

The year 2005 was the 60th anniversary of the end of the Second World War. For some time, UN Secretary General Kofi Annan had been advocating reform of the UN, which had played a definite role in the formation of the postwar world order, and also raising the issue of UNSC reform. Japan was shouldering about 20 percent of the UN's finances at the time, the second largest share after the United States, so it was calling for UNSC expansion and permanent membership for Japan. When Secretary General Annan made remarks supporting a UNSC permanent seat for Japan in this context, California-based ethnic Chinese groups started a petition drive on the Internet to oppose it. This petition drive then spread on major media sites in China, such as Sina, Sohu, and NetEase without any sort of restriction, and the number of signatures suddenly jumped to the ten million range. Some believe this movement arose naturally (Mori 2006), but it clearly would not have happened without the CCPCC Propaganda Department's permission. This can also be interpreted as an effort by the Jiang Zemin faction to shake up the Hu Jintao/Wen Jiabao mainstream faction that was inclined toward a flexible Japan policy. Politburo Standing Committee member Li Changchun, who was close to Jiang, was reportedly connected to the management of this effort (Shimizu 2008). Regardless of the tensions in Japan–China relations, Premier Wen presented three principles to improve relations at a March 14, 2005 press conference following the close of the NPC: reciprocal visits by leaders, strategic study on friendly relations, and the appropriate handling of history issues (Kazankai 2008, Document 232).

Anti-Japanese protests occurred as if by design in cities nationwide every Saturday beginning in April. First, a demonstration opposing Japan's UNSC permanent membership and a movement boycotting Japanese-made goods arose all of a sudden in places like Chengdu in Sichuan Province and Shenzhen in Guangdong Province on Saturday April 2. There was violence, and broken windows at a Japanese supermarket in Chengdu. Calm returned the following day, but an anti-Japanese protest on the order of 10,000 people happened once again in the capital, Beijing, one week later on Saturday April 9; stones were thrown at the Japanese embassy, and the police did nothing to stop it. Organizing and participating in unauthorized movements, however, was suppressed, perhaps to avoid having these protests against Japan spread to mounting domestic issues. Another protest was announced one week later, this time in Shanghai. Information circulated that this had been suppressed temporarily, but a protest of tens of thousands did occur on April 16; some of the crowd got out of control, throwing stones at the Japanese Consulate General in Shanghai and committing acts of violence at Japanese restaurants. That the Minister of Public Security, responsible for keeping the peace, was Zhou Yongkang, close to the Jiang Zemin faction, was probably not unrelated to these kinds of movements.

BOX 6.1 CHINA'S TOP LEADERS' VIEW OF JAPAN

Since China is a regime of single-party rule by the CCP, there is a large role for individual top leaders in each and every policy decision.

Mao Zedong had said that the CCP was able to come to power because of Japanese aggression against China. Perhaps because it helped the CCP to side-step the KMT's severe attacks against it. Thus, Mao had a strong realist aspect regarding Japan. This was also apparent at the time of normalization of diplomatic relations, when Mao's primary intention was to threaten the Soviets. Zhou Enlai had studied in Japan, and as could be understood from the enthusiasm he showed for normalizing relations, it is conjectured that he had special thoughts on improving relations with Japan.

Deng Xiaoping, too, had an advanced international sensibility from his experience living in France, and his pragmatism was frequently evident. He made Japan the model for China's development after seeing evidence of Japan's modernity all around him on his 1978 visit there. He was quick to decide to introduce loans from Japan at the time of later economic difficulties; no vestiges of the memories of history could be seen then.

Hu Yaobang fell from power in early 1987 after taking a magnanimous attitude toward university student demands for democracy; allegedly one factor for his fall was that he had too much backing from relations with Japan. He had enjoyed a strong relationship of trust with Prime Minister Nakasone Yasuhiro, had emphasized youth exchanges, and had tried to build Japan–China relations oriented to the future. For that reason alone, Hu's downfall came as a giant blow to Japan–China relations.

In contrast, Jiang Zemin was a leader who did not hide his animosity toward Japan. He was considerably friendlier to the United States, judging from his words and actions. When he went to Japan in 1998, he tenaciously stuck to speaking about prewar history issues, even at the imperial banquet. There are various rumors about Jiang's relationship with Japan: he was bitten by a Japanese military dog when he was a child, or his real father was a *hanjian* (traitor to his race) who was a cadre of the Nanking government of Wang Jingwei that collaborated with Japan, as was discussed in the Prologue.

Hu Jintao actively sought a breakthrough in relations with Japan, aiming for a future-oriented relationship, repressing the inclination toward the history issue, and advancing a strategic mutually beneficial relationship. Though it is conjecture, there is one point of historical background. Under Hu Yaobang, his boss, he worked hard as the one responsible on the Chinese side for Japan–China youth exchanges in the mid-1980s. At that time, future Premier Li Keqiang and Politburo member Li Yuanchao, among others, were Communist Youth League connections who worked under Hu Jintao. Even Premier Wen Jiabao tried to advance future-oriented relations with Japan, as can be seen in his 2007 speech to the Diet.

Regarding Xi Jinping, almost no connections to Japan have been identified, at least according to what has been made public. The fact is, his father, Xi Zhongxun, was Hu Yaobang's biggest backer, but the situation changes greatly with the era, and one cannot simply draw those connections. Xi's policy style emphasizes balance, and it does not appear that his views on Japan have firmed up yet.

After that, the central government's approach was to completely suppress anti-Japanese demonstrations, a move spearheaded by the Hu/Wen mainstream faction. A meeting to report on the emergency situation, convening 3,500 central executives, was held in Beijing on April 19, and Foreign Minister Li Zhaoxing strongly called for plans to calm the situation. Why Li was made to play this role is unclear, but his presence as foreign minister subsequently grew weaker. It should be noted that he was an important executive in the Jiang Zemin era. Prime Minister Koizumi was strongly critical of the situation in China, but he arranged a place for a summit meeting with President Hu Jintao on the sidelines of the Asian-African Summit held in Jakarta on April 23. The two leaders agreed that building stable Japan–China relations was vital, and Hu Jintao expressed "five insists" related to this point: reaffirming the three political documents, adhering to the perception of history and future-orientation, properly handling the Taiwan issue, maintaining the political situation for Japan–China friendship, and enhancing exchanges and cooperation (Kazankai 2008, Document 234).

Vice Premier Wu Yi visited Japan on May 17 to restore relations, but she canceled her meeting with Prime Minister Koizumi, perhaps because of remarks he made immediately beforehand about Yasukuni visits. Meanwhile, Jiang Zemin reportedly visited the Nanjing Massacre Memorial Hall to criticize Japan's former militarism on May 4, the day that memorializes the May Fourth Movement, the origin of nationalism movements in China's modern history (Shimizu 2008). Just by looking at this chain of events, one can understand that there was a large divide on Japan policy even in the inner circle of China's leadership. There was no way to achieve an improvement in Japan–China relations except to wait for Prime Minister Koizumi's tenure to end. China appeared to give up trying to improve ties during the Koizumi era. Then, as if fixated on the post-Koizumi period, Hu Jintao met with representatives of seven Japan–China friendship groups led by former Prime Minister Hashimoto on March 31, 2006, and he clearly indicated that stopping Yasukuni visits was a precondition to improving relations. The Bush administration was also concerned about the discord between Japan and China over the Yasukuni visits during this period. Then Deputy Secretary of State Robert Zoellick mentioned the possibility of joint historical research by experts from Japan, China, and the United States several times, but there was no concrete progress.

3 Formation, development, and limits of strategic mutually beneficial relations

Abe's visit to China and strategic mutually beneficial relations

Hu Jintao's diplomacy, excluding diplomacy toward Japan, got fully started in 2005. He was appointed president and began supervising diplomatic policy in 2003, but he was completely surrounded by Jiang Zemin's forces at that stage, so aside from the Six-Party Talks, Hu's diplomacy was unable to develop on all fronts. However, Hu began to make his mark on domestic and foreign policy once Jiang yielded his post as CCP CMC Chairman at the fourth plenary session of the 16th CCP Central Committee in September 2004, and following that, Hu automatically succeeded to the post of Chairman of the State CMC at the NPC in March 2005. In other words, one could say that, under these conditions, the Hu/Wen mainstream faction and its Japan policy in particular suffered a severe counterattack from Jiang Zemin and the old guard faction. In the same period, Hu Jintao dismissed Hong Kong Chief Executive Tung Chee-hwa, who had extremely strong ties to Jiang, two years before the end of his full term. Also, with respect to relations with Taiwan, Hu enacted the Anti-Secession Law, which substance-wise called for maintaining the status quo and improving relations, and so he switched to a policy that differed from that of the Jiang Zemin era, which had sought to hurry unification with Taiwan as the highest priority. "Building a harmonious (*hexie*) society" is the phrase symbolizing the basis of Hu Jintao era policy; even regarding diplomacy, "harmonious" diplomacy that pushes for international cooperation on all fronts was presented in the latter half of 2005.

Japan–China relations began moving in secret, aiming at a post-Koizumi period. At the center of these efforts was the Comprehensive Policy Dialogue (Strategic

Dialogue) held intermittently beginning in May 2005 between Administrative Vice Foreign Minister Yachi Shotaro, close to Chief Cabinet Secretary Abe Shinzo, the leading candidate to become the next prime minister, and Vice Foreign Minister Dai Bingguo, an associate of Hu Jintao and responsible for diplomacy issues. (The second round was held in June 2005, the third in October 2005, the fourth in February 2006, the fifth in May 2006, and the sixth in September 2006.) These strategic talks were sometimes held in the hometown of the chairmen in order to bolster mutual relations of trust (Shimizu 2008). China's Foreign Minister was Li Zhaoxing and the MFA Party Secretary was Dai Bingguo, so it meant that there were essentially two foreign ministers because of factional disputes. But, on April 21, 2005, right after the meeting to report on the situation held after the anti-Japanese protests, Dai was installed as director of the CCPCC's office of the foreign affairs leading group, essentially becoming the top foreign minister.

BOX 6.2 "1972 SYSTEM" AND "STRATEGIC MUTUALLY BENEFICIAL RELATIONS"

Japan–China relations after diplomatic normalization is called the "1972 System" (or "'72 System" for short). The origin of the term "'72 System" is unclear, but its first use may have been at the Japan–China Youth Forum sponsored by the Institute of Japan Studies (IJS) of the Chinese Academy of Social Sciences (CASS) that was held April 30–May 1, 1997 in an author's report titled, "Changes in the '1972 System' and the Road to Developing Harmonious Relations" (CASS IJS "*Riben Xuekan* [Japanese Studies]" 1997 No. 5 [September]). Discussions about the "1972 System" later arose between Japan, China, and Taiwan—it came to be debated as a concept that should be protected in China, broken in Taiwan, and rebuilt as situations changed in Japan.

The basis of the "'72 System" is found in the shared perception regarding the history and Taiwan issues. For the history issue, this means the correct understanding and stance on prewar Japan's China policy; for the Taiwan issue, this means the position of firmly respecting the "one China" principle and not supporting "two Chinas" or "Taiwanese independence." These two principles for history and Taiwan basically remain unchanged even today.

However, an excessive focus on history weakens the perspective on the present and the future, likely resulting in attention being paid only to whether reflections regarding history are done properly or not and perceptions regarding history are changing or not. If that is all that is done, then the meaning of Japan–China relations does not go beyond the bilateral relationship. Also, the baseline for the Taiwan issue has not changed, but large changes can be seen in Taiwan itself compared to 1972. Since 1986, Taiwan began democratizing and the KMT's authoritarian rule came to an end. As a result, one can no longer ignore the will of the people concerning the future of Taiwan. Of course, one must not interfere in domestic politics, but from the perspective of regional stability, the peace and stability of the Taiwan Strait is also important to Japan.

In addition to these two major principles of history and Taiwan, the "1972 System" is supported by the domestic and international conditions of the time. In Japan, this was the existence of a war generation that upheld the perception of history and their strong hopes for "friendship," a strong political constituency leading from the Tanaka Kakuei faction to the Keiseikai. Internationally, there was the union of Japan, China, and the United States against the erstwhile Soviet enemy during the Cold War system, and in that context, the existence of a kind of tacit political agreement that Japan and the United States together supported the modernization of China, which was a developing country. With generational change and the end of the Cold War, however, a new framework for the "1972 System" became necessary in the 1990s.

That is the broad background that gave rise in 2006 to the mutually beneficial relationship based on common strategic interests between Japan and China. As recorded in the main text, reciprocal visits by the leaders expanded from 2006 to 2008, through which they aimed to make relations big-picture and future-oriented (strategic), win–win (mutually beneficial), and moreover more multilateral in intent by thinking of the bilateral relationship in the regional and global contexts.

Prime Minister Koizumi made his sixth—and what would become his last in office—visit to Yasukuni on August 15, 2006, and later, he stepped down on September 26. It was the end of the long Koizumi era that stretched five years and five months. In his place, Abe Shinzo took office as the new prime minister. The only other candidate, former Chief Cabinet Secretary Fukuda Yasuo, stated in July that he would not run, and so that is how it was anticipated at that stage that Abe would be prime minister.

Abe's first trip overseas as prime minister was an "ice-breaking" visit to China October 8–9, 2006, soon after he assumed office. Seizing the opportunity, Abe visited South Korea on October 9–10, too. That this was conceived in the Yachi-Dai Strategic Dialogue goes without saying. Arriving in Beijing on October 8, Abe first met with Hu Jintao. Hu said that the Yasukuni issue had hurt Japan–China relations, to which Abe responded rather vaguely, "I have decided not to mention whether I have gone or not, or whether I will go or not." China did not pursue the matter further. Abe's visit to China was a risky bet politically at home, but China also took a big risk accepting his visit with such a vague stance on the Yasukuni issue (Kokubun 2008a).

The content of the meeting was made public in a joint press statement and it included some extremely new substance for Japan–China relations historically. It was a new concept for Japan–China relations, expressed as "a mutually beneficial relationship based on common strategic interests." The statement gave minimal treatment to the two major issues that had been the staple of bilateral relations—the perception of history and Taiwan—and, with the expression "strategic," brought prominence to the ideas of future- and big picture-oriented. Addressing the history issue, it stated that Japan had been walking the path of a peaceful country in the 60 years after the war and it would continue to do so in the future, a determination that China appreciated positively. It broadened Japan–China relations from a bilateral-oriented relationship premised on the existing "neighborly friendship" to a concept more multilateral in orientation that would deal with common regional tasks through cooperation. On the Taiwan issue, China essentially came to acquiesce to the status quo after the Anti-Secession Law, and so the statement was in step with this.

Why had Abe's visit to China that aimed at such a bold policy switch become possible? Of course, the results of the vice foreign ministerial Strategic Dialogue were predicate on the approval of both leaders, and there was also the existence of both countries' domestic situations. Speaking about the Japanese side, Prime Minister Abe was viewed as a hardliner on China, and that one aspect alone made it easier to emphasize a policy change. On October 5, 2006, soon after assuming office, Abe as prime minister acknowledged the 1995 Murayama Statement and even touched on the responsibility that his grandfather, former Prime Minister Kishi Nobusuke, had in starting the war. He also pursued partnership with the United States, conveying his intention to visit China in advance, a gesture that the Bush administration, its hands full with Iraq and the Middle East, is said to have welcomed. However, in light of the domestic political balance, Abe reportedly visited Yasukuni in secret in April 2006 when he was then chief cabinet secretary.

The larger shift came on the Chinese side. The Hu Jintao leadership, which had been unable to adequately demonstrate its leadership ability because of the weakness of its power base at the first session of the NPC in 2003, rallied ahead of the 17th CCP National Congress of 2007. Shanghai Party Secretary Chen Liangyu, the most powerful man in Shanghai and someone widely discussed as a future leader with close ties to Jiang Zemin, was suddenly dismissed on corruption charges in September 2006. Then Vice President Zeng Qinghong, a long-time associate of Jiang's, played a large role in persuading Jiang to let this happen. In exchange, the man installed as the new Shanghai party secretary was Xi Jinping, whom Zeng recommended. It is said that this was a balanced personnel move for Jiang and Hu. However, the incident resulted in weakening the authority of the Jiang Zemin faction. By so doing, the Hu/Wen mainstream faction gained strength, the impediments on its Japan policy diminished, and it set out at once on a reconciliation policy toward Japan using the opportunity of Koizumi's resignation and Abe's start as prime minister (Kokubun 2008a; Shimizu 2008). China sounded out Japan on an Abe visit a few days after the Chen Liangyu incident became public. Abe actually visited in the afternoon on October 8, the first day of the sixth plenary session of the 16th CCP Central Committee, and so by handling relations with Japan, the biggest pending issue, Hu Jintao showed off his grasp on diplomatic authority at home and abroad.

From Wen Jiabao's visit to Japan to Fukuda's visit to China

Premier Wen Jiabao made an official visit to Japan April 11–13, 2007, returning the favor for Abe's visit to China. Dubbed the "ice-thawing" trip, this visit to Japan would clarify the specific content of the strategic mutually beneficial relationship. According to the joint press statement this time, a mutually beneficial relationship based on common strategic interests was described as:

> both countries will fully develop mutually beneficial cooperation for the future at various levels, such as the bilateral, regional and international levels, that will contribute to the benefit of both countries, Asia and the world. In this context, both countries will benefit mutually and expand their common interests. In so doing, Japan–China relations will be elevated to new heights.
>
> *(Kazankai 2008, Document 243)*

Clearly, this was a transformation from the bilateralism premised on "neighborly friendship" since 1972 to a concept incorporating future-orientation, multilateralism, as well as a strategic sense.

In the spirit of the new relationship, the two sides incorporated specific proposals rooted in the main theme of expanding exchange and dialogue into programs on everything from exchanges and dialogue of the leaders, cabinet ministers, and high-level officials to mutual exchanges and visits of youths. Touting the importance of security exchanges and dialogue, the joint statement included reciprocal visits by the Chinese navy and Maritime Self-Defense Forces (MSDF) and the promotion of cooperation on North Korean issues. In the area of mutual cooperation, they would move ahead focusing on environmental protection cooperation (such as the prevention of water and air pollution, the building of recycling societies, the prevention of drifting marine litter, and measures for tackling acid rain and yellow sand) and energy cooperation (such as model projects for the promotion of energy conservation and environmental businesses). They agreed to set up an Energy Ministerial Policy Dialogue. Furthermore they promised to cooperate in such fields as agriculture, intellectual property rights, Ibis protection, pharmaceutical products, small- and medium-size enterprises, information and communications technology, finance, and criminal justice.

The highlight of Premier Wen's visit to Japan was his April 12 speech to the Diet. Since it was broadcast live in China via the Internet, in a sense, it also targeted the Chinese domestic audience. The content was groundbreaking. Wen minimized mention of the Taiwan and history issues in his speech, saying that Japan's government and leaders have on many occasions since the normalization of Japan–China diplomatic relations expressed deep remorse and apology, which the Chinese government and people appreciate, and they also appreciate Japan's peaceful development after the war. He then proposed four principles for raising Japan–China relations to a new stage: mutual trust, a big picture perspective, common development based on equality and mutual benefit, and strengthening exchanges with an eye on the future (Kazankai 2008, Document 245).

This was the most tranquil period for Japan–China relations in recent times. The start of joint research on Japan–China history (chaired by University of Tokyo Professor Kitaoka Shinichi and Director of the Institute of Modern History, CASS Bu Ping) and Defense Minister Cao Gangchuan's visit to Japan (during which there was agreement to hold regular defense exchanges) were important. Even on the economic front, China replaced the United States as Japan's largest trading partner in Japan's trade figures for fiscal year 2006. Meanwhile, Japan's political situation became fluid; the Abe cabinet stepped down after a year and the Fukuda Yasuo cabinet started on September 26. Fukuda had long emphasized relations with China, so he basically followed the strategic mutually beneficial relations that was the Abe administration's line toward China. On September 29, soon after Fukuda took office, Japan and China both welcomed the 35th anniversary of the normalization of diplomatic relations. In celebration, direct flights from Tokyo's Haneda Airport to Shanghai's Hongqiao Airport were inaugurated.

Prime Minister Fukuda went to China December 27–30, 2007. During his state visit, christened the "spring herald" trip, the two countries exchanged the following as concrete policies for strategic mutually beneficial relations: a joint communiqué on cooperation in the fields of energy and the environment; a memorandum relating to Japan–China youth exchange and friendship activities; a joint statement on scientific and technical cooperation on the problem of climate change; and an implementing arrangement for cooperation in the area of magnetic fusion energy research and development and related fields. Concerning the East China Sea, which was giving rise to increasing frictions, both leaders agreed on the common recognition of "a sea of peace, cooperation, and friendship." Prime Minister Fukuda gave a speech at Beijing University on December 28 titled, "Forging the Future Together" (Kazankai 2008, Document 251).

Poisoned frozen dumplings incident

It appeared that Japan–China relations were on track: reciprocal visits by leaders were becoming routine and the substance of strategic mutually beneficial relations was growing more specific. However, an unforeseen incident was lying in wait— what is called the poisoned frozen dumplings incident. In January 2008, ten people in three families from Chiba and Hyogo prefectures fell ill, the children even losing consciousness, from food poisoning caused by the same brand of Chinese-made frozen dumplings. The cause was not residual agricultural chemicals; rather an organic phosphorus pesticide, methamidophos, had been mixed into the dumplings. China banned the use of methamidophos in 2007 because of its high toxicity.

The issue was at what stage the dumplings were adulterated. The Chinese side, including the factory, maintained from the start that the probability the adulteration happened in China was low. Even when a team of Japanese government investigators went to the processing facilities February 5–6, the Chinese side remarked that the possibility of contamination in China was low. Yu Xinmin, the deputy director of the criminal investigation bureau of China's Ministry of Public Security, went to Japan on February 20 to cooperate with Japan's National Policy Agency (NPA) on the future course of the investigation. The following day, NPA Commissioner General Yoshimura Hiroto revealed at a press conference that methamidophos was detected from the inside of a sealed package of dumplings, and that moreover, the purity was substandard when compared to Japanese quality. NPA Deputy Commissioner General Ando Takaharu visited China February 25–27, and Deputy Director Yu once again said at a press conference on February 28 that there was little chance that the adulteration happened in China, openly showing his distrust of the Japanese police and press. Commissioner General Yoshimura soon held a press briefing to present a rebuttal. Failing to reach a conclusion and with President Hu Jintao's visit to Japan approaching, the issue was gradually quieted down. But the incident gave a tremendous shock to Japanese housewives, and Chinese-made frozen dumplings completely disappeared from supermarkets for a time afterwards.

After summer, things began to move. After the incident happened in Japan, cases of food poisoning emerged among Chinese who ate the dumplings of Tianyang Foods, the recalled brand; this information was reportedly conveyed to Japan via diplomatic channels. Because of this, it is said that Deputy Director Yu Xinmin and other executives involved on the Chinese side were dismissed. Then, when the incident was all but forgotten, a former Tianyang Foods employee was arrested in March 2010 on suspicion of contaminating products with methamidophos. It was reported that personal dissatisfaction with his pay was his excuse.

There were continuous troubles with food products in China around the time of the incident. A large number of dogs and cats died in the United States in 2007 after eating pet food using Chinese-made ingredients. In 2008, the same year as the frozen dumplings incident, there were multiple incidents involving infants who got kidney stones after drinking Chinese-made powdered milk that had the chemical substance melamine. The sanitary control of food products was later added as an important item in strategic mutually beneficial relations. The frozen dumplings incident could also be said to symbolize the challenges of strategic mutually beneficial relations.

Hu Jintao's visit to Japan

2008 was the year of the Beijing Olympics. Olympic torch relay events happened all over the world; a group of overseas refugees supporting Tibetan independence took this opportunity to expand their protest activities. The torch relay that took place in Nagano, Japan was placed on high alert. At the same time, large-scale rioting was happening in Tibet, too. These were a series of movements that tried to capture the world's interest on the Tibet issue at the time of the opening of the Olympics. The U.S. government called on the Chinese government and the 14th

Dalai Lama to pursue dialogue. In part because of this, an informal dialogue was held in May but produced no concrete results.

President Hu Jintao's visit to Japan took place in the tense atmosphere following wide coverage of the poisoned frozen dumplings incident and the Tibet issue. Hu was welcomed as a state guest during his May 5–10 visit, dubbed the "warm spring" trip. As a state guest, he had three meetings with the Emperor: a welcoming ceremony, an imperial banquet, and a farewell meeting. At the imperial banquet, Hu remarked that the Emperor's 1992 visit to China was a "beautiful memory" and "a beautiful episode in the history of Japan–China relations"; he hardly touched on history, perhaps reflecting on Jiang Zemin's excessive references to the history issue ten years before (Kazankai 2008, Document 261). There was significance couched in Hu's remarks. As stated in the previous chapter, former Foreign Minister Qian Qichen published his own memoirs in which he noted that China, isolated by the Tiananmen Incident, used the Emperor's 1992 visit to China for a diplomatic breakthrough (Sen 2006). Based on that, there were some critics in Japan who feared Hu's state visit to Japan would also be used politically. In other words, it is thought that Hu made his remarks in light of these circumstances.

During that visit, a "Joint Statement between the Government of Japan and the Government of the People's Republic of China on Comprehensive Promotion of a 'Mutually Beneficial Relationship Based on Common Strategic Interests'" was issued, joining the 1972 Joint Communiqué of the Government of Japan and the Government of the People's Republic of China, the 1978 Treaty of Peace and Friendship between Japan and the People's Republic of China, and the 1998 Japan–China Joint Declaration as one of the "four basic documents." In this statement, too, references to history and Taiwan were minimized, China positively evaluated Japan's postwar line of peaceful development, and agreed on Japan gaining a more suitable status in the international community, including the United Nations. Regarding strategic mutually beneficial relations, the two sides decided to build frameworks for cooperation and dialogue in line with the following five pillars: (1) enhancement of mutual trust in the political area through reciprocal high-level visits and security dialogues; (2) promotion of media, sports, and youth people-to-people and cultural exchanges as well as sentiments of friendship between the peoples; (3) enhancement of mutually beneficial cooperation on energy, the environment, food and product safety, trade and investment, intellectual property rights, and resource development in the East China Sea; (4) contribution to the Asia–Pacific region through such aspects as the Six-Party Talks and East Asian regional cooperation; and (5) contribution to the resolution of global issues, such as climate change, energy security, poverty, and contagious diseases (Kazankai 2008, Document 257).

In this way, Hu Jintao's visit to Japan took place in extremely harsh conditions but basically was completed successfully. It meant that, in a manner of speaking, the "test drive" period for strategic mutually beneficial relations that had gotten its start in 2006 was complete. In a sense, if Japan–China relations post-diplomatic normalization is said to be the "1972 System" of bilateralism, it suggested that the new relationship stood at the starting point of the "2006 System" based on multilateralism. The reality of Japan–China relations, however, did not advance smoothly in the expected direction. Strategic mutually beneficial relations have faced large difficulties since its inception.

In fact, during this visit to Japan, both countries reached an important agreement concerning the joint development of the East China Sea gas fields (Kazankai 2008, Document 263, 264). And yet, it was not made public at that time because, it is said, there was a strong backlash on this issue from hardliners in China, so Hu did not want to be seen as having made broad compromises on this trip. It was June 18 that the agreement was made public. The contents of the agreement were that Japan and China would jointly develop the northern part of Asunaro (Chinese name: Longjing) straddling the median line, permit Japanese corporations to invest in Shirakaba, which China already had been developing, and continue cooperating elsewhere. It was a groundbreaking agreement, but later it was vehemently criticized in China for having conceded too much to Japan. After various serious problems arose in Japan–China relations, progress on concrete discussions slowed to a crawl (Shimizu 2009).

4 Japan–China GDP trading places and Senkaku Islands

Great Sichuan Earthquake and Beijing Olympics

Hu Jintao returned to Beijing from Osaka on May 10, 2008. Two days later, a massive earthquake of magnitude 8.0 struck Wenchuan County, Sichuan Province. Nearly 90,000 people, more than a fifth of them school children, were reportedly killed or missing. Immediately, Premier Wen Jiabao flew to the disaster area that day; President Hu went five days later. The Chinese government requested Japan first of all to send an international rescue team; the first squad landed in Beijing on May 15 and arrived on site the following day. Requesting a rescue team from Japan first was a direct instruction from Hu, but it was a Japanese suggestion (Shimizu 2009). The search and rescue team was unable to locate any survivors, since 72 hours had passed by the time it arrived on site. However, the photograph of the Japanese rescue team, lined up facing the deceased bodies of a mother and her baby they had found, silently paying their respects, was disseminated by the Chinese national media (see photo at front of this chapter), and there was a moment when the media and Internet were deluged with articles and opinions greatly admiring the Japanese squad's polite courtesy. The very fact that such a photograph was widely disseminated would not be possible unless the definite will of the leader was at work. Hu Jintao, who went to Japan to attend the G-8 Hokkaido Toyako Summit, met with representatives of the international rescue team in Sapporo on July 8.

Needless to say, the Great Sichuan Earthquake shook China's domestic and foreign policies. The cold eye the international community had cast on China because of the Tibet issue changed to looks of sympathy after the earthquake. So then, about three months later, the Beijing Olympics—the long awaited dream of the Chinese people—was held August 8–24. Japanese Prime Minister Fukuda, U.S. President Bush, French President Nicolas Sarkozy, ROK President Lee Myung-bak, and a suitable number of other current and former leaders attended the opening ceremony. The Beijing Olympics was the perfect opportunity to enhance national prestige, and the opening ceremony staged by Zhang Yimou, the world famous movie director, was lauded for portraying Chinese history as if through a large-scale scroll painting. In the end, China took 51 gold medals, beating the United States for the first time, and from this point, too, it was also an ideal chance to bolster national prestige. Furthermore, Vice President Xi Jinping, who was eyed as the next highest leader, was in charge of overall Olympics preparations.

On September 1 Prime Minister Fukuda, who had been the biggest promoter of strategic mutually beneficial relations with China, expressed his intention to resign immediately amid a low support rate, as if out of consideration for the general election that would follow. The LDP put forward Aso Taro for party president as the face of its election campaign, and the Aso cabinet started on September 24. Whereas China had increased its global presence with the Beijing Olympics, Japan had entered a vortex, a period of political transition in which administrations seemed to change every year. Seeking to further enhance its national prestige, China successfully launched its third manned spacecraft *Shenzhou* 7 on September 25.

Financial crisis and hardline diplomacy

The world was facing an unprecedented economic crisis weeks after the curtain fell on the Beijing Olympics. The September 15 bankruptcy of Lehman Brothers, one of the major U.S. securities firms, set off a worldwide financial panic. In the United States, subprime loans—housing loans targeting low income borrowers—started going bad the year before, and the housing bubble began to collapse, which was linked to the "Lehman shock." The drop in the U.S. economy had an enormous impact on Japan and the global economy, and subsequently every country was hard pressed to respond.

Among them, China's response showed relatively little agitation, perhaps because of its self-confidence after the Beijing Olympics. China's decisions were rapid. On November 9, as the world was worrying about a response, the Standing Committee of the State Council approved an economic stimulus package through 2010 of four trillion yuan (about 56 trillion yen or $586 billion) as an emergency measure to counter the post-Lehman shock financial crisis. Popular debate, legislative approval, and other preparations to enact such an enormous fiscal package usually takes time in a democratic country, but it took very little time for China's political system to make a decision.

The decision came just ahead of the G-20 Finance Ministers and Central Bank Governors meeting held in São Paulo, Brazil, giving a sudden boost to China's standing and influence at this group comprising the G-7 (Europe, the United States, Canada, and Japan), the BRICs (Brazil, Russia, India, China), and other emerging market economies. President Hu Jintao, himself, attended the G-20 financial summit, a new framework of 19 countries and two European Union (EU) bodies, held in Washington D.C. on November 14, and here China expanded its influence. At the time, China's foreign currency reserves had already surpassed Japan's and were the largest in the world, and China was also the largest holder of U.S. Treasury securities, overtaking Japan.

Reflecting such a reality, a debate grew lively in the English-speaking world in *Foreign Affairs* and other publications over whether or not the era was transitioning from the neoliberal "Washington Consensus" to a "Beijing Consensus" founded on state capitalism. The negative opinion held the majority and even China, itself, officially denied it. In addition to this debate, a popular argument held that the world would be led in the future by the U.S.–China "G-2," not by the current G-7/G-8 industrial nations. Both the United States and China officially denied this argument, but for China, there was an aspect of national prestige and stimulating its sense of nationalism.

Such global trends gave heart to nationalist hardliners in China in 2009–10. An unprecedented situation occurred in March 2009 when Chinese vessels surrounded a U.S. navy acoustic measuring vessel in the South China Sea. China faced off against the developed countries at the 15th Conference of the Parties to the United Nations Framework Convention on Climate Change (COP 15) held in Copenhagen in December 2009, firmly asserting its position as a developing country with respect to setting numerical targets for warming reductions. China started making comments in 2010, ranking the South China Sea issue a "core interest" on par with Taiwan and Tibet. The military's growing influence appears in the background of China's harder line, suggesting a departure from Deng Xiaoping's dying instructions of *taoguang yanghui* ("hide your strength and bide your time"). Abroad, China's hardline diplomatic stance came to be called "assertive" and sometimes "aggressive."

Start of a Democratic Party administration

Amid the global financial crisis, as China's presence, influence, and assertiveness all grew stronger, in contrast, Japan's domestic political situation became more fluid and its presence in the world grew fainter. Inaugurated soon after the Lehman shock, the Aso administration could not help but be absorbed in dealing with the unprecedented global economic crisis. However, Aso made relatively clear statements concerning Japan's diplomatic policy on political security. Soon after becoming prime minister, Aso gave a public address at the United Nations in which he called the solidarity of countries sharing "fundamental values" the basic policy of his diplomacy. It was an extension of the "Arc of Freedom and Prosperity" that Aso had stressed as foreign minister in the Abe cabinet. Since the concept at its core embraced universal values such as freedom and democracy, some in China denounced it as encirclement. The Fukuda administration had not taken up the policy, but the Aso administration revived it. Prime Minister Aso called for cooperative relations with India, saying that it was not aimed against any specific country. He showed an active stance on China diplomacy, too. He participated in the 30th anniversary ceremony of the conclusion of the Japan–China Treaty of Peace and Friendship held in Beijing in October 2008, and in April 2009 made an official visit to China, where he emphasized the continuation of strategic mutually beneficial relations and particularly advocated the necessity of business exchanges.

The Aso administration originally was to have started with Aso as the face of the LDP in the general election, but that election was postponed, and moreover the prime minister's support ratings had fallen rapidly because of his occasional problematic remark. In that context, the Aso administration finally held a general election on August 30, 2009, but it was too late to be of use for his party. The LDP suffered an historically large loss and the DPJ won a big victory, garnering a stable majority of seats. The Aso cabinet ended with less than one year in office, replaced on September 16 with the inauguration of the DPJ's Hatoyama Yukio cabinet. Faithful to its "manifesto" (the DPJ's election pledges), the Hatoyama cabinet strengthened its anti-LDP character and its support rating was high at first, exceeding 70 percent in almost every public opinion survey.

On the domestic policy front, Hatoyama refused the bureaucracy-led style of policymaking of the LDP era, trying constantly to implement leadership by politicians and to minimize involvement by bureaucrats. On the security front, he reset the existing policy for the transfer of the Futenma Air Base to Henoko, Nago City and began to insist on moving this U.S. military base outside the prefecture to reduce the burden on Okinawa. "Trust me," Hatoyama had told U.S. President Barack Obama in their November 13 summit meeting, promising to resolve the issue within the year. He later decided to come to a conclusion on a new location for the facility by the end of May 2010. But, in reality, there was no progress on any kind of specific policy. Hatoyama's support ratings plummeted as the Japan–U.S. alliance was being shaken.

On the other hand, touting his "Spirit of Yuai (fraternity)," Hatoyama emphasized relations with Asian countries, with China and South Korea center stage, and put forward his own ideal of an "East Asian Community." From the start of his administration, Hatoyama proposed an East Asian Community based on the EU model. Right after becoming prime minister, he visited New York on September 21, 2009 to attend the UN General Assembly, where he revealed his concept in talks with President Hu Jintao, remarking that he wanted to turn the East China Sea into a "Sea of Yuai." China highly praised Hatoyama's thoughts and beliefs, and, needless to say, had high expectations for him.

However, on June 2, 2009 the Hatoyama administration announced its resignation at an assembly of DPJ members from both houses. In the end, it was unable to stop its loss of cohesion, linked to the Social Democratic Party's departure from the coalition and Hatoyama's own political financing problems. It wound up a short-lived administration at just nine months. A DPJ presidential election was held on June 4; the winner, Kan Naoto, took office as prime minister on June 8.

Chinese trawler collision incident in the Senkakus

The year 2010 was a critical juncture in Japan–China relations. China surpassed Japan in terms of GDP, snatching the rank of world's second largest economy from Japan, a position that Japan had defended for more than 40 years, ever since it had overtaken then-West Germany to claim the number two spot in 1968. This was the moment when the power shift between Japan and China became evident. In 2010, China strengthened its assertiveness with respect to international issues, as stated above, and the influence of party hardliners and the military seemed to increase. Amid such circumstances, an incident that made waves between Japan and China occurred in the waters off the Senkaku Islands on September 7. A Japanese Coast Guard patrol boat was in the process of warning a Chinese fishing trawler for having entered Japanese territorial waters and conducting illegal operations, when the trawler rammed two patrol boats, and so, the captain was arrested on charges of interfering with a public servant in the execution of his duties.

The arrested captain was taken to Ishigaki Island for further questioning and the rest of the crew was transferred to Ishigaki Port. The captain was sent for prosecution to the Ishigaki branch of the Naha District Public Prosecutors Office on September 9, and his detention was prolonged. Partially pressured by Internet popular opinion, China forcefully demanded everyone's release and called for an apology and indemnity. In the early hours of September 12, State Councillor Dai Bingguo called in Japanese Ambassador to China Niwa Uichiro to protest. The next day, the Japanese side first released all the crew except for the captain, sending them home aboard a chartered plane, and also returned the fishing trawler. But, it decided on September 19 to extend the captain's detention for another ten days, appearing to appeal to legal proceedings to the very end. In response, China continued such actions as sending patrol boats to patrol the area. The incident saw a temporary resolution, however, when the trawler captain was sent back to his home in Fuzhou, Fujian Province aboard a chartered plane after the Naha District prosecutor suddenly released him without indictment "by its own decision" on September 24. There was an outburst of criticism against this sudden decision from all over Japan, not just from the opposition parties or the media. Prime Minister Kan was in the United States at the time to attend the UN General Assembly. It was Chief Cabinet Secretary Sengoku Yoshito who managed this incident, reportedly accomplishing the key role in the related policy processes. Back home, the trawler captain was treated as a local hero, but reportedly his activities were later restricted.

Meanwhile, China took retaliatory measures, such as canceling ministerial visits, suppressing tourism, and canceling invitational travel for university students to the Shanghai Exposition. But, the most serious of the measures were restrictions on the export of rare earth elements bound for Japan starting around September 20, and the detention of four employees of the construction firm Fujita on the excuse that they entered a military-controlled zone. Since many countries of the world largely rely on China for rare earth elements, the export limits became a big issue globally.

One cannot definitively link the Fujita employee and fishing trawler incidents, though certain aspects make it hard to see it as mere coincidence. After the trawler captain's release on September 24, at first three Fujita employees were released on September 30, then the last one was released later on October 9. Prime Minister Kan and Premier Wen had a short discussion on the sidelines of the October 4 ASEM in Brussels, agreeing to return to the starting point of strategic mutually beneficial relations.

Anti-China protests organized by conservative groups "Ganbare Nippon! National Action Committee" and "Executive Committee to Defend the Senkaku Islands" sprang up throughout Japan after the first part of October, the largest with several thousand people. As if in opposition to these, anti-Japan demonstrations sporadically broke out in several specified cities in China after October 16. Many demonstrations took place especially in Sichuan Province—Chengdu, Chongqing, and Deyang. All were but a few thousand people, but since all the protests had been formally petitioned for, even foreign journalists were able to gather there to report. In other words, it is conjectured that these demonstrations were either organized by the government or approved by the authorities, and that locals, blindly following and participating, swelled the ranks. As stated above, Chinese diplomacy was more assertive in 2010 than ever before; it appears that the mobilization of anti-Japanese protests was related to the rise of conservative factions in the intra-party power structure, extolling a Chinese model to oppose the Hu/Wen mainstream faction. In other words, these protests were also an attack on the mainstream faction that compromised with Japan on strategic mutually beneficial relations.

Later, charges were filed against a Coast Guard official for leaking the video of the Chinese trawler collision on the Internet at the start of November, but on the whole, the affair was moving toward a conclusion. Prime Minister Kan and Premier Wen had a ten-minute talk at the East Asian Summit in Hanoi, Vietnam on October 30, where they again agreed to affirm strategic mutually beneficial relations. Prime Minister Kan and President Hu held a 20-minute discussion on the sidelines of the Yokohama APEC Summit on November 13, and, as expected, agreed on affirming the starting point of strategic mutually beneficial relations and the importance of expanding exchanges.

Unlike the LDP that had been in power for decades, the DPJ had not adequately established diplomatic connections with foreign countries. Even so, once an issue cropped up, the DPJ administration would advance its leadership by politician in the policy decision-making process, work a policy concept that sought to minimize the involvement of bureaucrats and bureaucratic institutions, and lay bare the difficulty of managing diplomacy. Yet, one could say that these tensions in the East China Sea, such as had never existed before, inevitably put Japan's security emphasis on the defense of the southwest islands and not just on North Korea, and, at the same time, foreshadowed the emphasis on the Asia-Pacific in the U.S. national defense strategy that became clear later. In that sense, you could say that China itself had ushered in a scenario that it had wanted to avoid (Anami 2012).

From Great Eastern Japan Earthquake to start of the Noda administration

The Great Eastern Japan Earthquake struck on March 11, 2011, with the largest magnitude ever measured in history at 9.0. The ensuing tsunami caused tremendous damage and destruction, and the Pacific coastal region centered on Tohoku suffered calamity. Because of this, the Tokyo Electric Power Company's Fukushima Daiichi nuclear power station lost all power and a meltdown of the reactor core occurred after the cooling systems stopped operating. In the end, the Great Eastern Japan Earthquake was a catastrophic event that claimed close to 20,000 victims, counting the dead and missing.

China's response was quick. President Hu Jintao sent a telegram to the Emperor with condolences and expressions of sympathy, and Premier Wen Jiabao immediately sent a telegram expressing sympathy and offered all necessary assistance. They decided to dispatch an international rescue team on March 12, and 15 people actually arrived the following day. The official media emphasized that it was time to return the favor for Japanese assistance and cooperation at the time of the Great Sichuan Earthquake. Material assistance from China reached a considerable amount while, at the same time, there was an expansion of disaster relief collections in China, primarily from the people. An enormous pump truck donated by China's Sany Heavy Industries Group Company was very actively used in operations to remove water at the Fukushima nuclear plant.

The Great Eastern Japan Earthquake was a tragedy for Japan, but it was also an opportunity in Japan–China relations, calming both countries' public opinion that had been heated by the fishing trawler collision incident in the waters off the Senkaku Islands. Also, the calm actions of the Japanese people and society toward the Great Eastern Japan Earthquake and the Fukushima Daiichi nuclear plant, their mutual assistance, and the spirit of the victims all made a large, positive impression on the Chinese people. Visiting some disaster sites in May 2011, Premier Wen greatly admired the calmness and fortitude of the Japanese people who had experienced the disaster firsthand.

Thereafter, relative calm started to return to Japan–China relations. But once the Great Eastern Japan Earthquake began to settle down momentarily, Japan's political situation once again became fluid over Prime Minister Kan's response to the crisis. Prime Minister Kan formally announced his resignation on August 26, an election for DPJ president was held on August 29, and the Noda Yoshihiko cabinet was inaugurated on September 2. China had some concerns about Prime Minister Noda's past conduct at first, but these were later resolved through a series of leader exchanges.

Prime Minister Noda and President Hu had their first summit meeting on the sidelines of the G-20 Cannes Summit in France on November 3. Noda reaffirmed strategic mutually beneficial relations in addition to expressing gratitude for Chinese assistance at the time of disaster. At the November 12 Noda-Hu summit on the sidelines of the Hawaii APEC Summit, they reaffirmed the development of relations. Furthermore, they held a Japan–China–South Korea summit in Bali, Indonesia on November 19, and Noda met separately with Premier Wen. Prime Minister Noda then made an official visit to China December 25–26, where he emphasized bolstering the political relationship of trust in his meetings with President Hu and Premier Wen, and had an exchange of views on such topics as the situation on the Korean peninsula following the death of Kim Jong-il, chairman of North Korea's National Defense Commission. Again, Prime Minister Noda and President Hu made use of some spare time to have informal talks on the sidelines of the Nuclear Security Summit held in Seoul at the end of March 2012.

In this way, they were able to mend Japan–China relations from the start of the Noda administration, as if completely wiping away the effects of the 2010 incident near the Senkaku Islands.

Senkakus purchase

Tokyo Governor Ishihara Shintaro, visiting Washington D.C. in April 2012, suddenly announced plans for the metropolitan government to purchase three of the Senkaku Islands—Uotsuri-shima, Kita-kojima, and Minami-kojima—and later initiated fundraising plans for that purpose. An MFA spokesperson criticized these unilateral measures as illegal and invalid, but China did not make bigger moves than that. In June, members of "Ganbare Nippon! National Action Committee" and a group of Diet members conducted survey activities in the area around the Senkaku Islands, and later seven members of the Tokyo Metropolitan Assembly surveyed the area. Meanwhile, the Noda administration was exploring the possibility for the country to purchase the three islands as a way to calm the Senkakus situation; it blocked Tokyo's plans after firming up its own plans for nationalization on July 6 (*Asahi Shimbun* 07/07/2012). On July 9, U.S. State Department Press Secretary Victoria Nuland made an announcement favorable to Japan that the Senkaku Islands fell under the scope of the Japan–U.S. Security Treaty.

Even amid such moves by Japan, China's response was relatively relaxed on the whole, though a fisheries supervisory vessel temporarily trespassed in Japanese territorial waters in the vicinity of the Senkaku Islands. Japan had explained to China that the plan for nationalization was to help stabilize the situation, and it might have succeeded. But, as discussed below, there is a strong possibility that the issue was associated with an intra-party power struggle ahead of the 18th CCP National Congress. Meanwhile, Russian Prime Minister Dmitry Medvedev diverted Japan by suddenly visiting Kunashiri Island, one of the four Northern Territories, on July 3. Also, South Korean President Lee Myung-bak suddenly visited Takeshima (Korean name: Dokdo) on August 10. Amid these conditions, the Chinese Internet community was full of criticisms of its government's sluggish moves, but the PRC government's own reaction was relatively calm.

The situation shifted after members of the Action Committee for Defending the Diaoyu Islands headed for the Senkakus on August 12. A boat carrying the 14 Hong Kong activists arrived at the Senkaku Islands on August 15 and seven members landed, shrugging off warnings by the Japanese Coast Guard. The Okinawa prefectural police immediately arrested all 14 activists. As if to protest, anti-Japanese demonstrations occurred in China that day, spreading across the country the next. It was as if a flood of strong anti-Japanese criticism was about to burst forth. Fearing the situation would snowball, the Japanese government decided to forcibly repatriate all 14 activists on August 17. On August 18, however, 150 people including Diet members left port heading for the Senkaku Islands and landed on Uotsurishima on August 19. In response, the protests in China expanded and became violent, damaging Japanese supermarkets and restaurants in Guangzhou, Shenzhen, Qingdao, and Shenyang, while public security officers just silently watched it happen.

Such demonstrations and violence were later calmed, but in the meantime, the Japanese flags were stolen from the diplomatic vehicle of Japanese Ambassador to China Niwa Uichiro on August 27. Seeking to calm the situation, Parliamentary Senior Vice-Minister for Foreign Affairs Yamaguchi Tsuyoshi visited China and delivered a personal letter from Prime Minister Noda to President Hu Jintao. The letter said that Prime Minister Noda and Governor Ishihara had met on August 19, and because Ishihara said he was even prepared for war with China, Noda firmly decided to nationalize the Senkakus (Sunohara 2013).

Prime Minister Noda and President Hu Jintao had a 15-minute pull-aside talk at the APEC Summit on September 9. Replying to Hu's sharp criticism that Japan's purchase of the islands would be illegal and invalid, Noda stated that nationalization was to stabilize the situation and requested a big-picture response. The Japanese government decided on September 10 to purchase the three Senkaku islands, actually buying them on September 11 from the landowner for 2.05 billion yen ($26.2 million). China reacted by expressing the view that a decision to nationalize just after meeting with President Hu went against courtesy. Japan's understanding was that, because Japan had previously told China of its plans to purchase the islands, China held the pull-aside meeting between the leaders at APEC as a reminder of the risks before the purchase.

There were more vehement anti-Japanese demonstrations in China right after this, and at the same time, Chinese maritime surveillance vessels and fishery inspection boats began appearing one after another in the vicinity of the Senkaku Islands and the surrounding waters. A large-scale demonstration occurred in front of the Japanese embassy in Beijing on September 15. On the same day, demonstrations took place in more than 50 cities all over China; some turned violent, destroying and looting Japanese-owned supermarkets and department stores. The protestors called for a boycott of Japanese goods; sometimes Japanese cars were destroyed, and there were also incidents of violence against Chinese nationals driving Japanese brand cars. September 18 was the anniversary of the Manchurian (Mukden) Incident; intense anti-Japanese demonstrations erupted on this day, too, but depending on the location, there were also occurrences very much like the Great Proletarian Cultural Revolution, with portraits of Mao Zedong being hung out. In a complete about-face, however, an order suspending the protests was issued on September 19 and the situation returned to normal quite suddenly after that. Meeting with visiting U.S. Secretary of Defense Leon Panetta on that day, Vice President Xi Jinping criticized Japan for going against the outcomes of the world war against fascism (WWII) and for taking actions counter to the postwar order. Even afterwards, Chinese maritime surveillance vessels and fishery inspection boats made repeated incursions in the vicinity of the Senkaku Islands and the surrounding waters.

Having approved of the vehement demonstrations and subsequent violence, China's intention was clear: it was seeking to overturn Japan's long-standing position of denying that a territorial issue existed. Japan did not change its position, however, and remained consistent, which gave rise to further pressure tactics by the Chinese side. But, because of the strong potential for anti-Japanese protests in China to turn into anti-government protests if left unaddressed, the government approved of the demonstrations even as it suppressed them. Generally speaking, a mobilizer is at the core of a demonstration, but many blind followers also participate, people discontented with a mounting number of social problems—a situation that would certainly become dangerous for the central government if left unresolved.

Amid this chain of events, one question remains: China had been relatively quiet since Ishihara's April remarks, so why did it suddenly become hardline in mid-August? One theory looks at the linkage to the 18th CCP National Congress in China that autumn.

Chongqing Party Secretary Bo Xilai was stripped of power in February, in what is called the Chongqing incident. The Chongqing incident revolves around an associate of Bo's, Wang Lijun, Chongqing's deputy mayor and head of the local public security bureau. Entangled in the scandal surrounding Bo and his wife, Wang fled to the U.S. consulate general in Chengdu, yet he was handed over to the Chinese authorities in the end. Bo Xilai had been expected to join the Central Politburo Standing Committee, meaning that he would have taken part in the

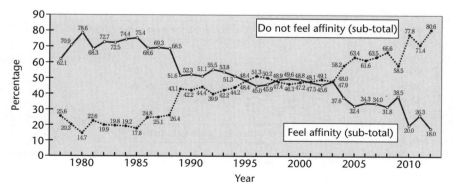

FIGURE 6.2 Japanese opinion: affinity towards China.

Source: Cabinet Office, Government of Japan "Public Opinion Survey on Diplomacy" [2012] http://survey.gov-online.go.jp/h24/h24-gaiko/2-1.html.

highest level of power at the 18th CCP National Congress that autumn. But his situation within the party changed overnight because of the incident. Bo reportedly had the strong backing of Jiang Zemin's faction and stood in opposition to Hu Jintao's faction. After the Chongqing incident, Hu's power base grew stronger and his mainstream faction, which had been advancing a reconciliation policy toward Japan, took a relatively wait-and-see posture on the Senkakus.

However, at the Beidaihe meeting in the first half of August, where final personnel decisions are made for the CCP National Congress, conservative factions led by Jiang's faction reportedly attacked the Hu leadership, saying that China's response to the Senkaku Islands was weak-kneed when compared to the moves Russia and South Korea made on their territorial issues. Before the Beidaihe meeting, it was thought that the mainstream faction would have an overwhelming victory in terms of CCP National Congress personnel, but reportedly there was a strong roll-back by the Jiang Zemin faction after the attack. In other words, there is a strong possibility that conservative factions used the Senkakus situation as fodder for attacking the mainstream faction. Similarly on the Japanese side, diplomacy had not been developing on solid domestic political foundations. The Noda administration suffered stinging attacks, including on its response to the Senkakus situation, from the LDP and other opposition parties. Diplomacy is an extension of domestic politics; it must be said that domestic politics in both Japan and China exerted an extremely large influence on bilateral relations.

Prime Minister Noda ordered the dissolution of the House of Representatives in November 2012, as he had long pledged publicly to do. The results of the general election held on December 16: LDP—294 seats; DPJ—57 seats; Japan Restoration Party—54 seats; New Komeito—31 seats; Your Party—18 seats; Tomorrow Party of Japan—nine seats; Japanese Communist Party—eight seats; Social Democratic Party—two seats; New Party Daichi—one seat; People's New Party—one seat; and unaffiliated—five seats. The LDP–New Komeito coalition had a

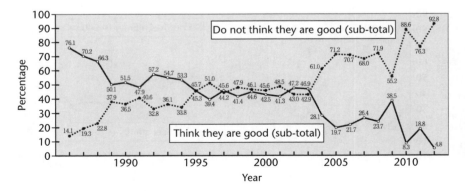

FIGURE 6.3 Japanese opinion: current relations between Japan and China.

Source: Cabinet Office, Government of Japan "Public Opinion Survey on Diplomacy" [2012] http://survey.gov-online.go.jp/h24/h24-gaiko/zh/z12.html.

huge win with 325 seats, once again returning to power; the DPJ was diminished from 230 seats before the dissolution to 57 afterwards. Preceding the general election, Abe Shinzo had been elected again in the party presidential election held on September 26 in conjunction with the completion of LDP President Tanigaki Sadakazu's term. And so, after the general election, the second Abe Shinzo cabinet was formed on December 26.

Cited and referenced materials

Anami Yusuke, 2012, "Senryakuteki gokeikankei no mosaku to higashishinakai mondai 2006–2008 nen [Groping for a Strategic, Mutually Beneficial Relationship and the East China Sea Issue, 2006–2008]," in Takahara Akio, Hattori Ryuji, eds., *Nitchu kankeishi 1972–2012 I: Seiji* [A History of Japan–China Relations 1972–2012, Vol. I: Politics], University of Tokyo Press.

Ba Ritsusei [Ma Licheng] (Yako Kimie, tr.), 2004, *Nihon ha mou chugoku ni shazai shinakuteii* [Japan No Longer Needs to Apologize to China], Bungeishunju.

Ji Inko [Shi Yinhong] (China News Service, tr.), 2004, *Chunichikankei ni taisuru senryakuteki shinshiko* [Strategic New Thinking on Sino-Japanese Relations], Nihon Kyohosha [The Duan Press].

Kamo Tomoki, 2012, "Koizumi naikaku to nashonarizumu no koyo [The Koizumi Cabinet and the Promotion of Nationalism]," in Takahara Akio, Hattori Ryuji, eds., *Nitchu kankeishi 1972–2012 I: Seiji* [A History of Japan–China Relations 1972–2012, Vol. I: Politics], University of Tokyo Press.

Kazankai, 2008, *Nitchu kankei kihon shiryoshu 1972–2008 nen* [Collection of Basic Documents in Japan–China Relations, 1972–2008], Kazankai Foundation.

Kokubun Ryosei, 2008a, "Nitchukankei to kokunaiseiji no sogorenkan [The Interrelationship of Japan–China Relations and Domestic Politics]," in *Hogaku kenkyu* [Journal of Law, Politics, and Sociology], Keio University Press, Vol. 81, No. 6.

Kokubun Ryosei, 2008b, "Shin nitchuyuko 21 seiki iinkai [The New Japan–China Friendship Committee for the 21st Century]," in *Toa*, Kazankai Foundation, No. 495.

Mori Kazuko, 2006, *Nitchu kankei* [Japan–China Relations], Iwanami Shoten.

Sen Kichin [Qian Qichen] (Hamamoto Ryoichi, tr.), 2006, *Sen Kishin kaikoroku* [Memoirs of Qian Qichen], Toyo Shoin.

Shimizu Yoshikazu, 2008, *"Chugoku mondai" no uchimaku* [The Inner Workings of the "China Issue"], Chikumashobo.

Shimizu Yoshikazu, 2009, *"Chugoku mondai" no kakushin* [The Core of the "China Issue"], Chikumashobo.

Sunohara Tsuyoshi, 2013, *Anto senkaku kokuyuka* [Secret Battle: The Nationalization of the Senkakus], Shinchosha Publishing.

Yomiuri Shimbun Seiji-bu, 2006, *Gaiko o kenka ni shita otoko* [The Man who Turned Diplomacy into a Fight], Shinchosha Publishing.

Yu Binko [Yu Minhao], 2007, "Chugoku no taigaikeizaiseisaku ketteikatei ni kansuru ichi kosatsu [An Analysis of China's Foreign Policy Decision-Making Process]," in *Hogaku seijigaku ronkyu* [Journal of Law and Political Studies], Keio University Graduate School of Law, No. 75.

7

THE CURRENT STATE OF JAPAN–CHINA RELATIONS

Navigating a fragile relationship

FIGURE 7.1 Prime Minister Abe Shinzo (on left) and President Xi Jinping meet for talks ahead of the APEC summit (November 10, 2014, Beijing).

Source: ©Jiji Press.

Since late 2012 and the launch of new administrations in both countries, Japan–China relations have been shaken by territory and history issues and the founding of a new regional financial institution. All were issues that, if mistakes had been made in responding to them, might have destabilized not only the bilateral relationship but the entire East Asian region. Even as they stood firm in their respective positions on these issues, however, the Japanese and Chinese governments groped for prudent responses to avoid causing relations to worsen decisively.

1 Start of new administrations and stagnation of Japan–China relations

Initial contact and setback under the second Abe administration

The LDP led by Abe Shinzo won 294 seats in the 46th general election held in December 2012, securing a stable single-party majority; the seat count totaled 325 when combined with the 31 seats of the New Komeito, which joined the ruling coalition. It was a landslide victory giving control of two-thirds of the seats of the House of Representatives, and as a result, Abe Shinzo achieved a comeback, becoming prime minister on December 26—the second to serve non-consecutive terms since Yoshida Shigeru.

Even as China reacted calmly to the start of the second Abe administration, it soon sent a reminder about the Senkaku Islands issue. On the day of the administration's inauguration, an MFA spokesperson stated that Japan must show sincerity when engaging in dialogue on the Senkakus issue, stressing that the Senkaku Islands are China's inherent territory (PD 12/27/2012).

Political contact between Japan and China under the second Abe administration began January 25, 2013 with the visit to China by Yamaguchi Natsuo, chief representative of the New Komeito, who delivered a personal letter from Abe. China took this New Komeito delegation seriously, and General Secretary Xi Jinping himself attended the meeting. Xi pointed out the importance of the historical four basic documents in Japan–China relations to Chief Representative Yamaguchi, and on the Senkaku Islands issue, Xi stated, "our positions and opinions differ, but we should control and resolve the issue through dialogue and consultation." In this way, both countries groped for an approach through the good offices of the New Komeito.

However, this political contact between Japan and China hit a setback immediately upon Yamaguchi's return home. A troubling incident happened in the East China Sea on January 30, 2013: a frigate of the People's Liberation Army Navy (PLAN) locked its fire-control radar, a radar system used to aim weapons, onto the MSDF destroyer *Yudachi*. Defense Minister Onodera Itsunori publicly disclosed this fact on February 5. The Ministry of Defense released this information together with suspicions that a PLAN frigate had also locked its fire-control radar on a patrol helicopter from the MSDF destroyer *Onami* in the East China Sea on January 19 (MOD website).

China criticized Japan's response, and both the MFA and Ministry of National Defense (MND) denied the Japanese statements (PD 2/9/2013). Thereafter, the *People's Daily* began to frequently run editorials criticizing the Abe administration's stance on constitutional revision and the history issue. And so, the first political contact between Japan and China under the Abe administration broke off.

China's political situation was complicated around this time. The new central leadership with Xi Jinping as general secretary got its start at the 18th CCP National Congress in November 2012. Ahead of this, a fierce power struggle was unfolding with the Jiang Zemin faction, and Bo Xilai, once expected to become a member of the Politburo, was stripped of power because of the Chongqing incident. At the time, it was conjectured that the newly formed Xi Jinping administration was too preoccupied with the ongoing power struggle to handle relations with Japan.

Growing security issue tensions

Japan–China relations saw an increasing degree of tensions focused on security issues following the radar lock-on incident. Vessels of the China Coast Guard, newly established after the integration of four existing maritime law enforcement agencies, committed frequent incursions into the territorial waters around the Senkakus in July 2013. Also, PLAN ships transited the waters between the Okinawan main island and Miyakojima to conduct active military exercises in the western Pacific Ocean. At the time of the exercises, an MND spokesperson asserted that China's actions did not violate international law and, in addition, unilaterally criticized monitoring activities. Thereafter, Y-8 airborne early-warning aircraft and H-6 bombers affiliated with the PLA Air Force began to conduct flights into the western Pacific by passing between the main island of Okinawa and Miyakojima. The number of times SDF planes had to scramble against Chinese aircraft rapidly increased (NIDS 2014).

In November 2013, soon after the Third Plenum of the 18th CCP Central Committee closed, China announced plans for an East China Sea Air Defense Identification Zone in a manner that included the Senkaku Islands as its own territory. The gist was that China unilaterally would require that aircraft flying in airspace over the high seas comply with its procedures, or else Chinese armed forces would take "emergency defensive measures." Japan thought this was inappropriate and violated the basic principle of freedom of flight over the high seas that was a general principle of international law (NIDS 2014). The Xi Jinping administration is thought to have approved such a sudden declaration to gain the military's support in the intra-party power struggle. It is a topic deserving of further study and clarification.

Prime Minister Abe's Yasukuni Shrine visit

Abe Shinzo visited the Yasukuni Shrine for the first time since becoming prime minister on December 26, 2013. It had been seven years and four months since an incumbent prime minister had last visited Yasukuni: Prime Minister Koizumi Junichiro on August 15, 2006 (Yomiuri 12/27/2013). An MFA spokesperson immediately issued a comment criticizing the visit and stressed that a series of Japanese actions were causing Japan–China relations to worsen (PD 12/27/2013). Notwithstanding such a rebuke, there was no criticism stronger than this within China, to say nothing of large-scale anti-Japanese demonstrations.

2 Political bargaining over Japan–China summit at Beijing APEC

Evolution of China's operations toward Japan

The biggest question in Japan–China relations in 2014 was whether or not the leaders would meet on the sidelines of the APEC Economic Leader's Meeting scheduled to be held in Beijing in November. For that purpose, Japan and China both rolled out various political tactics on this matter.

China's operations toward Japan in this period can be categorized into four main methods. The first was to mobilize international public opinion critical of Japan. Heartened by the fact that even the United States partly joined in the criticism of Japan over the issue of Prime Minister Abe's Yasukuni Shrine visit, China used the issue as material to publicize Japan's "turn to the right" and to spread its anti-Japanese propaganda throughout the world. Within one month following the visit, Chinese ambassadors from 73 countries and regional or international institutions put on a relentless exhibition critical of Japan, writing submissions for the local media and giving interviews (Yomiuri Shimbun Seiji-bu 2015).

The second method was to put pressure on politicians from the ruling LDP and New Komeito. China arranged for NPC Standing Committee Chairman Zhang Dejiang, the third ranking CCP member, to meet on May 5, 2014 with LDP Vice President Komura Masahiko, who was visiting China leading a non-partisan delegation as the Chairman of the Japan–China Friendship Parliamentarians' Union (Yomiuri 5/6/2014). Noda Takeshi, heading the delegation of the LDP Asian-African Problems Study Group, met on May 9 with fourth-ranked Yu Zhengsheng, chairman of the People's Political Consultative Conference (PD 5/10/2014; Yomiuri 5/10/2014). State Council Vice Premier Liu Yandong, a Politburo member, met with transport minister Ota Akihiro of the New Komeito on June 27. This was the first meeting between an incumbent Japanese cabinet minister in the second Abe administration and a Chinese official above the vice premier level (Mainichi 6/28/2014; PD 6/28/2014).

The third method of operations toward Japan were moves toward the Japanese business and financial community. Then Keidanren Chairman Yonekura Hiromasa met with Vice President Li Yuanchao on May 28, 2014 (Mainichi 5/29/2014; PD 5/29/2014). That September, China agreed to have State Council Vice Premier Wang Yang meet with the largest delegation of executives from the top Japanese corporations to ever visit China, led by Cho Fujio, chairman of the JCEA, and which included Sakakibara Sadayuki, the new chairman of Keidanren. (Yomiuri 9/24/2014, 9/25/2014; PD 9/25/2014).

The fourth method of operations toward Japan was to send leading figures from the "Crown Prince Party" (the children of high-level CCP officials), people rumored to be close to Xi Jinping, to Japan to make contact with key administration officials, including Prime Minister Abe himself. In April 2014, Hu Deping, former General Secretary Hu Yaobang's eldest son, met with Prime Minister Abe, Chief Cabinet Secretary Suga Yoshihide, Foreign Minister Kishida Fumio, LDP Vice President Komura Masahiko, and others (Sankei 4/9/2014, 4/10/2014, 4/15/2014). Li Xiaolin, chairwoman of the Chinese People's Association for Friendship with Foreign Countries and daughter of Li Xiannian, who served as PRC president in the 1980s, went to Japan in October. In her meeting with Prime Minister Abe, Li commended the improvement in bilateral relations under the first Abe administration and sounded him out on making another visit to China (Yomiuri Shimbun Seiji-bu 2015).

By resorting to these various methods, China groped for a way to realize a summit meeting with Prime Minister Abe at APEC, with the prerequisite being to draw out some kind of compromise from Japan regarding the history and Senkakus issues. This also signified a change in what had been China's posture toward Japan up to 2013. Xi Jinping had been strengthening his power base within the CCP during this period, as indicated in the confinement of Xu Caihou, former vice chairman of the CCP CMC, and Zhou Yongkang, former member of the Politburo's Standing Committee. Through such moves to strengthen his power base, Xi is thought to have given himself more room to be able to develop a positive policy toward Japan. As argued in the previous chapter, the Jiang Zemin faction had been attacking the mainstream faction relentlessly, employing anti-Japanese demonstrations to sow confusion in Japan–China relations. The man at the center of the Jiang faction who controlled the public security apparatus at the time was Zhou Yongkang. It is hard to believe that the confinement of Zhou and others in the Jiang faction was unrelated to Xi Jinping's policy of improving relations with Japan.

Evolution of the Abe administration's breakthrough diplomacy toward China

For its part, Japan also desired to break the deadlock in Japan–China relations. Prime Minister Abe suggested his intention to improve relations by stating, "my door for dialogue is always open," in his policy speech to the 186th session of the Diet on January 24, 2014, one month after his Yasukuni visit. That key administration officials including Prime Minister Abe later accepted meetings with the Chinese side, responding to the start of China's positive operations toward Japan, is further evidence of this. The man most active as the central figure in the Abe administration's China policy was Yachi Shotaro, who was appointed secretary general of the National Security Secretariat (NSS), which was set up in January 2014.

Former Prime Minister Fukuda Yasuo, well-connected to key Chinese figures as the board chairman of the BOAO Forum for Asia, went to China in July 2014.

At the time, Prime Minister Abe is said to have entrusted Fukuda with a message on improving Japan–China relations, and Yachi accompanied him on the trip to China to underscore the importance of that message. As a result, China, sensing the degree of Japan's sincerity, arranged for Xi Jinping himself to meet with Fukuda (Yomiuri Shimbun Seiji-bu 2015).

Soon after Abe met with Li Xiaolin, NSS Secretary General Yachi secretly visited China and had a meeting with State Councilor Yang Jiechi on October 11. Sparked by Yachi's visit, MOFA and MFA repeatedly held secret coordination meetings in Beijing and Tokyo for the purpose of realizing a Japan–China summit meeting. And then on November 7, Yachi and Yang drafted a document titled "Regarding Discussions toward Improving Japan–China Relations" (referenced later as four items of common ground).

The content of this document is as follows:

1. Both sides would observe the four basic documents between Japan and China (1972 Joint Communiqué, 1978 Peace Treaty, 1998 Joint Declaration, and 2008 Joint Statement) and develop a strategic mutually beneficial relationship;
2. Both sides shared some recognition concerning the history issue;
3. Both sides would avert the rise of unforeseen circumstances by constructing a crisis management mechanism and through dialogue and consultation on the premise that they had different views as to issues of the East China Sea and the Senkaku Islands;
4. Both sides would, by utilizing various multilateral and bilateral channels, resume dialogue in political, diplomatic, and security fields and build a political relationship of mutual trust.

(MOFA website)

That this content was issued before the summit meeting was unprecedented. Ambiguous expressions that both sides could claim as they saw fit were scattered throughout this agreed document, yet even if both sides "shared a recognition," it did not mean a resolution to the pending issues between Japan and China, such as the Senkakus and history issues.

Realization of Japan–China summit meeting

A Japan–China summit meeting was realized between Abe and Xi Jinping on November 10, 2014, preceding the APEC Economic Leaders' Meeting. Showing a desire to improve Japan–China ties, Abe proposed rebuilding the relationship on the concept of Mutually Beneficial Relationship based on Common Strategic Interests. He pointed out the importance of four points: 1) promoting mutual understanding between citizens; 2) further deepening economic relations; 3) cooperating in the East China Sea; and 4) stabilizing the security environment in East Asia. Abe sought to promote dialogue and cooperation in the security field, such as early implementation of a maritime communication mechanism between the defense authorities. In response, Xi Jinping agreed with developing Japan–China ties based on strategic mutually beneficial relations, yet he sought Japan's resolution of a series of issues based on the spirit of the "four items of common ground" previously announced. Moreover, saying the history issue was a matter concerning the feelings of the more than 1.3 billion Chinese people, he noted that he hoped Japan would squarely face the history issue and continue to follow the path of a peaceful nation. Meanwhile, he stated that there was already agreement regarding the maritime crisis management mechanism and that going forward he wanted them to continue communicating at the working level (MOFA website; PD 11/11/2014). The meeting was over in just 25 minutes; neither side directly mentioned the standoff over the Senkaku Islands or Prime Minister Abe's visit to Yasukuni Shrine.

If nothing else, this summit meeting opened a window for dialogue, thereby extricating Japan–China relations during the second Abe administration from its worst status.

3 Japan–China relations 70 years after the war's end

Battle over the Abe statement

In 2015, the 70th anniversary of the end of the war, the following three issues became the focus: Prime Minister Abe's statement issued 70 years after the war (Abe Statement); the South China Sea issue and Japan's legislation for peace and security that recognized the limited exercise of the right of collective self-defense; and the establishment of the Asian Infrastructure Investment Bank (AIIB).

Abe formally announced on January 5, 2015 that he would work on preparing a prime ministerial statement. An experts panel to study the content for a statement 70 years after the war, the "Advisory Panel on the History of the 20th Century and on Japan's Role and World Order in the 21st Century" (advisory panel), held its first session on February 25. This panel, a private advisory body to Prime Minister Abe, comprised 16 members, experienced individuals drawn from academia, business, and the media. The 1995 Murayama Statement and 2005 Koizumi Statement were drawn up only by the prime ministers' close associates. Even though the author of the Abe Statement would ostensibly be the prime minister, the advisory panel was created in order to give the statement "objectivity" based on discussion from various points of view.

On March 3, 2015, Yu Zhengsheng met with LDP Secretary General Tanigaki Sadakazu and New Komeito Secretary General Inoue Yoshihisa, who were visiting China to resume the "Japan–China Ruling Party Exchange Conference" that had been suspended in 2009. Yu touched on the history issue, stating, "I would like for the Japanese side to have the correct understanding of history." For their part, Tanigaki stated that the Abe Statement would not cause China worries and Inoue explained the Abe administration's position that it would be a continuation of the previous cabinet statements overall (PD 3/24/2015; Mainichi 3/25/2015.

Abe and Xi held their second meeting on April 22, 2015, at the ceremony commemorating the 60th anniversary of the Asian-African Conference held in Bandung. Perhaps out of consideration for the nature of the conference, Abe did not mention "*owabi*" (apology) in his speech the previous day. China's state-run media was somewhat critical of this; though he was absent and did not hear Abe's speech, Xi Jinping did attend the Japan–China summit. Xi pointed out to Abe that Japan must face history squarely, because the history issue was a major matter of principle concerning the political basis of Japan–China relations. Abe stated that he was upholding the understanding of previous cabinets, including the Murayama and Koizumi statements (MOFA website; PD 4/23/2015).

After his return home from Bandung, Prime Minister Abe went to the United States to give a speech to the U.S. Congress. It was the first time for a Japanese prime minister to give an address to a joint meeting of Congress, and so it attracted much attention at home and abroad as something that might prefigure the content of the Abe Statement. In the speech, Abe mentioned "deep repentance" and "deep remorse" but avoided the terms "*owabi*" (apology) and "*shinryaku*" (aggression) in relation to the history issue. Many in the U.S. government and Congress gave the speech high praise.

On May 23, Xi Jinping himself met with a large delegation to China of about 3,000 Japanese led by Nikai Toshihiro, chairman of the LDP General Council. Pointing out the importance of Japan–China friendship, Xi said:

> Any attempt to distort and beautify the history of Japanese militaristic aggression will not be tolerated by the Chinese people or the people of other victimized Asian countries. It is believable that any Japanese people with a sense of justice and conscience will not tolerate it either.

A series of shots from the meeting appeared the next day on the front page of the *People's Daily* (PD 5/24/2015).

The Advisory Panel's report was issued ahead of the Abe Statement. Although some of the members held dissenting views, the report clearly stated:

> after the Manchurian Incident, Japan expanded its aggression against the continent, deviated from the post-World War I shift towards self-determination, outlawry of war, democratization, and an emphasis on economic development, lost sight of the global trends, and caused much harm to various countries, largely in Asia, through a reckless war. In China in particular, this created many victims across wide areas.
>
> *(Report of the Advisory Panel)*

The Abe Statement, issued August 14, incorporated all four keywords that had become the focus of attention—*hansei* (remorse), *owabi* (apology), *shinryaku* (aggression), and *shokuminchi shihai* (colonial rule)—fundamentally on the basis of the panel's report. It displayed consideration with respect to China, expressing a "heartfelt gratitude" for "the Chinese people who underwent all the sufferings of the war" and "the former POWs who experienced unbearable sufferings caused by the Japanese military" who, with a spirit of tolerance, made every effort for reconciliation with Japan (Kantei website).

China's response to the Abe Statement was restrained. After the statement's release, China summoned Japanese Ambassador to China Kitera Masato to the foreign ministry and conveyed the Chinese side's "solemn position," but it did not use strong words of criticism. It is worth noting that the MFA spokesperson mentioned "taking history as a mirror to guide the future," but did not denounce the statement itself.

Peace and security legislation and South China Sea issue

China from early on had been paying attention to Japanese domestic trends regarding the right of collective self-defense. The Abe cabinet enacted a cabinet decision on July 1, 2014 changing the interpretation of the constitution that would enable exercising the right of collective self-defense to a limited extent. On June 26, right before this cabinet decision, an MND spokesman stated, "any military policy change by Japan mustn't jeopardize the sovereignty, security and interests of its neighboring countries." Furthermore, after the cabinet decision, the MFA spokesperson also stated, "[we have been] requesting that the Japanese side not harm China's sovereignty and security interests" (CNS 6/26/2014; PDO 7/2/2014). Since then, movements in Japan, in South Korea, and in other neighboring countries opposing the right of collective self-defense have been featured a great deal in the *People's Daily*, *People's Liberation Army Daily*, and other Chinese state-run media. On the other hand, despite the increasingly fierce debate within Japan over the Legislation for Peace and Security (hereafter "security legislation") since the start of 2015, China's leaders and government officials rarely take the opportunity to openly comment on this issue, and it appears that there may be a consensus not to criticize Japan formally.

As criticism grew stronger in Japan against the security legislation, in July one could see changes in the Abe administration's stance of restraining its words and actions critical of China. The Abe administration publicly announced that China was constructing a new deep sea platform in gas fields near the Japan–China median line in the East China Sea. Moreover, Defense Minister Nakatani Gen expressed security concerns, suggesting the potential for China to set up a radar and a helipad on this platform to enable the takeoff and landing of helicopters and unmanned surveillance craft. Prime Minister Abe, too, mentioned the increase in China's military power and the increase in the number of SDF emergency scrambles to counter Chinese aircraft as the upper house was deliberating the security legislation. Nevertheless, China's posture concerning the security legislation remained all the more restrained.

On September 19, after the passage of two bills related to the security legislation, the MFA called it "an unprecedented move taken by post-war Japan in the military and security fields" that is "making the international community question whether Japan is going to drop its exclusive defense policy and deviate from the path of peaceful development it has been following after WWII." It sought to restrain the Japanese side, saying that China urges Japan "to learn hard lessons from history, take seriously the concerns of its Asian neighbors, act with discretion on military and security issues, and stick to the path of peaceful development." In contrast, the MND spokesperson did not touch on this issue at the press conference held September 24 (Asahi 9/19/2015; PLAD 9/25/2015; PRC MFA website).

What piqued Chinese interest in this issue was that about this time, the United States conducted a "freedom of navigation" (FON) operation in October 2015, concerned by China's unilateral change in the status quo of the South China Sea through its land reclamation and construction of military facilities on the reefs of the Spratly (Nansha) Islands. It appears that China was concerned about the possibility that Japan would participate with U.S. forces in activities in the South China Sea based on the security legislation.

At the second Japan–China High-Level Political Dialogue held October 13–14, 2015, Yang Jiechi said he hoped that Japan would act cautiously regarding the South China Sea issue. However, once the FON operation got under way, the Japanese side indicated a posture supportive of the actions of U.S. forces (MOD website; MOFA website). When informed of the possibility that Prime Minister Abe would raise the South China Sea issue at his meeting with State Council Premier Li Keqiang at the Japan–China–South Korea trilateral summit in Seoul in November after a three-and-a-half-year gap, Foreign Minister Wang Yi revealed his displeasure, saying "I wonder what Japan has to do with the South China Sea" (Sankei 11/1/2015). Abe is said to have raised the South China Sea issue at the November 1 meeting, but the substance was not made public. Meanwhile, with the security legislation in mind, Li Keqiang commented that he hoped Japan would take the concerns of Asian neighbors seriously and "contribute more to the peace and stability of the region" (PD 11/2/2015; Sankei 11/2/2015).

Abe indicated in a November 6 speech in Tokyo that he was thinking of raising the South China Sea issue at international fora such as the G-20 and the APEC leaders' summits. In response, the MFA spokesperson denounced him, saying Japan is not a party concerned in the South China Sea issue and it is not in a position to butt in (Sankei 11/7/2015; PLAD 11/14/2015). Meeting with U.S. President Obama at the APEC summit, Prime Minister Abe commented that he would deepen Japan–U.S. cooperation on the South China Sea issue and "would study" SDF operations in that maritime region.

In his meeting with President Benigno Aquino, III of the Philippines, Abe agreed to conclude an agreement on defense equipment and technology transfers, and he commented that unilateral actions that change the status quo and heighten tensions, such as large-scale land reclamation and the building of outposts in the South China Sea, were a cause of common concern to the international community (Mainichi

11/20/2015; MOFA website; Tokyo 11/20/2015). Responding to such Japanese moves, the MND spokesperson said, "Japan is not a relevant party in the South China Sea issue" and "We urge Japan to do more for peace and stability in the South China Sea and for improving Sino-Japanese relations."

In this way, even though China indicated interest in the security legislation from the start, it firmly maintained a wait-and-see posture basically until the bills were passed. However, at the same time as the U.S. military rolled out its FON operation and the Japanese government clarified its posture in support of the United States, once the possibility was suggested for the SDF's participation, China's sense of alarm became apparent and it moved to check that action.

Establishment of the AIIB

In October 2013, Xi Jinping proposed founding the AIIB. ASEAN countries, excluding Indonesia, agreed to the AIIB's establishment in October 2014 (Indonesia later became a member). The goal of the AIIB is to advance infrastructure projects in developing Asia, and thereby to increase the medium-term growth rate of the region's economy. Because aspects of the AIIB duplicate the role of the Asian Development Bank (ADB), of which Japan is the largest shareholder, the United States and Japan held a sense of wariness towards the AIIB from the start, viewing it as a challenge to the international economic system led by the United States and the West.

The issue of the AIIB's establishment came under further scrutiny beginning in 2015. China unveiled its "One Belt, One Road (*Yidai, Yilu*)" concept in March 2015, combining the existing "Silk Road Economic Belt" concept with the construction of a "21st Century Maritime Silk Road." The purpose is apparently threefold: 1) amid decelerating growth in China's domestic economy, to seek economic growth by orienting the excess productive capacity of domestic industries abroad; 2) to plan the expansion of Chinese investment overseas; and 3) to enhance China's power to influence the international community. The AIIB is believed to be the financial support for the "One Belt, One Road" concept, intended to bring such a Sino-centric economic bloc to fruition.

Britain's announcement that it would join the AIIB gave Japan and the United States quite a shock. Then, just as if the dam had broken, Germany, France, Italy, and others also announced they would join.

Meanwhile, China did not show any intention of excluded Japan from the AIIB. Finance Minister Lou Jiwei announced that "we are constantly informing Japan of the progress of deliberations" in an NPC media briefing on March 6, 2015. China's Ambassador to Japan Cheng Yonghua also said that China "welcomes Japan's participation" on March 27, right before the deadline. In contrast, Japan passed up joining the AIIB at the end of March 2015, the deadline to enter as one of the prospective founding members, giving the reason that the AIIB's management was non-transparent (Nikkei 3/6/2015; 3/27/2015; 3/31/2015).

But China sought Japan's AIIB membership all the more. At the Japan–China summit held in Bandung on April 22, Xi Jinping called on Japan to join, explaining that the AIIB "already has been universally welcomed by the international community." Abe pointed out the problem points, such as fair governance of the institution and borrowing countries' debt sustainability, even as he praised the AIIB's significance saying that "there is a high demand for infrastructure in Asia" (Mainichi 4/15/2015; Nikkei 4/15/2015; 4/23/2015; 4/29/2015).

A signing ceremony for the articles of agreement establishing the AIIB was held June 29, bringing together representatives of the 57 prospective founding member countries to the Great Hall of the People in Beijing. According to the agreement, voting rights are calculated based on a member's capital subscription; China was the top with 26.06 percent, so it holds veto power over important matters for which a supermajority of over 75 percent vote in agreement is necessary. In the meantime, although there was a debate in Japan over whether or not to join, the Abe administration put off membership in the end (Nikkei 6/29/2015 evening edition; 6/30/2015; Yomiuri Shimbun Seiji-bu 2015).

Cited and referenced materials

Asahi: *Asahi Shimbun* newspaper.
CNS: *Zhongguo Xinwen Wang* (China News Service).
Kantei website: Prime Minister of Japan and His Cabinet (www.kantei.go.jp).
Mainichi: *Mainichi Shimbun* newspaper.
MFA website: Ministry of Foreign Affairs of the People's Republic of China (www.fmprc. gov.cn/web/).
MNDN: *Guofangbu Wang* (Ministry of National Defense Network).
MOD website: Ministry of Defense of Japan (www.mod.go.jp).
MOFA website: Ministry of Foreign Affairs of Japan (www.mofa.go.jp).
NIDS: The National Institute for Defense Studies, ed., "East Asia Strategic Review 2014."
NIDS: The National Institute for Defense Studies, ed., "East Asia Strategic Review 2016."
Nikkei: *Nihon Keizai Shimbun* newspaper.
PD: *Renmin Ribao* (*The People's Daily*) newspaper.
PDO: *Renmin Wang* (People's Daily Online).
PLAD: *Jiefangjun Bao* (*People's Liberation Army Daily*) newspaper.
"Report of the Advisory Panel on the History of the 20th Century and on Japan's Role and the World Order in the 21st Century," August 6, 2016 www.kantei.go.jp/jp/singi/21c_koso/pdf/report_en.pdf (last accessed June 28, 2016).
Sankei: *Sankei Shimbun* newspaper.
Tokyo: *Tokyo Shimbun* newspaper.
Yomiuri: *Yomiuri Shimbun* newspaper.
Yomiuri Shimbun Seiji-bu, *Abe Kantei vs. Shu Kinpei—Gekika suru Nitchu Gaiko Senso* [The Abe Kantei vs Xi Jinping—The Intensifying Japan–China War of Diplomacy], Shinchosha 2015.

GUIDE TO FURTHER READING IN ENGLISH

Bush, Richard C. *The Perils of Proximity: China–Japan Security Relations*. Washington D.C.: Brookings Institution Press, 2010.

Curtis, Gerald L., Ryosei Kokubun, and Wang Jisi. *Getting the Triangle Straight: Managing China–Japan–US Relations*. Tokyo: Japan Center for International Exchange (JCIE), 2010.

Dobson, Hugo, and Glenn Hook, eds. *Japan and Britain in the Contemporary World: Responses to Common Issues*. London; New York: RoutledgeCurzon, 2003.

Drifte, Reinhard. *Japan's Security Relations with China since 1989: From Balancing to Bandwagoning?*. London; New York: Routledge, 2003.

Fogel, Joshua A. *The Cultural Dimension of Sino-Japanese Relations: Essays on the Nineteenth and Twentieth Centuries*. Armonk, N.Y.: M.E. Sharpe, 1995.

Fogel, Joshua A. *Maiden Voyage: The Senzaimaru and the Creation of Modern Sino-Japanese Relations*. Oakland, Calif.: University of California Press, 2014.

Fogel, Joshua A. *Between China and Japan: The Writings of Joshua Fogel*. Leiden: Brill Academic Pub., 2015.

Gries, Peter Hays. *China's New Nationalism: Pride, Politics, and Diplomacy*. Berkeley, Calif.: University of California Press, 2005.

Hagström, Linus. *Enigmatic Power?: Relational Power Analysis and Statecraft in Japan's China Policy*. Stockholm: Stockholm University, Dept. of Political Science, 2003.

Hook, Glenn D., and Harukiyo Hasegawa, eds. *Japanese Responses to Globalization: Politics, Security, Economics and Business*. Basingstoke; New York: Palgrave Macmillan, 2006.

Hsiung, James C. *China and Japan at Odds: Deciphering the Perpetual Conflict*. New York: Palgrave Macmillan, 2007.

Iriye, Akira. *China and Japan in the Global Setting*. Cambridge, Mass.: Harvard University Press, 1992.

Itoh, Mayumi. *Pioneers of Sino-Japanese Relations: Liao and Takasaki*. New York: Palgrave Macmillan, 2012.

Jansen, Marius B. *Japan and China: From War to Peace, 1894–1972*. Chicago: Rand McNally College Pub. Co., 1975.

King, Amy. *China–Japan Relations after World War II: Empire, Industry and War, 1949–1971*. Cambridge: Cambridge University Press, 2016.

Lam, Peng Er, ed. *Japan's Relations with China: Facing a Rising Power.* London; New York: Routledge, 2006.

Lee, Chae-Jin. *Japan Faces China: Political and Economic Relations in the Postwar Era.* Baltimore, Md.: Johns Hopkins University Press, 1976.

Ogata, Sadako. *Normalization with China: A Comparative Study of U.S. and Japanese Processes.* Berkeley, Calif.: Institute of East Asian Studies, University of California, 1988.

Rose, Caroline. *Interpreting History in Sino-Japanese Relations: A Case Study in Political Decision-making.* London; New York: Routledge, 1998.

Rose, Caroline. *Sino-Japanese Relations: Facing the Past, Looking to the Future?.* London; New York: RoutledgeCurzon, 2005.

Rose, Caroline, ed. *Sino-Japanese Relations: History, Politics, Economy and Security, 4 vols., Critical Concepts in Asian Studies.* Milton Park, Abingdon; New York: Routledge, 2011.

Ross, Robert S., and Zhu Feng, eds. *China's Ascent: Power, Security, and the Future of International Politics.* Ithaca, N.Y.: Cornell University Press, 2008.

Smith, Sheila A. *Intimate Rivals: Japanese Domestic Politics and a Rising China.* New York: Columbia University Press, 2015.

Söderberg, Marie, ed. *Chinese-Japanese Relations in the Twenty-first Century: Complementarity and Conflict.* London; New York: Routledge, 2002.

Soeya, Yoshihide. *Japan's Economic Diplomacy with China, 1945–1978.* Oxford: Clarendon Press; New York: Oxford University Press, 1998.

Swanström, Niklas, and Ryosei Kokubun, eds. *Sino-Japanese Relations: Rivals or Partners in Regional Cooperation?.* Singapore; Hackensack, N.J.: World Scientific, 2013.

Takahara, Akio. *The Politics of Wage Policy in Post-Revolutionary China.* Basingstoke: Macmillan Press, 1992.

Vogel, Ezra F., Yuan Ming, and Akihiko Tanaka, eds. *The Golden Age of the U.S.–China–Japan Triangle, 1972–1989.* Cambridge, Mass.: Harvard University Asia Center: Distributed by Harvard University Press, 2002.

Vogel, Ezra F., Yuan Ming, and Akihiko Tanaka, eds. *Age of Uncertainty: The U.S.–China–Japan Triangle from Tiananmen (1989) to 9/11 (2001).* Harvard East Asian Monographs Online, www.fas.harvard.edu/~asiactr/publications/pdfs/Vogel_Age_of_Uncertainty. pdf, Harvard University Asia Center, Cambridge, Mass., 2004, pp. 254–269.

Wan, Ming. *Sino-Japanese Relations: Interaction, Logic, and Transformation.* Washington D.C.: Woodrow Wilson Center Press; Stanford, Calif.: Stanford University Press, 2006.

Whiting, Allen Suess. *China Eyes Japan.* Berkeley, Calif.: University of California Press, 1989.

Yahuda, Michael B. *Sino-Japanese Relations after the Cold War: Two Tigers Sharing a Mountain.* London; New York: Routledge, 2014.

Yang, Daqing, et al., eds. *Toward a History Beyond Borders: Contentious Issues in Sino-Japanese Relations.* Cambridge, Mass.: Published by the Harvard University Asia Center: Distributed by Harvard University Press, 2012.

Zhao, Quangshen. *Japanese Policymaking: The Politics Behind Politics-Informal Mechanisms and the Making of China Policy.* Westport, Conn.: Praeger, 1993.

CHRONOLOGY OF KEY EVENTS

CHRONOLOGY TABLE

Year	Events
1840	June 28: Opium War starts between the United Kingdom (Britain) and the Qing Empire (China) (ends August 29, 1842).
1842	August 29: Treaty of Nanking; China agrees to open five treaty ports, where consular officials may reside, and to pay war indemnity.
1848	Expanded edition of Wei Yuan's *Haiguo Tuzhi* [*Illustrated Treatise on the Maritime Kingdoms*] completed; later disseminated in Japan.
1851	January 11: Taiping Rebellion (ends July 19, 1864).
1853	July 8: Perry's fleet arrives at Uraga, demands that Japan open to trade.
1856	October 23: Arrow War (Second Opium War) starts (ends October 25, 1860).
1858	May 28: China and Russia sign Treaty of Aigun.
	June: China signs Treaty of Tientsin with Britain (26th) and France (27th).
	July 29: Japan–U.S. Treaty of Amity and Commerce.
1859	June 28: Tokugawa shogunate declares ports of Kanagawa, Nagasaki, and Hakodate open to Western trade.
1860	October: China signs Treaty of Peking with Britain (24th) and France (25th).
1861	January 20: China establishes the *Zongli Geguo Shiwu Yamen* (*Zongli Yamen*), a government office in charge of foreign policy.
1862	China starts Tongzhi Restoration reforms (through 1874).
	May 27: Takasugi Shinsaku leaves Nagasaki aboard the *Chitose-maru*, arrives in Shanghai on June 3.
1864	*Zongli Yamen* translates *Elements of International Law* [*Wanguo Gongfa*] from English; later disseminated in Japan.
1868	January 3: *Osei Fukko* edict calls for restoring imperial rule in Japan; Meiji Government established.
1871	August 4: Denmark's Det Store Nordiske Telegrafselskab A/S constructs Shanghai–Nagasaki underwater telegraph line.
	September 13: Sino-Japanese Friendship and Trade Treaty.
	December: Miyako-jima castaways massacred by Paiwan tribesmen in southern Taiwan (Mudan Incident).

Year	Events
1874	May 22: Japan deploys troops to Taiwan.
	July 31: First Japanese envoy to China, Yanagihara Sakimitsu, takes office in Peking, establishes the legation in the Legation Quarter.
1875	May 7: Japan and Russia sign Treaty of Saint Petersburg (in Japanese, "The Treaty Exchanging Karafuto and Chishima").
1876	February 26: Treaty of Kanghwa (Japan–Korea Treaty of Amity).
	October 17: Japan declares sovereignty over Ogasawara (the Bonin Islands).
1877	December 28: First Chinese envoy to Japan, He Ruzhang, takes office and establishes temporary legation at *Zojoji* in Shiba, Tokyo; exchanges with Japanese literati at the legation start thereafter.
1879	April 4: Japan abolishes the Ryukyu domain, establishes Okinawa Prefecture.
1880	Huang Zunxian of the Chinese Legation in Japan delivers his *Chaoxian Celüe* [*Korea Stratagem*] to Korea's mission in Tokyo.
1881	February 24: China and Russia sign Treaty of Ili (Treaty of Saint Petersburg).
1882	July 23: Imo Incident in Hanseong (now Seoul), Korea.
1884	June 23: Sino-French War starts (ends June 9, 1885).
	December 4: Gapsin Coup in Hanseong.
1885	March 16: Fukuzawa Yukichi's "*Datsu-A Ron*" ["An Argument for Leaving Asia"] published anonymously in *Jiji Shimpo* without much fanfare.
	April 18: Japan and China conclude Treaty of Tientsin.
1886	August 13: Nagasaki–Qing Navy Incident.
1888	May 14: Japanese Army reorganized from regional commands into divisions.
1889	February 11: Constitution of the Empire of Japan.
1890	November 25: First Imperial Diet convenes.
	December 6: Yamagata Aritomo presents "line of sovereignty"/"line of interest" theory.
1894	March 29: Donghak Rebellion in Korea.
	July 16: Japan–Britain Treaty of Commerce and Navigation; agreement to abolish extraterritoriality (entered into force: July 17, 1899).
	July 25: Japanese fleet attacks Chinese warships (Battle of Pungdo).
	August 1: Japan and China declare war (First Sino-Japanese War).
1895	January 14: Japanese government incorporates Senkaku Islands into Okinawa Prefecture.
	April 17: First Sino-Japanese War ends with Treaty of Shimonoseki; China cedes Taiwan and Penghu, pays indemnity of 200 million taels.
	May 4: Japan returns Liaotung Peninsula to China upon intervention by Russia, France, and Germany on April 23 (The Triple Intervention).
	May 10: First Governor-General of Taiwan Kabayama Sukenori takes office.
1896	June 3: Sino-Russian Secret Treaty.
1898	March: Goto Shinpei installed as director of Civil Administration Bureau in Taiwan.
	June 11–September 23: Hundred Days of Reform in China.
	July 24: Japan incorporates Minami-Torishima into Ogasawara Subprefecture, Tokyo.
1899	May 18–July 29: First Hague Peace Conference.
1900	June 20: Boxer Rebellion (ends September 7, 1901).

continued

Year	Events

1901   January 29: Emperor Guangxu's New Reforms in China.

       September 7: Boxer Protocol (Xinchou Peace Treaty); Russia does not withdraw troops from Manchuria.

1902   January 30: Anglo-Japanese Treaty of Alliance.

1904   February 10: Japan declares war on Russia (Russo-Japanese War).

       February 12: China declares neutrality.

1905   January 22: The Russian Revolution (Bloody Sunday Massacre).

       February: Japan incorporates Takeshima into Shimane Prefecture.

       September 2: China abolishes civil service examination system; many Chinese students go to study "the West and Modernity" in Japan.

       September 5: Treaty of Portsmouth; Japan acquires Russia's South Manchuria concessions—South Manchurian Railway Company and Kwantung Leased Territory with Port Arthur (Lüshunkou) and Dalian.

       November 17: Second Japan–Korea Agreement; Japan makes Korea a protectorate, denying it diplomatic sovereignty and establishing Resident-General of Korea.

1906   Number of Chinese exchange students in Japan peaks.

1907   China and Japan conclude a special agreement designating five schools for Chinese exchange students in Japan, after quality of their education becomes an issue.

       July 24: Third Japan–Korea Agreement; disbands Korea's military, strengthens Japanese rule.

1908   March 19: Anti-Japanese movement in China because of *Daini Tatsu-maru* Incident.

1910   August 22: Japan–Korea Annexation Treaty.

1911   October 10: Xinhai Revolution (Chinese Revolution of 1911).

1912   January 1: Republic of China established.

       February 12: Fall of the Qing Dynasty.

       July 30: Emperor Meiji dies.

1913   October 6: Yuan Shikai officially becomes President of China; Japan recognizes the Republic of China.

1914   July 28: World War I starts (ends November 11, 1918).

       August 6: Republic of China declares neutrality.

       August 23: Japan declares war on Germany.

       September 2: Japan lands troops at Longkou in China's Shandong Province.

1915   January 18: Japan presents China with the Twenty-One Demands.

       May 7: Japan gives China final notice.

       May 9: China accepts the Twenty-One Demands ("Day of National Humiliation").

1916   June 6: Yuan Shikai dies.

1917   August 14: Republic of China enters World War I.

       November 2: Japan and United States conclude Ishii-Lansing Agreement.

1918   April–September: Japan provides Nishihara loans to Duan Qirui administration.

       May 16: Sino-Japanese military agreement.

       August 2: Japan participates in the Siberian Expedition.

       August 24: Republic of China also joins the Siberian Expedition.

1919   January 18–June 28: Paris Peace Conference.

       May 4: May Fourth Movement in Peking.

       October 10: Chinese Nationalist Party (*Kuomintang* or KMT) founded.

1920   January 10: League of Nations established; Japan and China are founding members.

       Japan incorporates Okinotori Islands into its territory.

Year	Events
1921	May 20: Republic of China concludes separate peace treaty with Germany.
	July 1: Chinese Communist Party (CCP) founded.
	November 12: Washington Conference (until February 6, 1922).
1922	February 6: Nine-Power Treaty (concerning China).
1923	September 1: Great Kanto Earthquake.
1924	January 20: First KMT National Congress; first KMT–CCP alliance formed.
	May 31: Sino-Soviet Agreement.
	July 1: U.S. Immigration Act; excludes Japanese.
	November 24: Sun Yat-sen gives Greater Asianism Lecture in Kobe.
1925	May 30: May Thirtieth Movement in Shanghai.
1926	July 9: Chiang Kai-shek leads KMT Revolutionary Army on Northern Expedition from Guangdong.
1927	April 18: Chiang establishes KMT government in Nanking.
	May 28: Japan's first Shandong Expedition.
1928	April 19: Japan's second Shandong Expedition.
	May 3: Japanese Army clashes with KMT Revolutionary Army (Jinan Incident).
	May 9: Japan's third Shandong Expedition.
	June 4: Kwantung Army assassinates Zhang Zuolin.
	June 9: KMT Revolutionary Army enters Peking; Northern Expedition ends.
	December 29: Zhang Xueliang allies with Chiang Kai-shek; China is unified.
1929	June 3: Japan recognizes the KMT government in Nanking.
	October 24: Great Depression.
1930	January 11: Japan lifts ban on gold exports; Showa Depression.
	May 6: Japan–China tariff agreement; China recovers tariff autonomy.
1931	September 18: Manchurian (Mukden) Incident.
	September 21: China appeals to League of Nations, Nine-Power Treaty.
1932	March 1: Manchukuo founded.
	October 1: Lytton Commission delivers its report to the Japanese government.
1933	March 27: Japan withdraws from League of Nations.
	May 31: Tanggu Truce.
1934	April 17: Foreign Ministry Information Division Chief Amo Eiji opposes other countries' assistance to China (Amo Statement).
1935	October 7: Hirota's Three Principles proposed.
	November 3: KMT government reforms paper currency.
1936	December 12: Zhang Xueliang arrests Chiang Kai-shek (Xi'an Incident).
1937	July 7: Marco Polo Bridge Incident in outskirts of Peking (Second Sino-Japanese War starts).
	August 13: Second Shanghai Incident.
	November 5: Trautmann peace efforts begin.
	November 6: Italy joins Japan–Germany Anti-Comintern Pact.
	November 20: KMT government relocates base to Chungking.
	December 13: Japanese military massacre in Nanking (Nanking Incident).
1938	January 16: First Konoe statement.
	November 3: Second Konoe statement.
	December 20: Wang Jingwei escapes from Chungking.

continued

Year	Events

1939   May 12–September 15: Nomonhan Incident; Japanese forces suffer crushing
         defeat.
       September 1: German forces invade Poland (World War II starts).
1940   March 30: Wang Jingwei organizes Nationalist government in Nanking.
       September 23: Japanese military occupies northern French Indochina.
1941   April 13: Japan-Soviet Neutrality Pact.
       July 28: Japanese military occupies southern French Indochina.
       October 18: Sorge Incident in Japan.
       December 8: Japan attacks Malay Peninsula, Pearl Harbor (Asia-Pacific War starts).
       December 9: Chungking government declares war on Japan, Germany, and Italy.
1942   January 1: Chungking government signs Statement by United Nations, becomes
         one of the "Big Four" Allied Powers.
1943   November 22–26: Cairo Conference (U.S.–UK–China).
       December 1: Cairo Declaration.
1944   January 24: Japanese Imperial Headquarters orders Operation Ichi-go (a strategy of
         crossing through mainland China).
1945   February 4–11: Yalta Conference (U.S.–UK–USSR).
       August 9 (pre-dawn): USSR enters war against Japan, occupies Manchuria.
       August 14: Japan accepts the Potsdam Declaration.
       August 15: Radio broadcast of surrender; end of the war.
       August 17: Higashikuni Naruhiko forms cabinet.
       September 2: Japan signs instrument of surrender.
       September 9: Formal ceremony for surrender of Japanese forces in the China
         Theater.
       October 9: Shidehara Kijuro forms cabinet.
       October 10: "Double Tenth Agreement" (minutes of talks by Mao Zedong and
         Chiang Kai-shek).
       October 24: United Nations (UN) established.
       October 25: Japanese administration of Taiwan ends.
1946   May 3: International Military Tribunal for the Far East (Tokyo Trials) (through
         November 12, 1948); the same day, Soviet administration of Manchuria to end.
       May 22: Yoshida Shigeru forms cabinet.
       July 12: Chinese Civil War erupts over continued Soviet administration of
         Manchuria.
       August: KMT and CCP both issue statements attacking the other party.
       November 15–December 25: KMT government holds national assembly.
1947   January 1: KMT government promulgates Constitution of the Republic of China
         (ROC) (enacted December 25).
       February 28: "228 Incident" in Taiwan.
       March 12: Truman Doctrine announced.
       May 24: Katayama Tetsu forms cabinet.
1948   January 6: U.S. Army Secretary Royall announces policy change for Japan's
         occupation.
       March 10: Ashida Hitoshi forms cabinet.
       May 10: ROC government places Taiwan under martial law based on Temporary
         Provisions Effective During the Period of Communist Rebellion.
       October 19: Yoshida Shigeru forms cabinet.

Year	Events
1949	August 1: Diet Members' League for the Promotion of Sino-Japanese Trade established (name later changed: "... of Japan–China Trade"). October 1: People's Republic of China (PRC) founded. December 7: ROC government moves capital to Taipei, Taiwan.
1950	January 6: Britain recognizes the PRC government. January 12: Acheson Line announced. February 14: Sino-Soviet Treaty of Friendship, Alliance, and Mutual Assistance. June 25: North Korean military crosses the 38th parallel (Korean War begins). August 1: MacArthur announces U.S. support for defending the Taiwan Strait. October 25: UN forces approach the Yalu (Amnok) River; Chinese People's Volunteer Army enters the war.
1951	February 1: UN recognizes China as an aggressor in Korea. September 4–8: San Francisco Peace Conference. September 8: Peace Treaty signed by Japan and 48 other countries (entered into force April 28, 1952); the same day, Japan–U.S. Security Treaty signed. December 24: Prime Minister Yoshida Shigeru sends letter to John Foster Dulles, consultant to the U.S. State Department (Yoshida letter).
1952	January 16: Yoshida letter made public. April: Moscow International Economic Conference held. April: Japan Council for the Promotion of International Trade established. April 28: Japan–ROC Peace Treaty (entered into force August 5). June 1: First Japan–China private trade agreement. July: CHINCOM (Coordinating Committee for Export to China) established. November 14: Japan joins COCOM (Coordinating Committee for Export to Communist Areas).
1953	July 27: Korean Armistice Agreement. October 29: Second Japan–China private trade agreement.
1954	September 3: Chinese forces shell Kinmen and Matsu islands (first Taiwan Strait Crisis). September 22: Japan Association for the Promotion of International Trade established. December 10: Hatoyama Ichiro forms cabinet.
1955	March 9: Third Japan–China private trade agreement negotiations (signed May 4). April 18–24: Asian-African Conference in Bandung, Indonesia. November 15: Liberal Party and Japan Democratic Party merge, forming the Liberal Democratic Party (LDP) ("conservative union").
1956	Summer: China releases over a thousand Japanese war criminals, who are repatriated aboard the *Koan-maru* in September. October 19: Japan-Soviet Joint Declaration (entered into force December 12). December 18: Japan joins the UN. December 23: Ishibashi Tanzan forms cabinet.
1957	February 25: Kishi Nobusuke forms cabinet. March 12: Committee for the Promotion of Sino-Japanese Cooperation established.

continued

Year	Events

1958   March 5: Fourth Japan–China private trade agreement.
    March 14: ROC government announces cancellation of Japan–ROC trade talks.
    May 2: Nagasaki Flag Incident.
    May 5–23: Second Session of the 8th CCP National Congress; Great Leap Forward policy decided.
    August 23: Chinese forces shell Kinmen Island.

1959   June 20: USSR notifies China it will abrogate the Agreement on New Technology for National Defense.
    September: Former Prime Minister Ishibashi Tanzan visits China, meets with Premier Zhou Enlai.

1960   January 19: New Japan–U.S. Security Treaty (Treaty of Mutual Cooperation and Security between Japan and the United States of America).
    July 19: Ikeda Hayato forms cabinet.
    August 27: Premier Zhou offers "Three Trade Principles."

1961   October 19: Premier Zhou criticizes First Secretary Khrushchev at 22nd Congress of the Communist Party of the Soviet Union (CPSU).

1962   January 11–February 7: CCP Central Committee enlarged working conference; President Liu Shaoqi criticizes Great Leap Forward, Mao Zedong makes self-criticism.
    September 19: Diet member Matsumura Kenzo visits China, meets with Premier Zhou Enlai; agreement on "Okazaki Plan."
    October 22–28: Cuban Missile Crisis.
    November 9: Liao Chengzhi and Takasaki Tatsunosuke sign "Memorandum on Japan–China Comprehensive Trade" (LT Trade begins).

1963   August 5: Partial Nuclear Test Ban Treaty (PTBT).
    October 7: Zhou Hongqing Incident.
    November 22: President Kennedy assassinated.

1964   January 27: France normalizes diplomatic relations with China.
    February 10: ROC government severs ties with France.
    February 23–27: Former Prime Minister Yoshida visits Taiwan, meets three times with Chiang Kai-shek.
    April 4: Yoshida sends letter agreeing to "Draft Outline for Measures toward Communist China" ("first Yoshida letter [1964]").
    May 7: "Yoshida letter (1964)."
    July 3: Foreign Minister Ohira Masayoshi visits Taiwan.
    July 19: Japan Communist Party (JCP) splits decisively with CPSU.
    August 2: North Vietnam torpedoes U.S. destroyer (Gulf of Tonkin Incident).
    October 10–24: Tokyo Olympics.
    October 16: China successfully tests nuclear bomb.
    November 9: Sato Eisaku forms cabinet.

1965   February 7: United States begins bombing North Vietnam.
    March 7: U.S. Marines land in Danang, South Vietnam (large-scale U.S. intervention starts).
    April: Japan–ROC yen loan negotiations conclude; agreement signed.

1966   March: JCP and CCP sever relations.
    May: Cultural Revolution begins in China.

Year	Events
1967	June 17: China successfully tests hydrogen bomb. August 8: Association of Southeast Asian Nations (ASEAN) formed. October 20: Former Prime Minister Yoshida Shigeru dies. November 12: Prime Minister Sato Eisaku visits United States; summit with President Johnson. November 15: Japan–U.S. Joint Statement; agreement on Okinawa reversion "within a few years," Ogasawara Islands reversion within one year.
1968	February 8: Negotiations to extend LT Trade start. March 6: Negotiations conclude; now called Japan–China "Memorandum Trade." July 1: Nuclear Non-Proliferation Treaty (NPT). Autumn: UN Economic Commission for Asia and the Far East (ECAFE) announces possibility of large-scale oil and natural gas reserves in East China Sea.
1969	March 2: Sino-Soviet border clash at Zhenbao (Damansky) Island. April 1–24: 9th CCP National Congress; party platform specifying the overthrow of "American imperialism" adopted. July 8: Sino-Soviet border clash at Bacha (Goldinsky) Island. July 25: President Nixon announces Guam Doctrine (later called Nixon Doctrine). August 13: Sino-Soviet border clash in Central Asia. November 12: Former President Liu Shaoqi dies of unnatural causes. November 17: Prime Minister Sato visits United States; summit with President Nixon. November 21: Japan–U.S. Joint Statement; emphasizes firmly maintaining the Japan–U.S. Security Treaty, includes "Korea clause," "Taiwan clause."
1970	April 19: Premier Zhou Enlai presents "Zhou's Four Principles" to Memorandum Trade delegation visiting China, led by Matsumura Kenzo. July: ROC government grants oil-drilling rights in vicinity of Senkaku Islands to U.S. Pacific Gulf Corporation. August 10: Foreign Minister Aichi Kiichi causes diplomatic stir by revealing in House of Councilors' special committee that Japan had protested this matter to Taiwan.
1971	April 7: U.S. table tennis team, playing in World Table Tennis Championships in Nagoya, is invited to China (Sino-U.S. "Ping-Pong Diplomacy"). June 17: Okinawa Reversion Agreement. July 9–11: U.S. National Security Advisor Kissinger's top-secret visit to China. July 15: President Nixon announces Kissinger's trip to China and plans for his own visit (first Nixon shock). August 15: President Nixon announces suspension of gold/dollar convertibility and imposition of 10 percent import surcharge (second Nixon shock). October 25: PRC's UN membership decided; statement on expulsion of ROC government from UN is released. November 24: Japan adopts "three non-nuclear principles" in Diet resolution. December 30: China asserts sovereignty over Senkaku Islands in foreign ministry statement.

continued

Year	Events

1972   February 21–27: President Nixon's Visit to China.

February 27: Sino–U.S. joint statement (Shanghai Communiqué).

May 15: Okinawa's sovereignty reverts to Japan; Okinawa Prefecture established.

July 7: Tanaka Kakuei forms cabinet.

July 27: Komeito Chairman Takeiri Yoshikatsu visits China, meets with Premier Zhou Enlai.

September 25: Prime Minister Tanaka Kakuei visits China.

September 29: Joint Communiqué of the Government of Japan and the Government of the People's Republic of China; normalization of Japan–China diplomatic relations. Foreign Minister Ohira announces Japan–ROC Peace Treaty lost its *raison d'être* and has ended. Late that night, Taiwan declares it will sever relations with Japan.

October 29: Japan–China Memorandum Trade Agreement.

November 21: Japan–China Economic Association established.

December 1: Japan's Interchange Association in Taipei and Taiwan's Association of East Asian Relations in Tokyo established.

1973   January 27: Paris Peace Accords concluded (fighting in Vietnam War ends).

April 16–May 18: Sino-Japanese Friendship Society delegation headed by Liao Chengzhi visits Japan.

September 21: Japan establishes diplomatic relations with Democratic Republic of Vietnam (North Vietnam).

October 17: Organization of Arab Petroleum Exporting Countries (OAPEC) forms an oil strategy during the 1973 Arab-Israeli War (Fourth Middle East War); first oil crisis.

1974   November: Preliminary negotiations on Japan–China Treaty of Peace and Friendship begin.

December 9: Miki Takeo forms cabinet.

1975   February 14: Third round of preliminary negotiations on Japan–China Treaty of Peace and Friendship starts in Tokyo.

April 25: Negotiations over Japan–China Treaty of Peace and Friendship begins in Beijing.

April 30: Fall of Saigon; Vietnam War ends.

September 24: Japan offers "Miyazawa's Four Principles" concerning Japan–China Treaty of Peace and Friendship.

1976   January 8: Premier Zhou Enlai dies.

September 9: CCP Chairman Mao Zedong dies.

October 7: China publicly announces Premier Hua Guofeng installed as CCP Chairman and "Gang of Four" arrested.

December 24: Fukuda Takeo forms cabinet.

1977   July 16–21: Third Plenum of 10th CCP Central Committee; Deng Xiaoping reinstated.

August 12–18: 11th CCP National Congress; Cultural Revolution declared over.

August 18: Prime Minister Fukuda Takeo announces three principles for Southeast Asian diplomacy (Fukuda Doctrine) in Manila.

Year	Events

1978 February 16: Japan–China long-term trade agreement.
April 12: Multiple PRC fishing vessels violate Senkaku Islands' territorial waters.
August 8: Foreign Minister Sonoda Sunao visits China.
August 12: Japan–China Treaty of Peace and Friendship (entered into force October 23).
October 22–29: Vice Premier Deng Xiaoping visits Japan.
December 7: Ohira Masayoshi forms cabinet.
December 15: U.S.–China Joint Communiqué; normalization of relations.
December 18–22: Third Plenum of 11th CCP Central Committee; starting point for PRC's modernization policies.
December 25: Vietnam invades Cambodia.

1979 January 1: U.S.–China diplomatic relations established.
January 16: Mohammad Reza Pahlavi, the Shah of Iran, seeks asylum in Egypt.
February 1: Ayatollah Ruhollah Moosavi Khomeini returns home to Iran, leading to Iranian Revolution; second oil crisis.
February 6: Vice Premier Deng Xiaoping visits Japan, meets with Prime Minister Ohira Masayoshi the following day.
February 17–March 16: China invades Vietnam as "punishment" (Sino-Vietnamese War).
December 5: Prime Minister Ohira visits China; the next day, he pledges government assistance of about 500 billion yen (official development assistance [ODA] to China starts).
December 27: USSR invades Afghanistan.

1980 May 8: Prime Minister Ohira meets with Premier Hua Guofeng in Yugoslavia.
May 27: Premier Hua visits Japan; Japan–China Agreement on Cooperation in the Field of Science and Technology signed.
July 9: Premier Hua visits Japan to attend Prime Minister Ohira Masayoshi's funeral.
July 17: Suzuki Zenko forms cabinet.

1981 January 19: China announces it will discontinue contract for second phase of construction of Shanghai Baoshan Iron and Steel Complex.
October: Prime Minister Suzuki Zenko meets Premier Zhao Ziyang in Cancun, Mexico.

1982 May 31: Premier Zhao visits Japan.
June 26: Newspaper reports that Japan's Ministry of Education rewrote Japanese "invasion of Northern China" as "advance into Northern China" in authorized school textbooks.
July 26: China protests to the Japanese government about textbook issue.
August 17: U.S.–China Joint Communiqué (second Shanghai Communiqué).
August 26: "Statement by Chief Cabinet Secretary Miyazawa Kiichi on History Textbooks."
September 1–11: 12th CCP National Congress; Hu Yaobang installed as CCP general secretary, independent foreign policy proposed.
September 8: China accepts Japanese views on history textbook issue.
September 26: Prime Minister Suzuki visits China, meets with Premier Zhao.
November 27: Nakasone Yasuhiro forms cabinet.

continued

Year	Events

1983   November 23–30: General Secretary Hu Yaobang visits Japan; meets with Prime Minister Nakasone (24th) and they decide to establish Japan–China Friendship Committee for the 21st Century. Hu gives speech in Diet (25th).

1984   March 23: Prime Minister Nakasone visits China, decides on second yen loan package (470 billion yen).
July 7: PRC Defense Minister Zhang Aiping visits Japan, meets with Japan Defense Agency (JDA) Director-General Kurihara Yuko (9th).
September: Chinese side invites 3,000 Japanese youth.
October 20: Third Plenum of 12th CCP Central Committee.

1985   August 15: Prime Minister Nakasone makes official visit to Yasukuni Shrine.
September 22: Plaza Accord; results in stronger yen/weaker U.S. dollar.
October: Prime Minister Nakasone meets Premier Zhao in the United States.

1986   June 7: China protests Japan's authorization of history textbooks.
July 7: Japanese government has authorized high school history textbook rewritten (second history textbook issue).
November 8: Prime Minister Nakasone visits China, meets with General Secretary Hu Yaobang.
December 9: Pro-democracy student demonstrations throughout China.
December 30: Nakasone cabinet abolishes limit on defense expenditures of 1 percent of gross national product (GNP).

1987   January 16: General Secretary Hu Yaobang retires.
February 26: Osaka High Court decision recognizes Taiwanese ownership of "Kokaryo" dormitory for Chinese exchange students.
May 29: JDA Director-General Kurihara makes first visit to China by a JDA head, meets with Defense Minister Zhang Aiping.
June 4: Deng Xiaoping complains about Japan breaking the defense spending limit and Kokaryo decision to visiting Komeito Secretary General Yano Junya.
November 6: Takeshita Noboru forms cabinet.

1988   January 13: Taiwanese President Chiang Ching-kuo dies; Vice President Lee Teng-hui installed as president.
August 25: Prime Minister Takeshita Noboru visits China, pledges third yen loan package of 810 billion yen.

1989   February 24: Foreign Minister Qian Qichen attends Emperor Hirohito's state funeral as PRC president's special envoy.
April 12: Premier Li Peng visits Japan.
April 15: Former General Secretary Hu Yaobang dies; start of protests by intellectuals and university students against political corruption and delay of political reform.
May 15: CPSU General Secretary Gorbachev visits China.
May 18: Normalization of Sino-Soviet relations announced.
June 2: Uno Sosuke forms cabinet.
June 4: CCP mobilizes the People's Liberation Army to suppress democracy movement of university students and citizens (Tiananmen Incident).
July 14: G-7 Summit of the Arch issues Declaration on China, criticizing Beijing.
August 9: Kaifu Toshiki forms cabinet.
September 25: Japan rescinds travel advisory to China.
November 6–7: First Asia-Pacific Economic Cooperation (APEC) ministerial meeting (APEC established).

Year	Events

1989   November 9: Berlin Wall falls.

December 2: U.S. President Bush and USSR General Secretary Gorbachev meet in Malta, confirm end of the Cold War (3rd).

1990   August 2: Iraqi forces invade Kuwait (Gulf Crisis).

September 30: Soviet Union and South Korea normalize diplomatic relations.

October 3: National unification of East and West Germany.

November 2: Japan lifts freeze on third ODA yen loan package to China.

November 12: Vice Premier Wu Xueqian attends Emperor Akihito's enthronement ceremony as PRC government's representative.

December: Japan concludes five-year extension of Japan–China long-term trade agreement.

1991   January 17–February 27: U.S.-led multinational forces begin aerial bombing of Iraq (Iraq War).

May 1: Taiwan abolishes the Period of Mobilization for the Suppression of Communist Rebellion Provisional Act (declares end of Chinese Civil War).

August 10–13: Prime Minister Kaifu Toshiki visits China; decides to provide fiscal year 1991 tranche of third ODA yen loan package as 130 billion yen lump sum.

August 19–22: Conservative coup d'état in USSR fails.

August 24: Gorbachev resigns as CPSU general secretary.

September 17: North and South Korea join UN simultaneously.

November 5: Miyazawa Kiichi forms cabinet.

December 25: Gorbachev resigns as president of USSR.

December 26: Dissolution of Soviet Union.

1992   January–February: Deng Xiaoping, China's most powerful leader, makes an inspection tour of southern China; declares policy switch to "Reform and Opening" (southern tour talks).

February 25: China enacts Law on the Territorial Sea; stipulates Senkaku (Diaoyu) Islands are its own national territory.

April 6–10: General Secretary Jiang Zemin visits Japan, officially invites Japanese Emperor to visit China.

June 20: Japan's ODA Charter (formerly ODA outline) approved by cabinet decision.

August 24: China and South Korea normalize diplomatic relations; also, Taiwan severs relations with South Korea.

October 12–18: 14th CCP National Congress; "socialist market economy" formalized.

October 23–28: Emperor Akihito and Empress Michiko visit China.

1993   March 12: North Korea announces withdrawal from NPT.

August 4: "Kono Statement" on comfort women issue released.

August 9: Hosokawa Morihiro forms cabinet (non–LDP coalition).

August 10: Prime Minister Hosokawa Morihiro acknowledges Second Sino-Japanese War as "war of aggression."

November 1: Treaty on European Union (Maastricht Treaty) enters into force.

November 19: Prime Minister Hosokawa meets with President Jiang Zemin at APEC in the United States.

continued

Year	Events
1994	March 20: Prime Minister Hosokawa visits China, meets with President Jiang and Premier Li Peng. April 28: Hata Tsutomu forms cabinet. June 13: North Korea announces withdrawal from International Atomic Energy Association. June 30: Murayama Tomiichi forms cabinet (LDP–Socialist Party–Sakigake coalition). July 25: ASEAN Regional Forum established. August: CCP Central Committee promulgates "Outline on Implementing Patriotism Education," policy for thorough patriotic education aimed at youth.
1995	January 17: Great Hanshin Earthquake. May 2–6: Prime Minister Murayama Tomiichi visits China, meets with President Jiang and Premier Li. June 7: Taiwanese President Lee Teng-hui makes first visit as president to United States. July 21–26 and August 15–25: Chinese conduct missile practice in Taiwan Strait. August 15: Murayama administration issues prime ministerial statement "On the occasion of the 50th anniversary of the war's end" ("Murayama Statement"). November 15–19: APEC Summit, Osaka; President Jiang visits Japan.
1996	January 11: Hashimoto Ryutaro forms cabinet. March 8 and March 12–20: Chinese forces conduct large-scale military exercises and missile launch testing in Taiwan Strait. March 23: Taiwan's first presidential election by direct popular vote; Lee Teng-hui wins. April 17: Japan–U.S. Joint Declaration on Security Alliance for the 21st Century issued at Hashimoto–Clinton summit. November 22–26: APEC Summit, Manila; Prime Minister Hashimoto meets with President Jiang.
1997	February 19: Deng Xiaoping dies. July 1: China recovers sovereignty over Hong Kong. July 2: Thai baht plunges; Asia Financial Crisis starts. September 4: Prime Minister Hashimoto visits China, meets with Premier Li; next day meets with President Jiang. September 12–18: 15th CCP National Congress. September 23: New "Guidelines for Japan–U.S. Defense Cooperation." October 26–November 3: President Jiang Zemin visits United States; Clinton–Jiang summit confirms building of a "constructive strategic partnership" (29th). December 15: Japanese, PRC, ROK leaders invited to the ASEAN Summit; ASEAN+3 becomes standard.
1998	February 3: Defense Minister Chi Haotian visits Japan (first such visit of PRC Defense Minister in 14 years), holds first Japan–China Defense Talks in 11 years with JDA Director-General Kyuma Fumio. May 1: Kyuma visits China (first for a JDA head since 1987). June 25–July 3: President Clinton visits China, issues "Three Noes"; the two sides reaffirm building a "constructive strategic partnership" (27th). July 30: Obuchi Keizo forms cabinet. November 25–30: President Jiang's state visit to Japan; "Japan–China Joint Declaration On Building a Partnership of Friendship and Cooperation for Peace and Development" issued.

Year	Events
1999	July 8: Prime Minister Obuchi Keizo visits China.
	November 28: First Japan–PRC–ROK leaders meeting held at ASEAN+3 in Manila.
2000	March 18: Chen Shui-bien of the pro-independence Democratic Progressive Party wins Taiwan's presidential election.
	April 5: Mori Yoshiro forms cabinet.
	May 20: Chen Shui-bien declares the "four noes and one without" in presidential inauguration speech.
	October: Premier Zhu Rongji visits Japan.
2001	January 20: George W. Bush inaugurated as U.S. president.
	April 1: U.S. surveillance plane collides with PRC military fighter jet over South China Sea, makes emergency landing on Hainan Island.
	April 22–26: Former President Lee Teng-hui goes to Kurashiki City, Japan for medical treatment of a heart ailment.
	April 26: Koizumi Junichiro forms cabinet.
	August 13: Prime Minister Koizumi Junichiro visits Yasukuni Shrine.
	September 11: Terrorist attacks on New York and Washington D.C. ("9/11").
	October 7: U.S. and UK forces commence military operations in Afghanistan (War in Afghanistan).
	October 8: Prime Minister Koizumi makes day-trip to China, visits Museum of the War of Chinese People's Resistance Against Japanese Aggression near Marco Polo Bridge, meets with Premier Zhu and President Jiang.
	November 10: China officially joins World Trade Organization (WTO).
2002	April 12: Prime Minister Koizumi visits China.
	April 21: Prime Minister Koizumi visits Yasukuni Shrine during annual spring festival.
	May 8: North Korean defectors rush into Japanese Consulate-General in Shenyang.
	November 8–14: 6th CCP National Congress; post of general secretary passes from Jiang Zemin to Hu Jintao.
2003	January 10: North Korea declares its withdrawal from the NPT.
	January 14: Prime Minister Koizumi's third Yasukuni Shrine visit.
	February 25: Prime Minister Koizumi attends ROK President Roh Moo-hyun's inauguration ceremony in Seoul, meets with him later.
	March 15: First Session of 10th National People's Congress; Hu Jintao elected president.
	March 20: United States and Britain attack Iraq (Iraq War begins).
	April 30: North Korea announces it possesses nuclear weapons.
	Late-May: Agreement to establish New Japan–China Friendship Committee for the 21st Century.
	June 6: President Roh's state visit to Japan; attends imperial banquet, meets next day with Prime Minister Koizumi.
	August: Ceremony commemorating 25th anniversary of Japan–China Treaty of Peace and Friendship in Beijing; former prime ministers Murayama and Hashimoto, and Chief Cabinet Secretary Fukuda Yasuo attend.
	August 27–29: Six-Party Talks on North Korean nuclear issue in Beijing.

continued

Year	Events

2004   January 1: Prime Minister Koizumi's fourth Yasukuni Shrine visit.
        July 21: Prime Minister Koizumi meets with President Roh; Japan–ROK shuttle
        diplomacy starts.
        November 21: Prime Minister Koizumi meets with President Hu Jintao in
        Santiago, Chile.
        November 30: Prime Minister Koizumi meets with Premier Wen Jiabao in
        Vientiane, Laos.
        December 17: President Roh visits Japan, meets with Prime Minister Koizumi.
2005   March 16: Shimane Prefectural Assembly adopts "Ordinance to Establish
        Takeshima Day."
        April 2–19: Demonstrations protesting Japan's aim of permanent membership on
        UN Security Council (UNSC) occur in Chengdu, Shenzhen, Beijing, other
        Chinese cities.
        June 20: Prime Minister Koizumi meets with President Roh in Seoul; afterwards,
        Japan–ROK shuttle diplomacy discontinued until April 2008.
        September 14: Special leaders' summit at UN General Assembly celebrating UN's
        60th anniversary; UN reforms, including UNSC permanent seat for Japan, not
        implemented.
        September 17: Prime Minister Koizumi's fifth Yasukuni Shrine visit.
2006   April 25: President Roh issues special statement on Japan–ROK relations.
        July 5: North Korea fires seven missiles into Sea of Japan.
        July 15: UNSC unanimously adopts resolution criticizing North Korea.
        August 15: Prime Minister Koizumi visits Yasukuni Shrine.
        September 24: Shanghai Party Secretary Chen Liangyu dismissed on corruption
        charges.
        September 26: Abe Shinzo forms cabinet.
        October: Japan–China joint history research starts.
        October 8–9: Prime Minister Abe Shinzo visits China, meets with President Hu;
        agreement on "Strategic Mutually Beneficial Relations."
        October 9: North Korea announces successful underground nuclear test.
        October 14: UNSC unanimously adopts North Korea sanctions resolution.
2007   April 11–13: Premier Wen makes state visit to Japan; gives speech in Diet, meets
        with Prime Minister Abe.
        September 26: Fukuda Yasuo administration established.
        October: 17th CCP National Congress; Xi Jinping becomes candidate for general
        secretary.
        December 27–30: Prime Minister Fukuda Yasuo makes state visit to China, meets
        with President Hu.
2008   January 30: Poisoned frozen dumplings incident in Japan.
        May 6–10: President Hu visits Japan; "Joint Statement between the Government
        of Japan and the Government of the People's Republic of China on Promoting
        a 'Mutually Beneficial Relationship Based on Common Strategic Interests'"
        issued.
        May 12: 8.0-magnitude earthquake in Wenchuan County, Sichuan Province.
        May 15: Japan's international emergency assistance team's first squad arrives in
        Beijing; on site the following day.

Year	Events

2008　June 18: Japan–China agreement on joint development of East China Sea gas fields.

July 7–9: Hokkaido Lake Toya G-7/G-8 Summit; President Hu Jintao visits Japan.

August 8–24: Beijing Olympics; Prime Minister Fukuda attends opening ceremony.

September 15: Major U.S. securities firm Lehman Brothers goes bankrupt, setting off global economic crisis ("Lehman shock").

September 24: Aso Taro forms cabinet.

October 23–25: Prime Minister Aso Taro visits China, meets with President Hu and Premier Wen.

December 13: Premier Wen visits Japan; first Japan–PRC–ROK trilateral summit held in Fukuoka.

2009　April 29–30: Prime Minister Aso visits China, meets with Premier Wen.

May 25: North Korea announces successful underground nuclear test.

September 16: Hatoyama Yukio forms cabinet (coalition of Democratic, Social Democratic, and People's New parties).

October: Prime Minister Hatoyama Yukio visits China.

2010　April 12: President Hu visits the United States, meets with President Obama.

April 14: 7.1-magnitude earthquake in Qinghai Province, China.

April 30: Shanghai Exposition.

May: Premier Wen visits Japan.

June 8: Kan Naoto forms cabinet.

September 7: Chinese fishing trawler collision incident in the Senkakus.

September 20: China restricts export of rare earth elements to Japan.

October 18: Fifth Plenary Session of 17th CCP Central Committee; Vice President Xi Jinping installed as Vice Chairman of Central Military Commission, becoming President Hu Jintao's de facto successor.

November: President Hu visits Japan.

2011　January: China's 2010 gross domestic product overtakes Japan's, PRC economy becomes world's second largest.

March 11: Great Eastern Japan Earthquake.

May: Premier Wen Jiabao visits Japan.

June 30: Beijing–Shanghai high-speed train starts operations.

September 2: Noda Yoshihiko forms cabinet.

September 29: China successfully launches first unmanned space lab module, "Tiangong 1."

December 25–26: Prime Minister Noda Yoshihiko visits China.

2012　February: Chongqing Party Secretary Bo Xilai stripped of power (Chongqing Incident).

March 13: U.S., Japan, and EU bring WTO case against China for its export restrictions on rare earth elements.

April: Tokyo Governor Ishihara Shintaro issues plan for Tokyo to purchase three Senkaku Islands: Uotsuri-shima, Kita-kojima, and Minami-kojima.

August 10: ROK President Lee Myung-bak visits Takeshima (Korean name: Dokdo).

continued

Year	Events
2012	August 15: Anti-Japanese demonstrations in China; spread nationwide the next day. September 9: Prime Minister Noda and President Hu meet in Vladivostok. September 10: Japanese government decides to purchase the three Senkaku Islands from landowner on September 11; right afterwards, vehement anti-Japanese demonstrations start again in China, maritime surveillance and fishery inspection vessels appear near Senkaku Islands. November 16: Prime Minister Noda dissolves House of Representatives. December 26: Abe Shinzo forms cabinet.
2013	February 5: Japanese government announces PRC navy warship locked its fire-control radar on Maritime Self-Defense Forces destroyer in international waters; issues protest to China. February 12: North Korea declares third underground nuclear test "a success." February 15: Prime Minister Abe officially announces Japan will join Trans-Pacific Partnership negotiations. March 5–17: First Session of 12th National People's Congress (NPC); Xi Jinping takes office as president, Li Keqiang as premier. June 7–8: President Obama and President Xi Jinping meet in California. July 21: LDP wins overwhelming victory in House of Councillors election. October 28: A car crashes, bursts into flames in front of Tiananmen Square in Beijing. November 9–12: Third Plenum of 18th CCP Central Committee. November 23: China announces plans for "East China Sea Air Defense Identification Zone" that include the Senkaku Islands in its proper territory. December 26: Prime Minister Abe visits Yasukuni Shrine.
2014	January 24: Prime Minister Abe hints at improving relations with China in policy speech to the 186th Diet session. April 8: Hu Deping, eldest son of former General Secretary Hu Yaobang, visits Japan, meets with Prime Minister Abe, Chief Cabinet Secretary Suga Yoshihide, and others. May 5: LDP Vice President Komura Masahiko visits China, meets with NPC Chairman Zhang Dejiang. July 1: Abe cabinet enacts cabinet decision reinterpreting the constitution to enable a limited exercise of the right of collective self-defense. July 28: Former Prime Minister Fukuda Yasuo visits China, meets with President Xi. November 7: Yachi Shotaro, secretary general of Japan's National Security Secretariat, visits China, meets with State Councilor Yang Jiechi, and they agree on "Regarding Discussions toward Improving Japan–China Relations." November 10: Prime Minister Abe and President Xi hold Japan–China summit at Beijing APEC.
2015	February 17: U.S. think tank, Center for Strategic and International Studies, publishes satellite imagery of construction of a man-made island in the South China Sea. April 22: Prime Minister Abe and President Xi hold second Japan–China summit at the 60th anniversary ceremony marking the Asian-African Conference held in Bandung. April 29: Prime Minister Abe visits United States, gives address to joint meeting of Congress. June 29: Signing ceremony for the Asian Infrastructure Investment Bank held at the Great Hall of the People in Beijing; Japan had not joined at end-March 2015.

Year	Events
2015	August 6: Prime Minister Abe's private "Advisory Panel on the History of the 20th Century and on Japan's Role and World Order in the 21st Century" issues report.
	August 14: Prime Minister Abe issues prime ministerial statement on the 70th anniversary of the end of the war; China's response is restrained.
	September 3: CCP holds military parade in Tiananmen Square, commemorating the 70th anniversary of its Anti-Japanese War victory; Russian President Vladimir Putin, ROK President Park Geun-hye, other leaders attend.
	October 27: United States conducts "freedom of navigation" operations, concerned by China's unilateral change in the status quo of the South China Sea.
	November 1: Japan–China–ROK Summit (Prime Minister Abe, Premier Li, President Park), Japan–China summit and foreign ministerial meetings, held in Seoul.

INDEX

INDEX OF NAMES